1,001
IDEAS
for PARTIES
FAIRS and
SUPPERS

By Ann Seranne and Eileen Gaden

THE BLENDER COOKBOOK

THE BEST OF NEAR EASTERN COOKERY

By Ann Seranne

THE ART OF EGG COOKERY

YOUR HOME FREEZER

DELECTABLE DESSERTS

THE COMPLETE BOOK OF HOME BAKING

THE COMPLETE BOOK OF HOME PRESERVING

THE EPICURE'S COMPANION
(With John Tebbel)

THE COMPLETE BOOK OF DESSERTS

ANN SERANNE and EILEEN GADEN

1,001
IDEAS
for PARTIES
FAIRS and
SUPPERS

Originally published under the title The Church and Club Woman's Companion

ILLUSTRATED WITH 126 PHOTOGRAPHS BY EILEEN GADEN

Doubleday & Company, Inc., Garden City, New York, 1964

CONTENTS

Flowers — Preservation of Flowers — A Living Memorial — A Rose Garden — A Biblical Garden — Flowers of the Bible — Trees of the Bible — Herbs of the Bible

Recipes for starred dishes can be found by referring to *Index of Recipes*

Introduction

This book is dedicated to the many thousands of women in America, who give so generously of their time, effort, and creativity, to further a cause that is near and dear to their hearts. It is hoped that it will be of help to both the experienced and the neophyte who, for the first time, is elected to head a committee or to execute one of the various fund-raising events in church or club activities.

The book is meant to be a general guide for good management and good organization, but in no way to thwart or curtail individualism. It must be kept in mind that there is more than one way of doing anything, and your way is best, providing you follow methods that are tried and true, adding to them your individual creative ideas.

No single event, from a simple breakfast to a comprehensive bazaar, need be followed to the letter; part can be culled from here and part from there, to add up to an original and noteworthy occasion. A glance at the Table of Contents will show how the book has been divided into chapters to provide the most versatility.

Food usually plays an important part in the success of any group get-together, and the food should be of the best homemade quality, attractively presented in an imaginative setting. Menus for national, international, and regional America are among the many suggested. Many of them are too comprehensive for the average church or club, either from the standpoint of kitchen facilities or from budget; but most can be simplified without detracting from the success of the event. Not only can they be simplified, they can be changed to suit the taste preferences of your particular audience. Many recipes for dishes to serve eight to twelve are given throughout the book, where appropriate, while the recipes in the recipe section are designed to feed about fifty. Only you can evaluate if the amount has been estimated as sufficient or too abundant for your guests. Much depends on whether you are serving a group of hungry men, a gathering of women, or a mixed party of parents and children.

At the end of the book will be found a buyer's guide or *Directory of Sources*, where food supplies and bazaar merchandise can be ordered, frequently at a discount for quantity orders. It is hoped that this special section will prove of value to organizations in suggesting new types of merchandise that will add up to more money in the till.

The authors wish to extend their thanks to The Church of The Ascension in New York City for the loan of the ecclesiastical receptacles used in the arrangements of altar flowers, and to Morehouse and Barlow, also in New York City, for the loan of the handsome candlesticks shown in the cover photograph.

ANN SERANNE *and* EILEEN GADEN

1,001
IDEAS
for PARTIES
FAIRS and
SUPPERS

CHAPTER 1

Meals for Church or Club Functions

One of the best ways of raising money for your church, club, or organization is to serve a meal. The meal can be as simple as fruit juice, coffeecake, and tea or coffee, served either before church or after church, or an elaborate buffet for two hundred, but the determining factor as to the extent of the occasion is, of course, your kitchen facilities.

Almost every organization has some means of preparing and serving tea or coffee, or perhaps a simple soup with sandwiches, cakes, pies, or cookies donated by members. Some have fully-equipped institutional kitchens while still others, realizing the value of having the facilities for "serving a crowd," are in the process of gradually enlarging, modernizing, and adding equipment to their present facilities.

THE KITCHEN CHAIRMAN

If you are a person interested in food, with a good organizational head on your shoulders, the chances are that, before long, your organization will ask you to become kitchen chairman for a specific duration of office. Perhaps you have had similar experience before, but if not, don't underestimate the responsibility you have accepted, for being in charge of the food for club or church functions is no small undertaking.

YOUR KITCHEN FACILITIES

If you are not thoroughly familiar with the kitchen facilities at your disposal, there is no better time to study it than *immediately*. Make an inventory of every piece of equipment, every cooking pot and pan, every cup, plate, and platter for serving. Draw yourself a small blueprint of how the kitchen is laid out and where the major equipment is located. You will need to know how much oven space you have, the size of that space, and how many baking pans, casseroles, or roasters it will accommodate. You will need to know how many top-of-the-stove units there are and what size kettles they will accommodate. Is your refrigerator large enough to accommodate arranged salads or cold desserts for immediate service to a large group? What mixing facilities do you have? How much working counter space? What kind and how many plates, cups and saucers, and serving dishes are in good condition to set a pretty table? Do you have a small freezer for holding a few gallons of ice cream?

You must know the answers to all these questions before you can plan the type of meal, the extent of the meal, and the actual menu. If, for example, you have a lot of top burners but only one oven, you will have to plan the majority of the food for top-of-the-stove cooking and save the oven for heating bread or keeping casseroles hot.

If you have plenty of refrigerator space, you can plan a cold dessert, dish it up in advance, and stack on the refrigerator shelves, ready for service. If this facility is inadequate, you had better stick to cakes and pies for dessert. Or you can plan to serve ice cream, keep it on dry ice, and serve it as needed.

If your kitchen is only adequate for serving food, and not for cooking it, you will have to plan your menu around dishes that members can make at home and bring with them. Sometimes this can result in extraordinarily successful meals, such as a cold buffet or a Swedish smorgasbord—all fun and all easy, providing they are carefully planned and organized.

In all but the most elaborately equipped kitchens, much thought will have to be given as to how much can be cooked in the kitchen and how much must be "farmed out."

THE COOKING COMMITTEE

Next in importance to the kitchen facilities is the kind of culinary assistance you can count on. The cooking committee should be responsible for purchasing, cooking, and serving the food. Other groups can be responsible for the décor, setting up, and cleaning up. A few experienced people on the cooking committee are much better than a lot of amateurs. With some good, responsible people helping you, plus some willing hands, ready to do as they are instructed, you can plan fairly extensive and imaginative undertakings, even with limited kitchen facilities.

IMAGINATION IMPORTANT

Though you plan the most simple foods, the success of your meal will depend on how well these dishes are cooked and seasoned and how attractively they are served. It takes an experienced palate to judge the final flavor of the dish, but one extra pair of hands (inexperienced but willing) is all that is needed to add that spray of parsley, a cluster of water cress, a radish rose, a slice of lemon to a casserole, platter, or individual dish. This colorful touch makes all the difference in the world between success and failure.

WHOM ARE YOU GOING TO FEED?

Before actually planning the menu, based on facilities and assistance, you must take into consideration the group that you are appealing to. You certainly wouldn't serve dainty tea sandwiches to a group of hungry men any more than you would serve corned-beef hash at a ladies' tea party. In mixed groups of adults you can plan more exotic menus than you can for family gatherings.

THE MENU AND THE MAIN COURSE

Basically your meal should be well balanced as to texture, proteins, carbohydrates, and vegetables. Begin your menu with a main dish and build around it. Casseroles and one-dish meals are more economical than turkey, ham, or beef, and are easier to serve, since no carving is necessary; such meals are also easy for members to cook at home and bring with them, providing you have means of reheating them just before serving. With a casserole, a salad, hot bread, dessert, and coffee, you can have many memorable occasions. Add a soup first course or an appetizer, if you wish, but, in general, keep the food simple.

The First Course

A first course to a meal is not absolutely necessary, yet it is a very congenial way of starting conversation and giving your guests something to nibble on while waiting for the main course. Such nibble foods as a bowl or basket of crisp celery, and olives, or an attractive container filled with fresh radishes and a side dish of butter curls or cream cheese is a bright, cheerful beginning to any meal. Such foods can be placed on the tables before the guests are seated. They must, however, look crisp, fresh, and appetizing, and, if possible, should be nested on a bed of ice cubes.

First-course soups may be cold, clear, hot, or hearty, but this depends entirely on what you plan to serve as a main course. Certainly you would not serve a cream soup before a casserole with a cream-sauce gravy or before chicken with pan gravy. Nor would you serve a hearty soup before a stew. If you plan on a cold soup, be sure you have the facilities to serve it cold and the same goes for a hot soup. Make certain that your hot soup can be served really piping hot.

Individual servings of fruit cup, half a grapefruit, shrimp cocktail take many hands to prepare and serve unless you have plenty of refrigeration space to house the individual dishes, prepared and ready for table.

Vegetables

Fresh vegetables are almost too good to be true. They take a lot of preparation time, a longer cooking period, and generally, more cooking space than frozen or canned. But whether you use fresh, canned, or frozen, do something special to them. Don't just cook and serve them according to package directions. Add a touch of herbs or spices. A few chopped nuts, toasted, slivered almonds, some sliced water chestnuts (available in cans) add extra flavor and crispness to string beans or brussels sprouts, or cook the vegetable with a little shredded lettuce, some shredded mint leaves, or a little minced onion. Top them with some sautéed sliced onions or mushrooms.

Salads

Actually vegetables are not needed in many meals if you serve a big green salad and hot bread. The greens can be prepared ahead of time and stored in the refrigerator. Don't add the dressing or toss the salad until just before serving. Again, if you do not have sufficient refrigeration to keep the greens crisp and cold, plan on salads that take up less space and may be dressed ahead of time. Such salads as vegetables vinaigrette—cucumbers, string beans, beets, and tomatoes—actually improve in flavor by giving them time to marinate in the dressing. Other salads that may be made in advance and take up less refrigeration space, or may be made by members at home and brought to the dinner, are potato, macaroni, or rice salads, and coleslaw.

Bread

Unless you plan to serve hot bread with the meal, put a crisp hard roll at each person's plate before the meal begins—preferably heated and placed on the table just before the guests sit down. Hot French bread, herbed or garlic, if you desire, is good accompaniment for hearty stews and casseroles, or with a tossed salad. If you do not have facilities for serving bread warm, you can place baskets of sliced bread on the table before the meal begins. But don't put big stacks of sandwich bread on the table. In every community there are stores that specialize in good, honest breads —loaves of rye, pumpernickel, oatmeal bread, et cetera. Some can be bought sliced; otherwise assign a good bread cutter to slice the loaves thinly with a serrated knife, butter them if you wish, and arrange a variety of breads attractively in baskets or more imaginative containers on the tables.

Homemade Bread

Hot baking-powder biscuits, corn muffins, or homemade yeast breads can do much to make a very ordinary meal a real occasion. If you have some good breadmakers in your community, ask them to contribute the bread.

Ham and Bean Supper

The simplest of meals—homemade baked beans, homemade Boston brown bread, salad, apple pie (again homemade with a rich flaky crust), and coffee are often so successful that they become annual events in a community, but the success is only based on the wonderful homemade quality of every dish. Any time your organization hits on a particular event that appeals to your audience, repeat it, make it an annual occasion. In Danville, Illinois, the Lincoln Methodist Church serves an annual Ham and Bean

Supper. With it they serve coleslaw and hot, homemade corn bread, and finish with a choice of home-baked apple or lemon meringue pié. The little "special" touch they add to the baked beans is finely chopped raw onion.

Desserts

Desserts, as simple as a big bowl of fresh fruits, or even a raw apple, pear, or peach per person, to be peeled and eaten out of hand, are good finales to almost any meal. Of more universal appeal, but harder on the waistline, are delicious home-baked and lavishly frosted cakes, pies, with or without ice cream, or ice cream and cookies. As we mentioned before, you cannot plan individual servings of cold puddings or fruit unless you have refrigeration space.

PLANNING AND EFFICIENCY VITAL

These qualifications for success are important in any venture, but in the planning, executing, and serving of a community meal, they are vital.

Sit down with paper and pencil and make a list of every item that is needed for the meal and in what quantity.

Next make a work chart, and decide on how many people you are going to need over what period of time to produce the meal easily and expertly. A few experienced people are always better than many inexperienced helpers. Figure out how much of the meal can be prepared in advance of the date of the event.

Make a list of every pot and pan, every serving dish, knife, fork, spoon, plate, cup, et cetera that will be needed and, unless you have your inventory of such supplies on hand, you'd better check them.

Plan your work areas and serving areas so that every detail is arranged in advance to assure that the entire affair from start to finish will run smoothly. Be sure you plan room to accommodate the dirty dishes from the first course before the second course is served.

GOOD BUYING IS IMPORTANT

When buying food for serving a quantity, it is costly to purchase supplies from your local market. Some supermarkets have departments that stock quantity foods, but, if possible, try to find a source of institutional foods in your locality, even if it means you have to enlist the aid of a station wagon to transport the produce back home. You will save a great deal of money by buying wisely. For specific food sources, see *Directory of Sources* at back of book.

WISE BUYING

Buying the right amount of food is important. If you overbuy and food goes to waste, your profit is considerably reduced. In the back of this book you will find a chart for *Purchasing Food for Fifty Servings*. We reprint it by permission of the New York State College of Home Economics, Cornell University, and recommend that you refer to it for buying the correct amount of all food supplies.

PRICING THE MEAL

The general rule is to charge three times (or sometimes four) the actual cost of the ingredients of the meal per person. Yet, because you don't have to charge for such items as overhead and help, which commercial restaurants must consider, you can serve far better meals than one can buy at any restaurant for twice the price. YOU CAN BE SURE OF SUCCESS if you serve good, honest food; flavorful dishes, well cooked, attractively garnished, and imaginatively served. The members of your community will soon learn that "eating out" can be a most enjoyable and inexpensive way to take their family to dinner and you may find that you will have to limit your occasions to a specific number of first-come guests, or repeat the occasion on two different days or evenings. There is no excuse for bad food, no matter how limited your kitchen facilities. If you persist in serving cold, greasy soup, made from a packaged mix, in paper cups, sandwiches of two pieces of soggy white bread put together with a slice of ham between, and a slice of bakers' pie, members of your community will attend your event only because it is an obligation they feel they must perform and not because they really want to. Many people, with not such a strong sense of obligation, won't show up at all. When you serve poor food, the whole meaning of your objective is lost, for—not only do you want to increase the funds in your organization's larder—you want to encourage conviviality and friendships among your members. And there is no better way to accomplish this than via the pleasant atmosphere of good food in attractive surroundings.

BREAKFASTS

Breakfasts are not only great money-makers but are an excellent way to give friends a few moments together, for new members to meet others, and to inspire greater conviviality among all ages. Many churches throughout the country serve breakfast either before or after service and visitors are welcome. It is a friendly way to give out-of-towners a pleasant memory to take home and, perhaps, to meet a few people with whom they have something in common.

Breakfasts can become a weekly event for your church even with the most limited kitchen facilities, for they can be simple affairs consisting of fruit juice, coffeecake, and coffee. The Sunday-breakfast chairman, can enlist the co-operation of one responsible person to take charge of one Sunday a month, or if there are enough women to go around, a different person could be in charge each week. If the hostess of the week is assisted by the person who will be in charge of the next breakfast, certain formulated methods of preparing and serving the breakfast can be passed on from one to another. Each hostess should be responsible for enlisting the help of the young women as assistants.

Keep the cost low and the food of high caliber and you will have an increasing number of members each week. A small amount of profit each week, can add up to a goodly sum at the end of the season, with no one person burdened with a tremendous amount of work or responsibility.

A FINGER-FOOD BREAKFAST OR BRUNCH FOR FIFTY

This breakfast has been designed to serve a crowd, with a minimum of cleaning up. No plates are needed for serving, and you can use paper cups and napkins. Most of the food can be contributed by members. Set up a series of card tables around a room large enough to accommodate the guests without crowding, and put several platters or trays of food on each table. Have one person responsible for replenishing the food on each table and let the guests move around the room, picking up and eating with their fingers the small tidbits set before them. They can mix and mingle as they nibble, returning as often as they wish to any table in the room. Serve the hot foods from electric skillets, warming dishes, or electric serving trays. Since the dishes can be replenished frequently, they need not be outsized, and if your kitchen is not equipped with warming dishes, you may be able to borrow what you need from various members.

Table 1

Iced orange juice in jugs with paper cups. Count on 3 gallons.

Table 2

Bowl of fresh, pitted dates. Count on 2 per person.

Platter of pineapple chunks on picks with thin slice of ham woven in between and mint sprig on end. Count on 1 per person. An attractive way to serve these pick-up foods is to insert the end of the picks in a pineapple, grapefruit, melon, or firm head of lettuce.

Table 3

A basket of tiny baking-powder biscuits, split and buttered, with a minute slice of ham (Virginia is best) in between. Count on 2 per person and reheat before serving.

Small, grilled sausages or franks on picks.

A warming dish or tray with angels on horseback. This is a drained oyster, wrapped in bacon, fastened with a pick, and baked in a hot oven until the bacon is crisp. Reheat before serving and keep hot. Count on 2 per person.

Table 4

A large basket or container piled high with teeny round doughnuts. Count on 2 per person.

Table 5

Buttered and toasted English muffins, cut into quarters, and spread with marmalade or topped with scrambled eggs. Count on 2 pieces per person.

Warming dish of miniature codfish balls on picks. Serve with catsup dip, if desired. Count on 3 per person.

Barbecued spareribs. Have ribs cut by butcher into 1-inch sections. Pile on rack in baking dish and bake in a 300° F. oven for 3 hours, discarding fat as it accumulates in bottom of pan. Reheat before serving, and serve with barbecue dip. Count on 2 per person.

Table 6

Large container of potato chips.

Fried chicken wings or drumsticks. Use only the meaty portion of the wings; before serving put a tiny lamb-chop frill on end bone. Serve warm or cold. Count on 1 per person.

Table 7

Trays of miniature or portion-cut coffeecakes.

Table 8

Tea, coffee, sugar, and milk with paper cups.

A PANCAKE OR WAFFLE BREAKFAST

This can be a traditional sit-down breakfast with pancakes or waffles prebaked and served hot from the oven, or—and much more fun—borrow enough griddles from members of the community and make the pancakes before the guests. Count on one person officiating at a griddle for each ten persons to be served. Check on electrical current before undertaking.

This can be done in two different ways. The "hostesses" can all be lined up behind a long table, each with their griddle and a pitcher of batter in front of her. Other tables to accommodate the guests can be set in advance with a fruit compote or glass of juice at each place. On the table should be placed a bowl of butter or whipped butter, a pitcher of maple syrup and another of honey. After a guest has finished his first course, he goes to a hostess for his hot cakes. If you feel you need additional garnishes you might have junior hostesses circulating around the room with trays of hot crisp bacon, frizzled ham, and sausages. Tea or coffee should also be served to the guests at the table.

The second way is to serve the pancakes or waffles buffet style and give each hostess her own table equipped with pitcher of batter, the griddle, pitchers of syrup and honey, plate of butter, and a warming dish of crisp bacon and hot sausages. Each hostess should have an assistant junior hostess to keep the supplies on her table replenished. Separate tables would be set up for guests to help themselves to juice and hot beverage. At least 2 people would be needed in the kitchen to make the batter and fry the bacon and sausages.

EASTER BREAKFASTS

Menu 1

MINTED PINEAPPLE CHUNKS

CREAMED EGGS AND MUSHROOMS

IN PATTY SHELLS OR ON TOAST

BEVERAGE

Minted Pineapple Chunks: Prepare fresh pineapple or defrost the frozen chunks. Sprinkle with sugar and moisten with a little pineapple juice and chill. Garnish each serving with a sprig of mint.

Menu 2

STEWED RHUBARB

SCRAMBLED EGGS WITH DICED HAM

HOT CORN BREAD

BEVERAGE

JUNE BREAKFASTS OR BRUNCHES

Menu 1

SLICED STRAWBERRIES WITH ORANGE JUICE

PAN-BROILED SMALL FISH WITH LEMON PARSLEY BUTTER

BOILED NEW POTATOES

JOHNNYCAKE

COFFEE

Strawberries with Orange Juice: Hull and halve beautiful strawberries, sprinkle with sugar, and moisten with orange juice. Chill until serving time. Count on 1 box strawberries (1 pound) for every 6 servings.

Pan-Broiled Fish: If you have large skillets and plenty of top-of-the-stove burners, pan-sautéed small fish are easier to serve than those baked or fried. Simply melt ½ stick butter in each large frying pan and when it is sizzling, dust the fish lightly with flour and place in the pan. If you have 4 burners and 4 12-inch skillets, you can cook 16 to 20 fish at one time. Let them cook over medium heat for 5 minutes, turn and cook for 5 minutes longer. Arrange on serving platter. Add ½ stick butter, juice of 1 lemon, and 2 tablespoons minced parsley to butter remaining in pan, swirl pan over heat until butter is melted, and pour juice over the fish.

Menu 2

PINEAPPLE JUICE GARNISHED WITH ORANGE SLICE OR STRAWBERRY

SHIRRED EGGS

HOT BAKING-POWDER BISCUITS AND HONEY

BEVERAGE

Shirred Eggs: Line muffin cups with aluminum foil. Brush with melted butter and break an egg into each cup. Sprinkle with grated cheese and bake in a preheated 350° F. oven for about 12 minutes.

SUMMER BREAKFASTS OR BUFFET BRUNCHES

MELON BOWL WITH MELON BALLS AND

STRAWBERRIES

QUICHE LORRAINE (CHEESE TART)*

SMOKED-FISH PLATTER   ASSORTED BUTTERED BREADS

SLICED CUCUMBERS

COFFEECAKE AND COFFEE

Melon Bowl: Cut a thin slice from one side of a watermelon so it will stand firmly. Cut a slice, about ¼ way down, from top of melon and remove flesh, leaving a wall about 1-inch thick. With a French ball scoop make small balls from the watermelon flesh and from a variety of melons—using the best in season—Persian, cantaloupe, casaba, honeydew. Combine the melon balls with strawberries, or other berries in season. Fill melon bowl with the mixed fruit, sprinkle with sugar, and pour over 1 quart orange juice. Garnish with mint and keep cold until serving time. Count on ½ cup mixed fruit per serving, or 1 gallon to serve 32. If the bowl will not hold an entire gallon of fruit, it can be refilled when necessary.

Smoked-Fish Platter: Arrange on large serving platters on table a variety of smoked fish, such as whitefish, butterfish, salmon, sturgeon. Garnish with plenty of lemon quarters and parsley clusters or water cress.

A SIMPLE SUMMER BREAKFAST

SLICED PEACHES

EGGS GOLDENROD ON TOAST

or

FRENCH TOAST

COFFEE

AN AUTUMN BREAKFAST OR BRUNCH

APPLE JUICE

CREAMED CHICKEN AND HAM ON WAFFLES

or

THIN PANCAKES STUFFED WITH CREAMED CHICKEN

BEVERAGE

FOUR WINTER BREAKFAST MENUS

Menu 1
STEWED FRUIT *or* HALF GRAPEFRUIT
CHEESE RAREBIT WITH TOAST AND BACON
BEVERAGE

Menu 2
MELON WEDGE *or* WINTER PEARS
CREAMED DRIED BEEF ON TOAST
or
SAUSAGE CAKES
TOAST AND CRANBERRY JELLY
BEVERAGE

Menu 3
BAKED APPLES WITH CREAM
CORNED-BEEF HASH WITH POACHED EGG
DOUGHNUTS AND STRAWBERRY JAM
BEVERAGE

Menu 4
SLICED BANANAS *or* PRUNES COOKED IN ORANGE JUICE
SCRAMBLED EGGS AND CHICKEN LIVERS
CORN MUFFINS
BEVERAGE

FISHERMAN'S BREAKFAST

BERRIES IN SEASON WITH CREAM

FISHERMAN'S PLATTER*

POTATO CHIPS *or* FRENCH FRIES

SLICED TOMATOES

BEVERAGE

A NEW ENGLAND BREAKFAST OR BRUNCH

CRANBERRY JUICE

CREAMED CODFISH WITH PARSLEY POTATOES

ANADAMA TOAST   PLUM JAM

BEVERAGE

Anadama bread is a cornmeal and molasses yeast bread, well known in New England states. If not available, toast thin slices of cornmeal bread.

A MARYLAND BREAKFAST

ORANGE JUICE WITH FRESH MINT

CRAB CAKES

FRIED TOMATOES

TOASTED ENGLISH MUFFINS   PEACH JAM

BEVERAGE

A PLANTATION BREAKFAST OR BRUNCH

CHILLED WATERMELON SLICE

HOMINY GRITS   FRIED BREAKFAST SAUSAGES

CANE SYRUP

HOT BUTTERMILK BISCUITS

CAFÉ AU LAIT

Hominy Grits: Follow the recipe for cooking hominy grits on back of box. Serve hot with a pat of butter. A 1-pound 8-ounce box of grits will serve 24.

Café au lait: This is simply strong coffee mixed half and half with hot milk.

A SCOTCH BREAKFAST OR BRUNCH

SLICED ORANGES GARNISHED WITH MINT

BROILED KIPPERS AND SCRAMBLED EGGS

or

CREAMED FINNAN HADDIE

HOT BUTTERED SCONES   MARMALADE *or* GOOSEBERRY JAM

BEVERAGE

Broiled Kippers: Allow half a kipper for each serving. Arrange on broiling pans, skin side up, and broil for 3 minutes. Turn carefully, brush with a little melted butter and continue to broil for 3 to 4 minutes longer. Serve with a pat of butter melted on top and sprinkle with minced parsley. Add a generous wedge of lemon for garnish.

MEXICAN BREAKFASTS OR BRUNCHES

Menu 1
SLICED AVOCADO WITH LEMON WEDGE

TAMALE PIE*

BAKED TOMATOES

TOSSED SALAD

COFFEE

Menu 2
MELON WEDGE WITH LIME QUARTER

MEXICAN SCRAMBLED EGGS

TORTILLAS

HOT CHOCOLATE

Mexican Scrambled Eggs: Scramble eggs, flavored with chili powder, chopped green onions, and parsley in butter.

Tortillas: These can be purchased in cans. Follow directions on container for heating or frying.

SOUP AND CHOWDER SUPPERS

An inexpensive way to please a lot of people, with a minimum of work and assistance is with a soup supper—or, perhaps, a series of midwinter soup suppers—at which you can serve a different hearty soup or chowder each time. We're not talking about soups from a can, but homemade soups—the kind that always taste better made in large quantities. They can all be made a day in advance and reheated to the simmering point before serving.

All you really need in the way of equipment are top-of-the-stove burners, the necessary preparation knives, soup ladles, and a heavy soup kettle. A 3-gallon kettle will hold enough soup to serve an 8-ounce portion to 48 people. If you have an oven, you can also plan to serve hot bread and, with a refrigerator, you can add a tossed salad.

For dessert, homemade cakes or pies are the best, for these can be made by individuals at home and brought to the occasion, ready to serve.

All the soup suggestions lend themselves nicely to themes for decorations but, since the menus are the utmost in simplicity, so should be the décor.

If you wish to serve an appetizer before the soup, we have suggested one which is in keeping with the region or country to which the soup is indigenous and complements the theme. However, nibble foods—such as bowls of radishes, celery, and olives—are hard to beat for ease of preparation and serving and do well to keep the guests satisfied until the soup can come piping hot from the kitchen. If you are planning on tables to seat from 8 to 12, perhaps you could borrow from members of your organization enough large soup tureens so that each table could serve their own soup from the tureen. Be sure the tureens are scalded with boiling water before putting the hot soup into them, to assure a really hot soup to your guests. While the soup is heating, line up the tureens on the counter and fill with boiling water. Let stand until ready to serve. Empty out the hot water and fill the tureens with the boiling soup.

FRENCH ONION SOUP SUPPER

ARTICHOKES REMOULADE

or

LIVER PÂTÉ*

FRENCH ONION SOUP

HOT FRENCH BREAD

POACHED PEARS WITH RASPBERRY SAUCE

or

CHOCOLATE CAKE *or* CHOCOLATE MOUSSE

COFFEE

ITALIAN MINESTRONE SOUP SUPPER

ANTIPASTO*

BREADSTICKS

ITALIAN MINESTRONE

HOT GARLIC BREAD

CHEESECAKE *or* BISCUIT TORTONI

COFFEE

A RUSSIAN SOUP SUPPER

SMOKED SALMON ON DARK PUMPERNICKEL BREAD

or

CREAM CHEESE AND RED CAVIAR CANAPÉS

BORSCH

HOT PIROSHKI*

COFFEECAKE

TEA

Smoked Salmon Canapés: (Serves 48) Trim and butter 24 slices dark pumpernickel bread. Cover with paper-thin slices of smoked salmon. One pound, if thinly sliced, is enough. Cut into quarters and serve 2 canapés with a wedge of lemon to each person.

Hot Piroshki: (Serves 48) The recipes for three different kinds of fillings for piroshki are given in back of the book—fish, cabbage, and meat. Ask 3 women to each contribute three dozen of a different flavor. Reheat before serving.

NEW ENGLAND CHOWDER SUPPER

DEVILED EGG ON LETTUCE

NEW ENGLAND CLAM *or* FISH CHOWDER

JOHNNYCAKE

BLUEBERRY PIE *or* PUMPKIN PIE (À LA MODE)

COFFEE

NEW ORLEANS BEAN SOUP SUPPER

SHRIMP COCKTAIL

LENTIL SOUP WITH HAM AND CHEESE

TOASTED FRENCH BREAD

TOSSED SALAD

PECAN *or* SWEET POTATO PIE

COFFEE

DEEP-SOUTH CORN CHOWDER SUPPER

SLICED TOMATOES WITH FRENCH DRESSING *or* MAYONNAISE

CORN CHOWDER

PILOT BISCUITS *or* SEA TOAST

PEACH *or* CHOCOLATE CREAM PIE

BEVERAGE

INTERNATIONAL DINNERS

Dinners, with the menu planned around the national dish of a country, are usually enjoyed by everyone. They are stimulating to the older members of the community and intriguing to the young, and everyone loves an adventure to another land. Flags, paper streamers to match the colors of the flags, flowers or fruit, travel posters, all contribute to the gaiety and interest of the occasion. For more details, see chapter on *Themes and Decorations.*

The national dish of most countries is often one of the most flavorful that the country has to offer and, fortunately, is economical, easy to make, and adapts nicely to quantity cooking and service. Again, appetizers have been suggested, but may be eliminated for the sake of economy or kitchen facilities. Also, a dish containing a cheese or other flavorful dip may be placed in the center of each table, or at intervals down a long table, and surrounded by an assortment of crackers, potato chips, or pretzels. (*See photo 23.*)

Desserts may be changed or simplified to ice cream with a fruit topping, served with a sugar cooky, a good finale to a dinner in any language.

A HUNGARIAN DINNER

CONSOMMÉ WITH LIVER DUMPLINGS

HUNGARIAN GOULASH*

or

CHICKEN PAPRIKASH*

BOILED POTATOES   BUTTERED STRING BEANS

DOBOSH TORTE *or* FRUIT COMPOTE

COFFEE

AN ITALIAN DINNER

DEEP-FRIED VEGETABLES*

or

ANTIPASTO

BREADSTICKS

CHICKEN TETRAZZINI*

or

CHICKEN CACCIATORA*

STEWED SUMMER SQUASH   COOKED RICE

TOSSED SALAD

BISCUIT TORTONI *or* ITALIAN WATER ICE AND COOKIES

COFFEE

Antipasto: Arrange on individual plates, very small portions or an assortment of Italian favorite appetizers, such as black olives, tuna packed in olive oil, *caponata*, pimiento slices, anchovies, radish roses, cabbage slaw, potato salad, sardines, and pickled peppers.

Deep-fried Vegetables: The Italian name for this appetizer is *Fritto Misto*, or mixed fry. The vegetables are dipped in batter, then fried in hot deep fat. Such an appetizer should only be attempted with adequate deep-fat frying equipment. The vegetables can be fried in advance and reheated in the oven before serving. Serve with lemon wedges, salt, and pepper. Recipe will be found in the recipe section.

A SCANDINAVIAN DINNER

SLICED CUCUMBERS WITH DILL DRESSING

PUMPERNICKEL BREAD FINGERS

SWEDISH MEAT BALLS IN CREAM GRAVY*

BOILED PARSLEY POTATOES   BUTTERED CABBAGE WEDGES

BEET SALAD

APPLECAKE or DANISH PASTRIES

COFFEE

A RUSSIAN DINNER

CREAM CHEESE AND RED CAVIAR APPETIZER*

BEEF STROGANOFF*

BUTTERED BROWN RICE   BUTTERED CARROTS

CHEESECAKE

TEA

A GERMAN DINNER

MOLDED CHEESE BALL* WITH CRACKERS

SAUERBRATEN WITH GRAVY*

POTATO PANCAKES   RED CABBAGE AND APPLE

BLACK CHERRY TARTS

TEA or COFFEE

AN IRISH DINNER

GREEN CHEESE DIP WITH POTATO CHIPS

IRISH STEW

WITH

BOILED POTATOES   BUTTERED CARROTS

COLESLAW

SHAMROCK CAKE *or* CLAY PIPE CAKE*

TEA

EAST INDIAN DINNER

MINTED BEEF CONSOMMÉ

CURRIED LAMB *or* CHICKEN

COOKED RICE   CHUTNEY

SLICED CUCUMBERS

FRUIT COMPOTE WITH SPICE CAKE SQUARES

TEA *or* COFFEE

Minted Beef Consommé: Use a good grade of canned beef consommé and serve piping hot in consommé cups sprinkled with finely chopped fresh mint or with crumbled dried mint.

A MEXICAN DINNER

GUACAMOLE* WITH FRITOS

CHILI CON CARNE*

COOKED RICE   KIDNEY BEANS

TOSSED SALAD

EUPHRATE *or* SESAME-SEED BISCUITS

MELON SLICE WITH LIME

COFFEE *or* HOT CHOCOLATE

A GREEK DINNER

ASSORTED OLIVES AND RADISH ROSES

LAMB STEW À LA GRECQUE*

RICE PILAF*

APPLE, RAISIN, AND HONEY TURNOVERS

COFFEE

Apple, Raisin, and Honey Turnovers: Almost every good cook has a recipe for apple turnovers. It is easy to give them a Greek flavor by adding some raisins, some chopped nuts, if desired, and part honey for sweetening. If more convenient, this dessert can be made in a large baking pan with the apple filling spread between two layers of pastry, sandwich style. After baking, it can be cut into squares. Serve with whipped or sour cream.

A SOUTH SEAS DINNER

PINEAPPLE JUICE

DEEP-FRIED SHRIMP *or* FISH STICKS

SOY SAUCE AND HOT MUSTARD SAUCE

HAWAIIAN HAM STEAKS*

CANDIED SWEET POTATOES

SPINACH COOKED WITH WATER CHESTNUTS

COCONUT ICE CREAM

TEA *or* COFFEE

A NEAR EAST DINNER

CUCUMBER APPETIZER*

or

LENTIL SOUP

SHISH KEBABS   RICE PILAF*

TOSSED SALAD

ORANGE CUSTARD *or* ORANGE ICE

COFFEE

A FRENCH DINNER

VICHYSSOISE

CHICKEN MARENGO*

or

LOBSTER NEWBURG*

PETITS POIS FRANÇAISES

TOSSED SALAD WITH CHEESE WEDGES

CHOCOLATE CAKE

or

CHOCOLATE MOUSSE

COFFEE

A SPANISH DINNER

MELON WEDGE

PAELLA VALENCIANA

TOSSED SALAD

EGGNOG ICE CREAM

or

SPANISH FRUITCAKE

COFFEE

A CARIBBEAN SUPPER

SLICED AVOCADO WITH LIME

ARROZ CON POLLO *or* JAMBALAYA*

TOSSED SALAD

BANANA ICE CREAM

or

BANANAS IN PINEAPPLE JUICE WITH SHREDDED COCONUT

COFFEE

A CHINESE SUPPER

EGG-DROP SOUP

or

BUTTERFLY SHRIMP

CHINESE STEAK WITH PEPPERS*

CHINESE CABBAGE *or* SWISS CHARD   COOKED RICE

ICE CREAM WITH PRESERVED KUMQUATS *or* MANDARIN ORANGE WEDGES

SUGAR COOKIES

TEA

Egg-Drop Soup: This is simply a good canned chicken or beef consommé into which beaten eggs are stirred just before serving. To serve 24, count on 4½ quarts of consommé. Beat 6 eggs. Bring consommé to a rapid boil and gradually pour in the eggs, whisking rapidly with a whisk. The eggs will form delicate threads.

REGIONAL AND SEASONAL MENUS

Many organizations base a yearly dinner around their local specialties. It might be fun, however, to upset the applecart and for a club in New England to stage a Texas Hash Party, while a group in Texas arranges for a Deep South Fish Fry.

Regional dinners lend themselves well to a theme, and decorations as well as food can augment the theme. When you think of New England, for instance, you think of fishing boats, fishing nets, lobster pots, clam rakes, and cranberry bogs. The South brings to mind the plantations and the cotton fields, while Texas recalls the open plains and cowboys and rodeos.

Seasonal dinners are, perhaps, the easiest of all; a few bunches of spring flowers or bundles of fall leaves, for example, are all that are needed to set the stage. Foods in season are plentiful and flavorful and less expensive than at other times of the year.

The following are only a few regional and seasonal menu suggestions that are suitable for serving a crowd.

A TEXAS DINNER

CHEESE DIP WITH SESAME SEEDS

FRITOS

TEXAS HASH*

BUTTERED CARROTS   STEAMED BROCCOLI

WHOLE-WHEAT BREAD

COLESLAW

PECAN PUDDING

COFFEE

A NEW ENGLAND DINNER

CLAM CONSOMMÉ *or* CHOWDER

NEW ENGLAND BOILED DINNER*

or

BOSTON BAKED BEANS*

STEAMED BROWN BREAD

BOSTON CREAM PIE, RICE *or* INDIAN PUDDING

TEA *or* COFFEE

A DEEP-SOUTH DINNER

MINIATURE CRAB CAKES

BRUNSWICK STEW*

or

SOUTHERN-FRIED CHICKEN *or* CHICKEN POT PIES*

HOT CORN BREAD

WATERMELON *or* LADY BALTIMORE CAKE

COFFEE

A NEW ORLEANS DINNER

CELERY, RADISHES, OLIVES

SHRIMP *or* FISH AND RICE LOUISIANA

PIMIENTO SALAD

HOT FRENCH BREAD

CHOCOLATE MOUSSE

or

ICE CREAM AND PRALINE COOKIES

COFFEE

A PENNSYLVANIA DINNER

CHICKEN NOODLE SOUP

or

PEPPERPOT SOUP

BAKED HAM *or* SPARERIBS

CANDIED SWEET POTATOES   LIMA BEANS

SWEET ROLLS

SHOOFLY PIE *or* DUTCH DOUGHNUTS

COFFEE

A WEST-COAST DINNER

AVOCADO COCKTAIL

SALMON CROQUETTES

or

ROAST TURKEY WITH STUFFING

BLACKBERRY JAM

BUTTERED PEAS *or* SUCCOTASH

APPLE PIE WITH CHEESE

or

BAKED PEARS *or* FRESH *or* CANNED FIGS

TEA *or* COFFEE

A SPRING MENU

RADISH ROSES *or* WATER-CRESS SOUP

BLANKET OF VEAL* *or* CHICKEN SALAD

STRAWBERRY SHORTCAKE

TEA *or* COFFEE

Water-Cress Soup: Heat beef or chicken consommé until steaming hot (choose beef, if the main dish is to be chicken). Into each cup, at serving time, drop a spray of water cress.

FALL MENUS

Menu 1

MELON SLICE

BAKED HAM *or* ROAST PORK

SWEET POTATO AND PECAN PUFFS   BUTTERED SPINACH

CANNED PEACHES WITH RASPBERRY SAUCE *or* APPLE COBBLER

TEA *or* COFFEE

Menu 2

CONSOMMÉ WITH RICE

STUFFED VEAL BIRDS*

BUTTERED CARROTS   CHEESED CAULIFLOWER

PUMPKIN PIE À LA MODE

TEA *or* COFFEE

Menu 3

CREAM OF MUSHROOM SOUP

CHEESE STRAWS

HAM IN MUSTARD SAUCE

BRUSSELS SPROUTS

BUTTERED NEW POTATOES

FRESH PEAR AND CHEESE

TEA *or* COFFEE

Menu 4

CELERY, RADISHES, OLIVES

or

CHEESE-STUFFED CELERY

or

PIMIENTO AND ANCHOVY CANAPÉS

HAMBURGERS ON TOAST WITH GRAVY

or

MAGNIFICENT MEAT BALLS

or

MEAT LOAF*

BUTTERED BROCCOLI

BAKED POTATOES AU GRATIN* *or* BAKED POTATO

BUTTERSCOTCH PIE

TEA *or* COFFEE

Hamburgers are in season all year round. To serve this menu for a spring supper, change the butterscotch pie to fresh cherry or rhubarb. For a summer menu, blueberry pie à la mode would be a good choice for dessert.

Pimiento and Anchovy Canapés: Cover buttered toast with canned, sliced pimiento. Cover pimiento with a latticework of flat anchovy fillets. Cut toast into 4 pieces and serve 2 pieces per person.

WINTER MENUS

Menu 1

ONION SOUP

BAKED SAUERKRAUT WITH SAUSAGES

BOILED POTATOES

BUTTERSCOTCH SAUCE AND DESSERT

TEA *or* COFFEE

Butterscotch Sauce and Dessert: A wonderfully easy and remarkably delicious butterscotch sauce can be made by cooking unopened cans of sweetened condensed milk in boiling water to cover for 2 hours. Cool cans before opening. The milk will have turned to a rich caramel sauce, which may be stored in the refrigerator. For a quick dessert: break ladyfingers or spongecake into serving dishes, cover with the caramel sauce, and sprinkle with pecan halves. Top with whipped cream.

Menu 2

STUFFED EGGS

LAMB STEW   PARSLEY POTATOES

SALAD AND CHEESE

APPLE AND ORANGE COMPOTE

TEA *or* COFFEE

Menu 3

TOMATO JUICE COCKTAIL

BEEF STEW

PARSLEY POTATOES   BUTTERED CARROTS

TOSSED SALAD

BAKED APPLES *or* MINCE PIE

TEA *or* COFFEE

Menu 4

CREAM OF LENTIL SOUP

OYSTER LOAF *or* SALMON LOAF

STUFFED TOMATOES

APPLE PIE À LA MODE

TEA *or* COFFEE

CHAPTER 2

Special Occasions

Teas, buffet suppers and luncheons, smorgasbord spreads and picnics are all means of gathering a group together for the friendliness and good companionship that inevitably results from the sharing of food. Themes, decorations, costumes, games, and entertainment can add to the pleasure and gaiety of the occasion. All are excellent ways to entertain a large group with comparative ease; all can be simple and informal, or as elaborate as you wish to make them.

TEA PARTIES

Teas are, perhaps, one of the most gracious yet easiest ways to supply a hot drink and simple refreshments at the conclusion of a committee meeting, to entertain visiting dignitaries, lecturers, the new minister and his wife, or to raise needed funds for a cause that is near and dear to one's heart.

The scope of a tea is limitless. It may be very informal for a dozen or so people, it may be more formal, when invitations are extended to your entire organization, church, or club, or it may be a formal tea, on which many months have been spent in planning its execution, such as an International Tea or a summer garden-party tea. These comprehensive tea occasions are usually fund-raising affairs and need adequate committees to handle the various aspects of decoration, food and service, entertainment, and publicity. Much of the organizational planning and advice given in the chapter on *Bazaars and Fairs* can be applied to a tea of such scope.

About the only differences between a formal and an informal tea are the elaborateness of the food and the table appointments.

Both tea and coffee are usually served and, in warm weather, iced tea or punch is always welcome. The tea and coffee services are placed at either end of the table and are served by friends of the hostess; it is considered an honor to be asked to "pour."

For its charm the tea table depends entirely on the attractiveness of the appointments. Set up a long table at one end of the room, closest to the kitchen or food supply. Select a pretty table covering of linen, damask, or other material. Decorative paper can be used, but would not be appropriate at a formal tea. Arrange a large bowl of fresh flowers in the center. At one end of the table, tea is served from a large tray holding the tea urn, the hot-water urn, milk or cream pitcher, sugar bowl and tongs, teaspoons and a tea strainer. You will also need a small plate to hold thin slices of lemon for those who prefer this to milk. Each slice may be studded with a clove, if desired. The coffee tray is placed at the other end with the coffee urn, large cream pitcher, large sugar bowl, and coffee spoons, and plates should be stacked on the table with a napkin on each.

The silver and dishes as well as the food should be dainty, colorful, and pleasingly arranged. The more formal the occasion, the more beautiful the table appointments.

As for the food served at any tea party, there are no hard and fast rules: toasted English muffins with marmalade or jam, and store cookies are quite acceptable for a moment of relaxation at the conclusion of a P.T.A. or committee meeting. Certain items, such as tiny baking-powder biscuits or toasted-cheese rolls, fall more readily into the informal than the formal category, while iced *petits fours*—by no means improper at any tea—are more suited to the strictly formal.

Food served at a tea may include any or all of the following:

Dainty sandwiches of assorted breads, such as nut, orange, date, and thinly sliced white and whole-wheat. The sandwiches may be ribbon, checkerboard, pinwheel, rolled, two-toned, or cut into various small shapes (crusts are always trimmed from tea sandwiches).

Cheese wafers, cheese straws, miniature cream puffs filled with cream cheese, mashed avocado, or chicken salad.

Small iced cakes or *petits fours*, miniature cupcakes, thinly sliced pound cake, small pastries, cookies, macaroons, shortbread.

Salted or spiced nuts, preserved ginger, candied peel, pastel mints, and stuffed or candied fruit.

A DOZEN TEA-SANDWICH RECIPES

Sandwiches, made in advance, should be wrapped in transparent film or in waxed paper, then in a damp cloth, and kept cold. Count on approximately 32 tea sandwiches per 1-pound loaf of thinly sliced bread.

Water-Cress or Asparagus Rolls

Roll trimmed bread slices with a rolling pin to flatten. Spread with mayonnaise, mixed with a little mustard. Place a tender stalk of cooked asparagus, trimmed to length, or a spray of water cress on each slice and roll up. Fasten with a toothpick and place rolls in a pan. Cover with a damp towel and chill for several hours. Remove picks before serving.

Crab-Meat or Lobster-Butter Sandwiches

Flake and finely chop 1 can Alaska King Crab, or ½ pound lump crab meat or cooked lobster meat. Gradually beat in 1 cup butter and flavor mixture with lemon juice and salt. Spread between thinly sliced bread, trim and cut into squares.

Avocado and Chive Sandwiches

Peel and remove seed from a ripe avocado. Mash with a silver fork, and mix into it 2 tablespoons chopped chives and 2 teaspoons lemon juice. Season with salt. Spread between thin slices whole-wheat bread (or use one slice whole wheat and one white), trim and cut into triangles.

Chicken Ham Filling

Mix 1½ cups cooked ground white meat of chicken with ½ cup ground cooked ham. Stir in ½ cup finely chopped almonds and 2 tablespoons drained crushed pineapple. Add enough mayonnaise to moisten to spreading consistency.

Cucumber Sandwiches

Peel and slice cucumbers very thinly and sprinkle with salt and chopped parsley. Arrange slices between two very thin, buttered slices of white bread. Trim and cut into rectangles. If desired, spread sides with mayonnaise and dip into minced parsley.

Cheese Nut Spread

Cream 8 ounces soft cream cheese and 2 tablespoons cream or sour cream. Stir in ¼ cup finely chopped pecans or walnuts.

Water-Cress Cheese Spread

Cream 8 ounces soft cream cheese and 2 tablespoons cream. Stir in ½ cup minced water-cress leaves.

Egg Spread

Press 6 hard-cooked egg yolks through a fine sieve and mix with 2 tablespoons each mayonnaise and cream. Season with celery salt.

Ham Nut Spread

Mix 1 cup ground cooked ham with ¼ cup mayonnaise, ½ teaspoon dry mustard, 1 tablespoon chopped chives, salt to taste, and ¼ cup chopped walnuts.

Mushroom Butter

Sauté ½ pound fresh mushrooms, sliced, in ¼ cup butter for 5 minutes, or until tender. Do not let them brown. Into container of an electric blender put mushrooms and pan juices. Add ½ cup soft butter, ¼ teaspoon freshly ground pepper, ¼ teaspoon salt, and 3 tablespoons chicken broth. Cover and blend on high speed for 20 seconds or until smooth, stopping to stir down if necessary. Chill and spread between thinly sliced bread. Trim and cut into small shapes.

Water-Cress Butter

Combine finely minced leaves from ½ bunch of water cress, ½ cup soft butter, 1 tablespoon lemon juice, and salt to taste. Chill and spread between thin slices of bread. Trim and cut into small shapes.

Nut Butter

Combine ¾ cup ground pecans or walnuts (3 ounces), ½ cup minced celery, ¼ teaspoon salt, and ½ cup soft butter. Chill and spread between thin slices of bread.

TEA FOR FIFTY SERVINGS

The most satisfactory solution to serving tea to a large group is to make a tea concentrate, which can be served from a tea urn and diluted to the proper strength with hot water from a large samovar.

For 50 servings, bring 6 cups freshly drawn cold water to a full rolling boil. Rinse teapot with boiling water, add ¼ pound good tea, and pour in the 6 cups boiling water. Cover and let brew for 5 minutes, stirring once or twice. Strain into serving teapot. Use 1 part tea to 8 parts very hot water.

For every 50 cups you should count on 1 pound lump sugar, 1½ pints milk, and 4 lemons, thinly sliced.

COFFEE FOR FORTY SERVINGS (Drip Method)

Most church and club organizations have large drip coffeepots. You will need 1 pound drip-grind coffee for every 40 cups. Place coffee in the coffee basket under the water spreader. Pour 8 quarts boiling water over the coffee, about 2 quarts at a time. Wait until the first amount has dripped through before adding more. Keep a large supply of boiling water on hand so you can make fresh batches as needed.

For every 40 cups, count on 1 quart coffee cream and ¾ pound granulated sugar.

STOCKPOT COFFEE FOR FORTY

With no other equipment than a coffee bag or piece of cheese-cloth and a large kettle containing 2 gallons of cold water, good coffee can be made. Just remember that coffee should NEVER be boiled. If it is, an undesirable flavor change takes place.

Put 1 pound coffee, regular grind, into a coffee bag, or a bag made of several thicknesses of cheesecloth. Lower it into the kettle of water and bring the water just to a boil three times, without actually letting it boil. Each time the water begins to bubble, remove kettle from heat, plunge bag up and down several times and let stand for 5 minutes before reheating.

INSTANT COFFEE FOR FORTY

Actually, the larger the quantity of instant coffee made, the better it is. Stir 4 ounces instant coffee (regular or espresso) into 2 gallons (8 quarts) boiling water. Keep hot, but do not let it boil.

TIPS ON MAKING GOOD COFFEE

1. Be sure the coffee maker is thoroughly clean. Rinse with hot water before using. Wash thoroughly after use, rinse with hot water, and dry.
2. Begin with freshly drawn cold water.
3. Serve coffee as soon as possible after brewing.
4. Use the correct amount of coffee: 2 level measuring table-spoons or one standard coffee measure to each ¾ standard measuring cup or 6 fluid ounces of water, as follows:

Average 5½ ounce Servings	Amount of Coffee	Amount of Water
20	½ pound	1 gallon (4 quarts)
40	1 pound	2 gallons (8 quarts)
100	2½ pounds	5 gallons (20 quarts)

ICED COFFEE

Make double-strength coffee. Use half as much water with the usual amount of coffee for 20, 40, or 100 servings. This extra strength allows for the dilution caused by the melting ice. Pour the hot coffee over ice cubes in tall glasses and serve black or with cream and sugar.

TEA AND ORANGE PUNCH
(Makes 4½ quarts)

1 *quart strong tea*
1 *quart orange juice*
1 *cup each lemon juice, grapefruit juice, raspberry juice*
3 *cups sugar syrup (boil half sugar and half water until clear)*
1 *quart ginger ale*

Combine ingredients and pour over block of ice. Garnish with orange slices.

GINGER PUNCH
(Makes 5 quarts)

2 *quarts sweet cider*　　　*Sprigs of mint*
1 *cup shredded pineapple*　2 *quarts ginger ale*
2 *oranges, thinly sliced*　1 *quart sparkling water*

Mix cider and prepared fruit. Chill. Pour into punch bowl with ice and add mint and remaining ingredients.

HOT CIDER PUNCH
(Makes 4 quarts)

1½ *cups brown sugar*　　　6 *sticks cinnamon*
2 *teaspoons whole cloves*　4 *quarts sweet cider*
2 *teaspoons whole allspice*

Mix brown sugar and spices. Add cider, bring to a boil, and simmer for 10 minutes. Strain through cheesecloth and reheat. Serve in mugs with a sprinkling of fresh nutmeg.

ORANGE GINGER PUNCH
(Makes 8 quarts)

¾ *gallon orange ice*   Cherries, strawberries, or
5 *quarts chilled ginger ale*   *orange slices*
Mint leaves

Spoon orange ice into punch bowl. Pour ginger ale over. Garnish with mint and fruit.

TEA AND COFFEE PARTY SUGGESTIONS

Most of the following ideas can be staged either indoors or out. Outdoor tea and coffee parties can be charmingly simple or elaborate, with roving musicians, pretty costumes, and entertainment —perhaps a juggler, magician, or a trained-animal act. Hang baskets of flowers from the trees and decorate with Japanese lanterns. Arrange small tea tables on the lawn under colorful umbrellas. Serve iced tea and coffee, lemonade or punch, with a variety of sandwiches and sweets.

TEAHOUSE OF THE AUGUST MOON

Transform room or garden into a Japanese teahouse, with bamboo screens, reed mats, and Japanese lanterns. Hang a full moon high in the "sky," and serve Japanese tea. Float a tiny blossom or a rose petal in each cup. Serve fortune cookies or trinket cakes. Japanese kimonos and coolie coats and hats for costumes if desired.

GYPSY TEA

Balloons and colorful paper streamers set the stage. Gay cotton cloths on individual tea tables. Have one or more costumed fortunetellers reading the tea leaves, and be sure to leave the leaves in the tea! Dress hostesses in white blouses, colorful dirndl skirts and lots of bangles and beads. Serve ribbon sandwiches, spiced nuts, and gaily frosted cupcakes.

A BOSTON TEA PARTY

Set up rough planks on horses for tea tables and use empty wooden crates for chairs. Hurricane lamps filled with flowers for table centerpiece. Serve tea from Early American or English teapots and keep the tea warm with tea cozies. Serve Boston brown bread and cream cheese, and lobster-butter sandwiches, blueberry tarts.

CLIPPER-SHIP TEA

Cover tea tables with elaborate silks and satins and let treasure chests spill jewelry and "gold" coins onto the tables. Dress hostesses in pirate costumes and serve herb-butter sandwiches, gingerbread, and spicy cookies.

ARABIAN NIGHTS' COFFEETIME

Decorate the room with travel posters, paper lanterns; use candlelight for illumination. Ask members to come in improvised costumes with gauze veils, pantaloons, and lots of costume jewelry. The score of *Kismet* would make appropriate background music.

OLD-TIME COFFEEHOUSE

Serve homemade pastries and coffee in mugs on checkered tablecloths; a candle in the center of each table.

COFFEE ROUND THE WORLD

Decorate with travel posters and serve cakes, pastries, and coffee from many lands, including large American cups of coffee as well as espresso, cappuccino, and café au lait.

A FRENCH SIDEWALK CAFÉ

Set small tables under colorful umbrellas with a small basket of flowers on each table. Serve café au lait, hot chocolate, and custard ice cream. Costume the hostesses in pretty French peasant dresses.

PICNICS AND BARBECUES

Summer outings to a picnic spot, a beach beside the ocean, or a sparkling lake, can be a most enjoyable way of getting a group together, without the work generally associated with more formal functions.

Keep your picnics simple—the simpler the better—for outdoor parties should be more fun than labor. An advance trip to the picnic area should be made to evaluate the cooking and serving facilities, the available space for games and sports, parking and rest-room facilities, and any rules or regulations connected with a public picnic ground. If the spot is near the water, you will need to know if bathhouses will be available. Once you return from your scouting trip, be sure to post conspicuously all the advantages of the place that has been selected. Let your members know how to dress, what to expect, and what games or other recreational activities they should be prepared for.

If there are no benches or stools at the picnic site, your members might like to bring along folding chairs or waterpoof cushions. If at the beach, suggest each member bring a blanket or terrycloth beach towel large enough to put the food on to protect it from the sand.

There's something about a summer outing that gives a healthy zest to appetites. So whether you plan a picnic, barbecue, or a sociable clambake, be sure to plan on plenty of food. Such food as raw vegetables—radishes, scallions, carrot sticks, cauliflower, cucumber sticks, cherry tomatoes—make refreshing picnic "nibble" food. Take along some salt or a bowl of mayonnaise into which the vegetables can be dipped. Bread-and-butter sandwiches, with side trays of cold cuts and sliced tomatoes, salad greens and macaroni salads, are often preferable to made-in-advance sandwiches, which can become crushed, wilted, and unappetizing during transportation. Set everything up smorgasbord style, and let everybody help himself. If you do make up sandwiches in advance, stick to sliced cold turkey or chicken, cold roast beef, baked ham, Swiss cheese, or thin Bermuda-onion sandwiches, which also travel well. And don't forget the pickles and olives—they're a MUST. Melons are a good idea for dessert. They stay cold and fresh. Take along sharp knives for slicing and let the melons be eaten out of hand. Chocolate cake, apple, blueberry, or cherry pies, and cookies are all fine picnic fare.

Plan and organize every detail of your summer outing. Enlist enough helpers to buy supplies, make and wrap the edibles, pack and transport the equipment to the picnic area, so that all will run smoothly and not too much work or responsibility will fall on the shoulders of just a few.

Enlist the men to help tote and officiate in other capacities. If the picnic site is equipped with barbecue pits, you may want to plan your menu around hamburgers, hot dogs, or fried chicken. Let the men officiate at the barbecue and be responsible for the transportation of the kindling, charcoal, and all necessary barbecue equipment. The amount of equipment will depend on the number of people you plan to serve efficiently and the number of barbecue cooks needed to cook or heat the food.

Be sure to have plenty of disposable napkins, cups, and plates.

Aluminum, plastic, or steel forks and spoons are much more satisfactory to eat from than the pressed-paper kind, yet are lightweight to transport to the picnic area.

Don't forget lots of large paper bags for garbage disposal and several rolls of paper towels for quick clean-up jobs.

Pack all foods, both hot and cold, in insulated carrying bags, or wrap containers of food in several thicknesses of newspapers. Carry beverages, hot and cold, to the picnic spot in large Thermos jugs.

Fresh vegetables and salad greens should be packed in plastic bags and kept cold, on ice if possible. Mix the greens with the dressing at the last minute, for there is nothing more disappointing than a warm or wilted salad. Dressings and sauces travel well in lightweight plastic containers. Have fruit thoroughly chilled, wrap it first in foil, then in several layers of newspapers to keep it cold and fresh.

Here are a few picnic suggestions for palatable portables:

STUFFED-TOMATO SANDWICHES
(Makes 12 stuffed-tomato sandwiches)

In a bowl beat 8 ounces soft cream cheese with 2 tablespoons chopped parsley, 1 tablespoon grated onion, ¼ cup drained pickle relish, and salt and pepper to taste. Cut large ripe beefsteak tomatoes into thick slices. Put slices together two by two, sandwich style, with about 1½ tablespoons of the filling between. Wrap individually in foil and chill.

STUFFED EGGS
(Serves 12)

Cut 12 hard-cooked eggs in half and scoop out yolks. Combine yolks with 1 cup shredded natural Cheddar cheese, 1 teaspoon dry mustard, ½ teaspoon Tabasco, ½ cup cream, ¾ teaspoon salt, and ⅓ cup finely chopped stuffed olives. Beat until smooth. Fill egg whites and put halves back together again. Wrap each egg in foil and chill.

POTATO FRANK SALAD
(Serves 12)

1 *pound frankfurters*
4 *pounds potatoes, cooked, peeled, and sliced*
1 *cup finely chopped celery*
1 *cup sliced radishes*
1 *large onion, finely chopped*

1 *cucumber, peeled, seeded, and chopped*
1½ *cups mayonnaise*
1 *tablespoon vinegar or lemon juice*
2 *teaspoons salt*
¼ *teaspoon pepper*

Simmer franks in boiling water for 10 minutes. Drain, cool, and slice. Combine sliced franks with potatoes in mixing bowl. Add celery, radishes, onion, and cucumber, and toss lightly. Combine mayonnaise, vinegar or lemon juice, salt and pepper. Pour dressing over salad mixture and mix well. Chill.

HAM-'N'-CABBAGE SALAD
(Serves 12)

6 *cups shredded cabbage*
2 *medium carrots, grated*
1 *green pepper, finely chopped*
1 *large onion, finely chopped*

½ *cup chopped parsley*
1 *pound sliced cooked ham, shredded*
1 *cup French dressing*
Salt and pepper to taste

In large mixing bowl toss together vegetables and meat. Add French dressing and toss well. Correct seasoning with salt and pepper.

GRILLED FRANKS

Slit the skin diagonally so the frankfurters won't burst in cooking. Place on broiling grill and broil over glowing coals until browned on both sides. Serve sizzling hot with hot buttered buns, mustard and pickle relish.

GRILLED KNACKWURST

Split knackwurst without cutting all the way through. Insert a strip of Cheddar or Swiss cheese, wrap each in a strip of bacon and secure with picks. Grill over glowing coals until bacon is cooked and cheese is melted. Serve with sauerkraut, if desired.

GRILLED HAM STEAKS

Combine 1 cup each molasses or honey and vinegar and 3 teaspoons dry mustard. Brush on individual ham steaks and grill for 3 to 5 minutes on each side, brushing often with the sauce. The sauce is sufficient quantity to glaze 24 individual ham-steak servings.

BARBECUE AND ICE-CREAM PICNIC

This is the kind of a party in which everyone participates. Only one outdoor grill is needed to feed many, but you will have to gather together one old-fashioned ice-cream freezer (gallon capacity) for every 16 guests. You'll also need quantities of crushed ice and rock salt. People wait their turn as the corn and chicken come hot off the grill. Let the children turn the crank of the ice-cream freezers, and the fathers can take over when the turning gets rough.

The Menu

CELERY, SCALLIONS, RADISHES

PRECOOKED BARBECUED CHICKEN

POTATO SALAD *or* POTATO CHIPS

SLICED BEEFSTEAK TOMATOES

CORN ON THE COB

HOMEMADE ICE CREAM

PRECOOKED CHICKEN

For 48 people, you'll need 12 broilers. Have each broiler cut into 4 pieces—two thigh-and-leg portions and two wing-and-breast portions. Sprinkle pieces with salt and pepper, and broil about 5 inches below the heat for 10 minutes on each side, beginning skin-side down. Baste occasionally with melted butter or hot oil. Cool chicken thoroughly, then wrap.

At serving time, dip each piece of chicken into barbecue sauce and heat on the grill, turning each piece once and basting again with sauce.

BARBECUE SAUCE
(For 48 servings)

4 *cloves garlic, minced* 1 *large onion, minced*
1 *cup vinegar or lemon juice* 2 *teaspoons dry mustard*
2 *cups cooking oil* ½ *cup tomato catsup*
2 *teaspoons salt* 1 *cup water*
1 *tablespoon prepared horse-*
   radish

Combine all ingredients and take in pint jars to the barbecue.

CORN ON THE COB

Count on 2 ears per person.

Strip husks and silk from corn. Spread corn with soft butter and dust with salt and paprika. Wrap each ear in aluminum foil. Place ears of corn on the grill and cook for 15 to 20 minutes, turning frequently.

THE CLAMBAKE

If one or more members of your organization have had experience conducting a clambake, you can do it yourself; otherwise you'd better plan to hire a bake master, for it is no easy task. Without a clambake master, you'll need a general director and several committees of both men and women. The male committees are responsible for gathering the driftwood, seaweed and rocks, building a fire, and supervising the bake. Female committees are responsible for purchasing all food and other supplies, scrubbing the clams and preparing the food, ready to put it on the fire.

A clambake isn't a clambake without lots of food, so count on a bushel of clams for 32 people or 1 quart clams per person and 1 lobster apiece.

The Menu

STEAMED CLAMS

LOBSTERS   FISH FILLETS

LINK SAUSAGES

WHITE AND SWEET POTATOES

ONIONS   CORN ON THE COB

QUARTERED CHICKENS

BREAD

WATERMELON

FOOD PREPARATION

Scrub clams with a stiff brush or hose off under heavy stream of water. Remove the heavy outer husks from the corn, leaving on the tender inner husks. Peel onions, scrub potatoes, and wrap fish fillets and sausages in pieces of cheesecloth, one serving per cheesecloth wrap, that is, one fish fillet and two sausages.

Miscellaneous items from attic and cellar can be used to add charm, color, and imaginative effects for any occasion.

1. Old-fashioned candlemaker is topped with artificial or fresh flowers and a spray of ivy. Candlemaker can hold water to keep fresh flowers alive.

2. Wooden bucket is piled high with colorful balls of assorted yarn. Wooden knitting needles and a few flower heads add interest. This might be used as a display at the knitting table of a fair.

3. Antique or dime-store lamp chimneys filled with fresh or artificial flowers make attractive table centerpieces.

4. Cranberry scoop is filled with shiny apples, ivy, and bayberry. Any fall fruit or vegetables could be used and a wooden cheese box or shaker box could replace the scoop. When used for a table centerpiece, the fruit might be eaten for dessert.

Roadside weeds, wild flowers, rocks, stumps, dried flowers, branches, berries, and leaves all make simple and inexpensive decorations.

5. Masses of goldenrod or other tall weeds such as bulrushes or pampas grass set into large containers make good arrangements for entrance to a hall; can transform a bare room into one of interest.

6. An old stump makes an intriguing centerpiece. Decorate it with ivy, moss, a few artificial butterflies or a real bird's nest.

7. An arrangement of dried flowers, leaves, berries, and pampas grass in a long wicker basket is a good centerpiece for a long table. Flowers and leaves can be gilded or spray-painted in various gay colors.

Fall or spring fruits and vegetables make striking displays for table centerpiece or for bazaar booths. The combination of colors can be purposely contrasting or subtly monochromatic.

8. Huge pumpkin is surrounded by a variety of squash. Green pepper and parsley add colorful touches.

9. Large garden cabbage, red or green, has spray of flowers tucked into leaves. Other fruit and vegetables complete the arrangement.

10. Baskets of fresh fruit for table centerpiece might be served as a final course to a luncheon or supper—the first course at breakfast.

11. A gypsy theme is always appealing to teen-agers. Toy tambourines, dime-store beads, play coins, and small bou quets of flowers make colorfu and gay table decorations.

12. Children are delighted by an arrangement of blocks, toys, and trinkets.

13. Toy cash registers topped with artificial flowers, play money, and ticker tape make an amusing and eye-catching display for any money-raising event.

14. An arrangement of saws, hammers, and other construction tools set against a painted stepladder is a meaningful décor for a Labor Day party or a father-and-son banquet. Supper tables might be made of planks set on ladders.

Oriental moods can be expressed with a minimum of colorful and inexpensive items.

15. Yellow mums, fortun cookies, fans, tiny umbrell set beneath a wind chin make a good vertical arrang ment against a colorful bac ground.

16. Small teakettles and cups filled with flowers make charming table centerpiece set beneath a small umbrella.

17. A French atmosphere is easily established by a basket of long loaves of French bread decorated with flowers and ribbon streamers.

18. Bullfighter's *banderilla*, made from wooden poles twisted with crepe paper, are stuck into a basket filled with crushed tissue paper and surrounded by straw or tissue-paper beads to illustrate a Mexican theme.

Straw hat filled with arcial or fresh fruit, leaves, d flowers set on a piece of striped material or table-th quickly establishes a ribbean theme.

20. Wooden shoes, "potted" with artificial tulips fashioned from self-sealing satintone ribbon, and a Dutch pipe carry out a Dutch theme and is also a good display for a flower or bulb table at a fair.

21. Simplicity is the basis of all Scandinavian décor. Tall tapers set into a simple wooden container of pine branches are particularly Danish in effect.

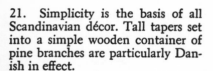

THE BAKE

Build a platform of stones from 10 to 12 feet in diameter. In the center build a tremendous pile of wood and stones: a layer of stones, a layer of wood, a layer of stones, a layer of wood, and a final layer of stones. The stones should be about the size of large melons. Have plenty of extra wood to add to the fire. The fire must burn furiously for about 3 hours, until the stones become red hot. Rake away the wood, leaving just the hot stones. With a large pitchfork put a layer of wet seaweed, about 1 foot deep, on the hot stones. The food is placed on the seaweed in layers, beginning first with the food that cooks the fastest—the clams and fish fillets, then the lobster and corn; chickens next, and finally the potatoes. A layer of seaweed should be put between each layer of food and the food covered with another thick layer of seaweed.

Cover the top layer of seaweed with a heavy tarpaulin, large enough to cover the pile of food and the stone platform. Seal the edges tightly with stones or preferably sand to keep in the heat and let the food bake for about 1 hour, or until potatoes on top of the pile of food are done. If a large kettle of butter is placed on top of the tarpaulin, it will melt as the food steams to savory perfection.

If desired, the lobster and corn can be cooked separately from the clams, fish, and potatoes in the bake. The chickens can be broiled over charcoal and added to the bake just long enough to reheat them.

There are many different ways of conducting a clambake; this is only one! Every coastal state will have its own method which is, of course, the only *correct* way. Some diehards will claim that chickens have no place in a clambake; others will be horrified at the inclusion of sausages. Many will insist that the fire must be built in a pit dug in the sand. No matter how the bake is conducted, and no matter what is included in the menu (leave out what you wish), a clambake is bound to be a lot of fun. The important thing to remember is to have plenty of food for everyone.

BUFFETS AND SMORGASBORDS

For organizations without extensive cooking facilities, the most successful group functions are generally planned around a buffet or a smorgasbord to which members each donate one dish to serve from 8 to 12. While similar in service, the distinguishing difference between the two meals is that at a buffet, everybody serves themselves to the same dishes; a smorgasbord is more elaborate and the table is set with a tremendous variety of dishes from which the guests can choose. In both, all dishes, hot and cold, including salads, rolls, and relishes are placed on the table. Dessert and coffee are usually served at another table or after the big table has been completely cleared of the dishes that make up the main part of the meal.

BUFFETS

Almost any meal, including breakfast, can be served buffet style. It is the most convenient way to serve relatively large groups of people. It is especially valuable for creating an atmosphere of informality and friendliness either among an intimate group or when strangers are present or for an occasion which mixes adults and children. The menu may be as simple or as elaborate as you wish to make it. It is generally limited to two courses, the main course and dessert, but a hot or cold consommé, tomato juice, or fruit-juice cocktail may be served, preferably in an annex room, before the guests gather in the dining room where the buffet table is set.

The success of such a party depends greatly on the attractiveness of the buffet, the arrangement and variety, and diversity of colors, flavors, and textures of the foods selected for the menu. The general effect should be one of harmony and organization, and no matter how ambitious you wish to make the affair, it is better to limit the number of dishes to those that can be nicely served than to have more food than can be served properly.

The table should be covered with cloth or paper. Gay colors can be introduced in both the table covering and the serving dishes, in the garnishings on the dishes, and in the centerpiece. Frequently a center composition of fruit, vegetables, gourds, and nuts is more suitable than the more formal flower arrangements.

The food on the buffet table should be arranged in the order in which it is ordinarily served; the meat first, then the vegetables, relishes, and salads. When no seating arrangements are provided, the plates are stacked at the beginning of the buffet table and the silverware, folded in a napkin, is placed last. When seating arrangements are part of the scheme, the tables should be set in advance with silver, napkins, water, rolls or bread, and butter. It is better to have assistants serve the hot beverage to the guests at the table and to clear the table while the guests return to the buffet, now set for dessert.

TEN TIPS FOR BUFFET SERVICE

1. Keep the service as simple as possible.
2. Avoid foods which are soupy on the plate or foods which require a special utensil such as a bread-and-butter knife.
3. Hot foods should be those that can be kept hot without spoiling flavor or consistency.
4. Garnish each dish imaginatively and attractively.
5. Include an assortment of pickles and relishes.
6. Include a platter of celery, radishes, and olives.
7. Serve hot foods in chafing dishes or in *réchauds* set over candles.
8. Serve cold foods cold, preferably on a bed of crushed ice.
9. A sweet jam or jelly makes a pleasing color and flavor note to most buffet menus.
10. Serve dessert as a separate course.

The Menu

Buffet menus can be as simple as a platter of sliced turkey, ham, and cheese, served with a big bowl of tossed green salad, potato salad, and buttered rolls or bread. Many of the menus given in the preceding chapter are suitable for buffets, but usually any first course is eliminated. If you wish to include a first course, make it something that can be sipped from a glass such as:

CONSOMME ON THE ROCKS FOR 100

You'll need 100 old-fashioned-type glasses and ice.

In large serving pitchers combine equal parts of chicken consommé and beef bouillon. For each 2 quarts stir in 1 tablespoon Worcestershire sauce. To serve: Put an ice cube into a glass, pour the consommé over the ice and garnish with a thin half slice of lemon. For 100 servings, count on 2 quarts each of chicken consommé and beef bouillon, 2 tablespoons Worcestershire sauce, and 6 lemons.

HOLIDAY HOT CONSOMME

Combine 4 parts chicken consommé and 1 part jellied madrilène. Add a few drops red food coloring. Heat and correct seasoning to taste. Serve 5 to 6 ounces per person with a thin half slice of lemon and a spray of parsley in each cup.

REVEILLON BUFFET SUPPER

Serve on Christmas Eve after midnight service.

FRENCH ONION SOUP

YULE LOG

COFFEE

AN EASTER BUFFET

EGGS À LA RUSSE

PUMPERNICKEL BREAD AND BUTTER SANDWICH FINGERS

BAKED HAM

PARSLEY NEW POTATOES   FRESH ASPARAGUS

SMALL BAKING-POWDER BISCUITS

LAMB CAKE

COFFEE

A THANKSGIVING BUFFET

CHICKEN CLAM CONSOMMÉ

ROAST TURKEY WITH OLD-FASHIONED BREAD STUFFING

PAN GRAVY

MASHED POTATOES AND TURNIPS   CREAMED ONIONS

BUTTERED BRUSSELS SPROUTS

SPICED CRAB APPLES   CANDIED CRANBERRIES

PUMPKIN PIE

COFFEE

CHICKEN CLAM CONSOMME

Combine equal parts chicken consommé and bottled clam juice, and flavor to taste with lemon juice. Serve with a sprinkling of chopped parsley and a side dish of pilot biscuits.

THE SMORGASBORD

For a smorgasbord, ask each member to make one dish to serve a predetermined number of people. Food supplies may be purchased out of a general fund and the dishes prepared at home by the members, but it is more profitable by far if each member is willing to contribute the ingredients that go into the dish in addition to the time it takes to make it.

You should know in advance who plans to contribute or make what dish, so you don't end up with a dozen potato salads and no dessert. The correct proportion of hot to cold and savory to sweet dishes must be planned. Many people have their own favorite smorgasbord-type casserole, salad, or dessert, which they might prefer to make, providing it fits into the over-all menu, otherwise supply them with a typed recipe to follow.

A smorgasbord is designed to be a feast to the eye as well as the appetite, so food should be deliberately planned to vary in color, shape, and texture. Guests help themselves buffet fashion.

The food should be arranged on the service table in such a way that guests can make their selection from among the many dishes quickly, without lingering too long and holding up service. The use of tiers on the table, built of wooden blocks, contributes to the speed of service as well as to the over-all display effect.

For a very large gathering it is wise to set up two tables, so that two lines may be served at once. Duplicate dishes should be placed on each table, so that the food served on one is identical with the other. For groups under fifty, where you have a great variety of dishes, you might serve the cold dishes first, then the hot. At a traditional Swedish smorgasbord, the meal always begins with bread, butter, and herring, followed by the cold foods, then the hot, and finally the dessert and beverage. Clean dishes are supplied with each course.

Tables should be available where guests may sit to enjoy the feast. Small tables are more popular than large, for it is easier for guests to sit down and arise from small tables. They also make for more intimate conversational groups, and one or more small tables can be put together for a hostess to entertain a group of personal friends.

If there is room, set up tables in an anteroom from which all breads and desserts can be dispatched. You should have a variety of at least three desserts; cut them into serving portions, arrange them on wagons, and let pretty-costumed waitresses roll them to the tables for the diners' selection.

For a large number of guests, give them numbers as they arrive and let them be served in that order, or schedule different sittings: one at five P.M., another at six, and a third, when necessary, at seven. Tickets, which you hope to sell in advance, could be a different color for each different seating.

Some organizations sponsor smorgasbords for as many as 500 guests. For such a large event, plans should be made at least two months in advance. Your president should call a meeting to "start the ball rolling." At this first get-together, the menu is planned, decorations discussed, date set, and subchairmen named.

The committee list should consist of an over-all chairman and assistant chairmen in charge of food purchasing, tickets and reservations, dining-room decorations, tables and service, hostess duties, clean-up, and publicity.

A church in Toledo, Ohio, serves an annual smorgasbord to over 500 people, with tables heavily laden with roast beef, baked ham, creamed chicken, fruit platters, shrimp, eight kinds of salads, relishes, deviled eggs, candied sweet potatoes, tomato pudding, succotash, broccoli, noodles with buttered crumbs, Swedish pancakes, orange sherbet, and angel-cake "snowballs." Sixty-five couples help prepare and serve the meal.

Almost any dish, hot or cold, is at home at a smorgasbord. It need not be Scandinavian in origin, but many with a Nordic flavor are particularly appealing.

In addition to platters of cold cuts, cheese, smoked fish, and stacks of buttered pumpernickel and rye bread, all or any of the following dishes are appropriate:

Fish Dishes: Pickled Herring, Herring and Beet Salad, Fried Sardines or Smelts, Lobster or Crab-Meat Salad, Fish in Aspic, Scalloped Salmon or Salmon Mousse, Creamed Fish au Gratin, and Anchovies.

Meat and Egg Dishes: Liver Sausage, Creamed Sweetbreads and Mushrooms in Patty Shells, Meatballs, Veal Birds, Chicken Salad, Meat Loaves, Ham Rolls Stuffed with Cheese or Liverwurst, Deviled Eggs, Sliced Tongue, Baked Ham, Roast Turkey, Creamed Chicken, Roast Spareribs, Jellied Pork and Veal, Broiled Sausages, Boiled Beef, and Kidney Stew.

Vegetable and Salad Dishes: Beets Vinaigrette, Stuffed Tomatoes or Onions, Cabbage Rolls, Tomato Aspic, Vegetable Salad in Mayonnaise, Tomatoes, Radishes, Celery and Olives, Cucumbers in French Dressing, Baked Beans, Coleslaw, Potato Salad, Macaroni Salad, Scalloped Potatoes, and Creamed Mushrooms.

Here are a few additional salads and casseroles, each to serve from 8 to 16.

LENTILS VINAIGRETTE
(Serves 12 to 16)

Cook 1 pound lentils in water to cover, for 45 to 60 minutes, or until lentils are tender. Drain and combine with 1 cup French Dressing. Season to taste with salt and pepper, and sprinkle with minced onion and parsley.

CHICKEN-LIVER SPREAD
(Makes 1 pint)

In small saucepan simmer ¾ pound chicken livers, 1 small onion, coarsely cut, and ½ cup chicken stock for 5 minutes. Empty mixture, including liquid, into container of an electric blender. Add ½ teaspoon paprika, ½ teaspoon curry powder, ½ teaspoon salt, 1 tablespoon Worcestershire sauce, and ⅛ teaspoon pepper. Cover and blend. Remove cover and, with motor on high, add 1 stick soft butter, chunk by chunk, stopping to stir down if necessary. Chill before serving.

LIVER PATE
(Makes about 1 pint)

1 *pound liverwurst*
1/8 *teaspoon thyme*
1 *tablespoon Worcestershire*
1/4 *cup sweet butter*
1/8 *teaspoon nutmeg*
1/2 *teaspoon clove*

1/4 *teaspoon pepper*
1 *tablespoon grated onion*
    and juice
1 1/2 *tablespoons chicken or*
    beef consommé

Beat all ingredients until smooth and creamy. Turn into a crock and chill until serving time.

HAM ROLLS

Spread ham slices with Chicken-Liver Spread or Liver Pâté and roll like tiny jelly rolls. Insert a sprig of parsley at each end. Arrange spiral fashion on large serving platter, and fill center of platter with radish roses, scallions, and salad greens. Recipes for Chicken-Liver Spread or Liver Pâté is sufficient stuffing for about 32 slices of ham.

PICKLED BEETS

Drain 2 cans sliced beets. Mix with 1/4 cup minced onion and 2 tablespoons chopped fresh dill. Pour over a dressing made of 4 tablespoons water, 2 tablespoons sugar, 1 teaspoon salt, and 1 cup vinegar. Chill, basting frequently with juice in dish.

SOUTHERN POT PIE
(Serves 12)

6 *tablespoons butter*
6 *tablespoons flour*
5 *cups chicken broth*
2 *cups diced chicken*
2 *cups diced ham*

2 *teaspoons salt*
1/4 *teaspoon pepper*
    Corn-batter topping (see
    below)

Melt butter and stir in flour. Gradually stir in chicken broth and cook, stirring, until sauce is smooth and thickened. Add chicken and ham and salt and pepper to taste. Pour into a baking pan (9 × 13 × 2 inches). Spread corn-batter topping over top and bake in a 400° F. oven for about 20 minutes, or until corn bread is nicely browned. Cut into 12 pieces and serve hot.

CORN-BATTER TOPPING

2 eggs
⅔ cup milk
½ cup melted shortening
1⅓ cups flour

⅔ cup corn meal
3 teaspoons baking powder
½ teaspoon salt

Beat eggs and stir in milk and shortening. Combine flour, corn meal, baking powder, and salt. Add all liquids to the dry ingredients and blend until dry ingredients are moistened. Do not stir smooth.

FIESTA CASSEROLE
(Serves 8 to 12)

8 slices bacon
2 cups chopped onion
2 large cloves garlic, minced
½ cup chopped green pepper
2 pounds ground beef
4 cans (1 pound each) kidney beans, undrained

2 cups canned tomatoes, drained and chopped
4 tablespoons tomato paste
3 tablespoons chili powder
1 teaspoon salt
½ teaspoon clove

Cut bacon slices into quarters and sauté in a 4-quart casserole until lightly browned. Add onion, garlic, green pepper, and beef, and sauté until lightly browned. Combine remaining ingredients and mix with meat mixture. Cover and bake in a 300° F. oven for 1½ hours.

CHICKEN IMPERIAL
(Serves 8)

6 cups cooked rice
2 teaspoons salt
¼ teaspoon pepper
¼ teaspoon marjoram
¼ teaspoon thyme

2 tablespoons chopped
  parsley
¼ teaspoon garlic powder
1 cup melted butter
4 broilers, split

Put cooked rice in a 3-quart shallow casserole. Combine salt, pepper, herbs, parsley, garlic powder, and butter. Arrange broilers, skin-side up, on rice and brush generously with the butter-herb mixture. Bake in a 325° F. oven for about 1 hour, or until chicken is tender and crusty. Brush with butter after 30 minutes' baking time, using all the remaining butter and herbs. Serve from the casserole.

COUNTRY STEW
(Serves 8)

7 tablespoons flour
1 teaspoon poultry seasoning
½ teaspoon pepper
2 teaspoons salt
4 pounds beef chuck, cut into
  1½-inch cubes
7 tablespoons butter or
  shortening

4 cups tomato juice
2 cups consommé
½ teaspoon thyme
½ teaspoon oregano
16 small white onions
2 cups sliced or diced carrots
2 packages frozen peas

Combine flour, poultry seasoning, pepper and salt in a paper bag. Add meat cubes and shake bag until all meat is well coated. In heavy flameproof casserole melt 5 tablespoons of the butter or shortening and in it brown meat cubes well on all sides (reserve remaining seasoned flour). Add tomato juice, consommé, thyme, and oregano. Cover and simmer for 2 hours. Add onions and carrots and continue to cook until vegetables are tender. Combine reserved flour mixture with remaining 2 tablespoons butter or shortening and stir into stew gravy. Cook, stirring, for 3 to 5 minutes. Cook peas separately according to package directions. Drain and arrange in a circle on top of the stew. Serve in the casserole.

ASPIC PIE
(Serves 8 to 10)

1 package lemon gelatin
1¼ cups hot water
1 can (8 ounces) tomato
    sauce
1 tablespoon vinegar

½ teaspoon salt
Few drops Tabasco
½ cup chopped celery
½ cup chopped stuffed olives
¼ cup minced onion

Dissolve lemon gelatin in the hot water. Stir in tomato sauce, vinegar, and seasoning. Chill until cool and beginning to set. Fold in celery, olives, and onion. Pour into 9-inch pie plate and chill until set. When set, top with a wreath of seafood salad (see below).

SEAFOOD SALAD

1 cup tuna flakes, crab meat,
    or cooked, diced shrimp
1 cup diced celery
1 teaspoon minced onion

1 teaspoon lemon juice
Salt and pepper to taste
Mayonnaise

Combine fish, celery, onion, and lemon juice and season to taste. Chill. Drain before serving and toss with just enough mayonnaise to hold the mixture together.

CREAMED OYSTERS
(Serves 16)

Serve on toast or in patty shells
1 quart freshly shucked oysters
1 pound mushrooms, sliced
4 tablespoons butter
1 cup water
1 tablespoon lemon juice
6 tablespoons butter
9 tablespoons flour
2 cups milk
2 cups cream
2 teaspoons salt
¼ teaspoon white pepper
2 tablespoons minced parsley

Simmer the oysters in their own juice for about 3 minutes, or until plump. Drain, reserving the liquid. Cut oysters in halves or quarters. Simmer mushrooms with the 4 tablespoons butter in water with lemon juice for 10 minutes. Drain and combine liquid with the oyster liquid. It should measure 1 pint.

In large saucepan melt the 6 tablespoons butter. Stir in flour and gradually stir in milk, cream, and reserved liquid. Cook, stirring, until sauce is smooth and thickened and stir in salt and pepper to taste. Stir in mushrooms, oysters, and parsley.

HOLIDAY HADDOCK AU GRATIN
(Serves 12)

4 pounds frozen haddock fillets, thawed
4 tablespoons butter
½ cup minced onion
4 tablespoons flour
2 teaspoons dry mustard
2 teaspoons salt, or to taste
¼ teaspoon pepper
½ teaspoon paprika
3 cups hot milk
1 cup grated Cheddar cheese

Arrange haddock fillets without overlapping in a buttered shallow baking pan or pans. In saucepan melt butter and in it sauté onion until onion is transparent. Stir in flour, mustard, salt, pepper, and paprika. Add milk and whisk over low heat until sauce is smooth and thickened. Add cheese and stir until cheese is melted. Spread the sauce over the fillets and bake in a 350° F. oven for 30 minutes.

BAKED COD
(Serves 8)

2 pounds cod fillets
2 cups milk
½ small onion
1 bay leaf
12 tablespoons butter
6 tablespoons flour
4 cups reserved broth plus
    milk or cream

4 hard-cooked eggs, sliced
2 teaspoons salt
½ teaspoon pepper
3 packages frozen chopped
    spinach
Grated cheese

Simmer cod fillets in the milk with onion and bay leaf for 8 to 10 minutes, or until flesh flakes easily. Strain, reserving broth. Discard onion and bay leaf and flake the fish. In saucepan melt half the butter. Stir in flour and cook, stirring, until mixture bubbles. Add reserved broth plus milk or cream to measure 4 cups and cook, stirring, until sauce is smooth and thickened. Stir in eggs and fish and half the salt and pepper. Cook spinach according to package directions. Drain and season with remaining butter, salt, and pepper. Spread spinach in bottom of a 3-quart casserole and top with the creamed fish and eggs. Sprinkle with grated cheese and bake in a 425° F. oven until top is lightly browned.

EGGS WITH SHRIMP AND MAYONNAISE
(Serves 8)

8 hard-cooked eggs
2 pounds shrimp, cooked,
    shelled and deveined
1 cup mayonnaise

1 cup cream, whipped
1 tablespoon lemon juice
4 tablespoons chopped chives
    or fresh dill

Halve eggs and arrange in center of a serving dish. Arrange shrimp in a circle around the eggs. Combine mayonnaise, cream, and lemon juice and pour over eggs. Garnish with chives or dill. Chill.

TUNA ITALIANO
(Serves 12)

1 pound elbow macaroni
4 cans (10½ ounces) cream of celery soup
2½ cups milk
3 cups grated Cheddar cheese
1 tablespoon Worcestershire sauce

½ teaspoon marjoram
Salt to taste
4 cans (7 ounces) tuna, drained and flaked
4 cups cooked peas
1 cup buttered bread crumbs

Cook macaroni according to package directions. Heat soup, milk, and cheese in saucepan. Season with Worcestershire, marjoram, and salt to taste. When cheese is melted, add tuna and peas. Arrange half the cooked drained macaroni in bottom of a greased 4-quart casserole. Pour over half the tuna-cheese mixture and repeat with remaining macaroni and sauce. Sprinkle top with bread crumbs and bake in a 325° F. oven for 30 minutes, or until crumbs are browned.

SEACOAST SALMON
(Serves 8)

2 cans (1 pound each) salmon, drained and flaked
4 tablespoons minced parsley
¼ teaspoon pepper
8 cups mashed potatoes

4 eggs, beaten
½ teaspoon salt
4 tablespoons minced onion
4 tablespoons butter

Combine salmon, parsley, pepper, and mashed potatoes. Stir in eggs, and salt to taste. Sauté onion in the butter until onion is transparent and stir onion and butter into fish-potato mixture. Turn mixture into a greased 3-quart casserole and bake in a 450° F. oven for 20 minutes, or until browned.

CABBAGE ROLLS
(Makes 32 rolls)

1 *head cabbage*	½ *cup cream*
1 *pound ground beef*	¼ *cup melted butter*
½ *pound ground pork*	1 *tablespoon brown sugar*
1 *tablespoon salt*	4 *cups beef stock, broth or*
½ *teaspoon pepper*	*water*
2 *eggs*	3 *tablespoons flour*
1 *teaspoon allspice*	1 *cup cream*
1 *small onion, grated*	

Discard discolored leaves from outside of cabbage. Place whole head in boiling, salted water and cook until leaves are limp and separate easily. Drain, discard core, and remove leaves, one by one, being careful not to tear them. Cut larger leaves in half. Combine beef, pork, salt, pepper, eggs, allspice, and grated onion with the ½ cup cream. Trim thick center vein out of cabbage leaves, put 2 tablespoons of the meat mixture on each leaf, fold sides of leaves over filling and roll up like a small cigar. In skillet melt butter and in it brown the rolls on all sides. Transfer to a heavy kettle or Dutch oven and sprinkle with brown sugar. Rinse out skillet with a little boiling water and pour over rolls. Add more bouillon and water to cover the rolls, cover kettle, and cook over low heat for 1 to 1¼ hours, basting occasionally. Arrange rolls in serving dish. Mix flour and the 1 cup cream and stir into pan juices. Simmer for 5 minutes, adding a little milk if the gravy is too thick. Correct seasoning and pour over rolls. Serve with boiled potatoes.

KING'S DELIGHT
(Serves 8)

1 cup minced onion
8 tablespoons butter
6 tablespoons flour
4 cups canned tomatoes
1 tablespoon Worcestershire
   sauce
1 teaspoon salt

1 teaspoon sugar
¼ teaspoon pepper
12 cups finely shredded
   cabbage
6 slices bread, cubed
½ pound Cheddar cheese,
   cubed

Sauté onion until tender in 6 tablespoons of the butter. Stir in flour and cook until flour is well blended. Stir in tomatoes, Worcestershire, salt, sugar, and pepper; cook, stirring, for 5 minutes, or until mixture is slightly thickened. Cook cabbage in a little salted water and drain or steam for 7 minutes. Brown bread cubes in remaining 2 tablespoons butter. Arrange layers of cabbage, tomato mixture, bread, and cheese in a 4-quart casserole, putting bread and cheese on top. Bake in a preheated 375° F. oven for 30 minutes.

BOSTON BAKED BEANS
(Serves 12)

2 pounds pea beans
1 pound fat salt pork
2 onions, if desired
2 teaspoons salt

½ cup light molasses
2 teaspoons dry mustard
2 cups reserved bean liquor

Wash beans and discard imperfect ones. Cover with cold water and soak overnight. Next day drain and cover with fresh water. Cook slowly for about 1 hour, or until tender. Drain, reserving the cooking water. Scald pork. Cut off ¼-inch slice of the fat and put into a 4-quart bean pot or casserole with the onions. Cut through rind of remaining pork every half inch, making cuts 1 inch deep.

Put beans in pot and bury pork in beans, leaving rind exposed. Combine salt, molasses, and mustard with the reserved bean liquor and pour over beans. Cover bean pot and bake in a 300° F. oven for 6 to 8 hours, adding a little more bean liquor if they get dry. Uncover for the last hour of baking so the rind will brown and crisp.

FRENCH BEAN CASSEROLE
(Serves 12)

4 packages frozen French cut green beans
2 cans (1 pound each) whole white onions
½ teaspoon oregano
1 teaspoon salt
¼ teaspoon pepper
⅔ cup cream
⅔ cup grated cheese

Cook beans according to package directions and drain. Drain onions and arrange vegetables in alternate layers in a 3-quart casserole, sprinkling each layer with oregano, salt, and pepper. Add cream and top with grated cheese. Bake in a 350° F. oven for 20 to 30 minutes before serving.

MEXICAN LIMA BEAN CASSEROLE
(Serves 12)

4 cups dried Lima beans
12 cups boiling water
1 pound salt pork
2 large onions, chopped
2 cloves garlic, minced
4 tablespoons butter
2 cans (10 ½ ounces) tomato soup
2 teaspoons prepared mustard
½ cup brown sugar
½ cup cider vinegar
2 teaspoons salt

Soak beans overnight in water to cover. Next day, drain, cover with the boiling water, and bring to a boil. Score pork at ¼-inch intervals almost through to rind and add to Lima beans. Reduce heat and cook slowly for 1½ hours. Drain, reserving the liquor.

Sauté onions and garlic in butter for 5 minutes, or until onion is transparent. Stir in tomato sauce and 1½ cups bean liquor, the mustard, sugar, vinegar, and salt. Fill a 4-quart casserole with alternate layers of beans and sauce and bury salt pork in center. Cover and bake in a 350° F. oven for 45 minutes. Uncover and continue to bake for 15 to 30 minutes longer.

PROGRESSIVE DINNERS

A progressive party needs a timetable and careful planning, but such events have been most successful with many church groups and other organizations. Each course is served at a different home and the menu usually consists of three courses—appetizer, main course, and dessert.

No home should be burdened with more than 10 to 12 guests for any one course and, if the homes are spaced at any distance from one another, cars will be required. Perhaps two carloads per house would be just right; again from 10 to 12 people. Therefore if 48 people subscribe to the party, you will need four homes serving the first course, four serving the main course, and four serving the dessert and coffee, or a total of 12 co-operating houses and hostesses. Each hostess should have one or more competent assistants.

You might have different menus, each specializing in the food of another country, and letting subscribers select the menu they would prefer. Or, if the same menu is planned for all participants, it is possible to divide the groups for the different courses, so that many people will have a chance to mingle. If you have eight carloads of guests, give each car a number and let cars one and two go to a designated home for the first course. For the second course, cars one and three would proceed to the next home, and finally, the people in cars one and four would enjoy the dessert together.

After dinner all the guests might gather at your hall or schoolroom for an evening of entertainment, dancing, a special movie, or a lecture.

CHAPTER 3

Parties for All Ages

Every organization, large or small, has worthwhile reasons for giving a party. A good party can benefit your organization financially and socially, and in a larger sense, it can benefit the community as well. Many warm friendships are started at such parties, many fine causes advanced, and the whole atmosphere of the community brightened. The relaxed sociability of a party will often be the basis for a closer relationship among the group long after the party is over. Both adults and children can enjoy and benefit from parties that are carefully planned to be as entertaining and as friendly as they can be.

TEN RULES FOR GOOD PARTIES

1. Start with a Plan

Whether your party is planned for adults or children, you must have a plan. Whether you are seven years old or seventy, a party is boring if there's no real reason for it, if guests are asked, then left to entertain themselves, if the decorations and food are mediocre, and if nobody seems to care whether the guests have a good time.

Whether you are planning a small party for a nursery-school group or a gala gathering that may include several chapters of a society, try to "walk through" the party and cover every last detail in your planning. Who will greet the guests? Where will they put their wraps? Will you have enough guests so that check stubs will be necessary? Will food be served immediately, or later, when the party is going well? What kind of music will you have? Will it be playing softly in the background, via a faithful phonograph, or will you have a good pianist who will play old songs for a sentimental songfest? How will you make announcements? If you are going to play games, who will announce the games and describe the rules? Who will be responsible for props, like the peanuts for the peanut race, the pads and pencils for the word games, the old clothes for the game of charades?

If the party is to be held outdoors, what will you do if it rains? If the party is for grownups, will you provide baby-sitting service in an adjoining room? This one idea may make the difference between poor attendance and a crowded party.

How will you make sure that shy people are drawn out of their shells? Who will introduce the strangers? Who will make sure that everyone gets to meet the guest of honor, if there is one?

You can see that the questions and answers are endless. Naturally, you can overdo the planning, so that the party runs on a clockwork schedule, with nobody relaxed enough to enjoy the fun —but it *is* better to have a flexible, but complete plan that covers every reasonable eventuality.

2. Plan First for Fun

Parties are for pleasure and every good party combines many elements to create an atmosphere of gaiety, warmth, joy, and fun. Perhaps the best way to plan a party for your organization is to think about the best party you ever went to—and what made it memorable. Was it that you knew you were wanted—the invitation extra special, the greeting at the door particularly affectionate, a special favor just for you? Or was it the food—a menu that combined foods you may never have tasted before, but turned out to be delicious? Maybe you met somebody wonderful at your favorite party—and that's why you remember it so vividly. Whatever the reason, almost every person on your planning committee has a good party to remember, to use as a guide in planning future parties.

In posters, announcements, invitations, stress the fun of the party as well as the purpose. Sell a little, so your guests will be anxious to come. Which invitation would *you* respond to with enthusiasm?

Come one, come all
BIG OYSTER-STEW DINNER DANCE
Friday, June 22
Parish Hall　　8 o'clock

OR

If you love oyster stew, lots of fun, and good music
don't miss our gala
SEAFOOD SHINDIG
Next Friday night　　Parish Hall　　8 o'clock
Hearty appetites required

If you judge every suggestion by asking the question, "Will it be fun for our guests?"—you're bound to plan a party that people will be talking about with pleasure for months.

3. Try to Know Your Guests

You don't have to know every last club member, or the names of all the parishioners, in order to plan a party they'd like. But it does help to give some thought to the kind of people they are —the things they respond to, their taste in fairly obvious things like homes, clothing, the subjects they like to talk about. If you're planning a party for the Altar Guild of a small country church, you'll plan a different party than you would if you were planning to entertain the Great Books Discussion Club in a large city. Both parties might be great fun—but they'd be different.

Naturally, the ages of your guests would influence the kind of party you would plan. That's why this chapter is divided into several sections—with tips for various age groups. Some ideas you'll find workable for almost every age group; others are just right for teens, terrible for toddlers, fair for adults. Your own knowledge of the group you're planning to entertain will help guide your selection of menu, games, entertainment, and themes from all the suggestions offered.

4. Know Why You're Giving the Party

Knowing *why* you are giving the party will help limit discussion to ideas that will further your goal. Your party may be planned to raise funds for a charity, or to pay for a new record player for your meeting hall, or merely to balance a shaky budget. Or, it may be just a get-together affair, with the accent on fun rather than finances. Certainly, if it's a party for children and teens, you can hardly expect it to raise huge sums, but on the other hand, it doesn't take a lot of money to pay for a party for youngsters.

Whatever the reason for the party—the retirement of your minister, the high school graduation, a holiday, a fund-raising affair —include the reason for the party in your announcements for it:

A DOLLAR FOR THE HOSPITAL FUND MEANS A
GREAT CHICKEN DINNER FOR YOU!

or

COME MEET YOUR NEW PRESIDENT AT TEA NEXT TUESDAY

If you want to raise funds, you'll keep the party costs down; ask for donations and volunteers, and charge more for everything. If the main purpose is to make friends, you'll plan games that force your guests to talk to each other, mingle, relax. If you're honoring a distinguished guest, you'll plan a dignified party, with a reception line. If your purpose is to delight the youngsters, you'll plan a wild circus of a party, with the accent on noise and excitement.

5. Choosing a Theme Helps Make Planning Easy

Perhaps your reason for giving the party will limit your choice of theme. Or, because your reason is one like "making friends" or "helping our members to get to know each other," you'll want to pick a theme that is universally appealing, but doesn't label your party as an appeal for friendship. Choosing a theme makes it easy to choose a menu, decorations, music, games, and, in some cases, costumes.

6. Publicize Your Party

If your purpose is to raise funds, or to acquire new members, you'll want to make sure that everybody knows about your party. Posters, newspaper publicity, announcements, perhaps even a mailing list, can be used to spread the good news. It helps your party planning to provide some way of estimating "acceptances" —either by advance sale of tickets, or by asking guests to sign an acceptance list at meetings. If you have enough workers to help, you might telephone members to ask if they are planning to come to the party. Handling this telephone call correctly can do much to insure their coming. The telephoners should say, "I do hope I'll see you at the Mexican Fiesta next week"—not, "We don't have an acceptance from you. Are you coming?"

7. A Party Should Look Like a Party

If you're giving a party in the school gym, or a barren hall, or a drab conference room, you can't expect to create a gala atmosphere without some kind of decorations. You needn't spend a lot of money. When the area is large, you can get lots of effect for little money, because guests won't notice small details. You want color, brightness, and gaiety. Crepe paper, balloons, paper mobiles, flower arrangements, are all fun to plan, especially when you have a definite theme to set your imagination to sparking. Even very small children respond to a table that's set nicely, with an attractive centerpiece.

Take a bon voyage party, for instance, given for members of a group that are planning a charter flight to Europe. Foreign posters are stapled to the wall; inexpensive model airplanes hang by invisible threads from the ceiling. Each table is set in the mood of a different country—a Spanish fringed shawl for a table cover on one, an arrangement of cheese and fruit on the French table, a long basket of Italian bread stretches across a third table.

Decorations can help set the party mood immediately. If guests enter to find a table beautifully set with a damask tablecloth, a flower arrangement that shows effort and art, a silver coffee service, and a gleaming punch bowl, they're bound to act differently than if they enter to discover red-checked tablecloths, corn husks trimming the tables, and sawdust on the floor.

8. Use Music to Add to the Fun

Once the fun gets going, you won't need any extra help, but start your party off on the right foot with music that follows your theme, and sounds like fun. If you've planned a circus party, you'll want band or circus music. If you want to encourage dancing, you'll pick records that make feet fly—carefully selected to fit the feet that are flying—young or old, fast or slow. Don't forget how much fun group singing is, making sure that a few of your volunteers have been prompted to get the singing started, and that the songs selected are easy to sing, with good, strong rhythm.

9. Have a Definite Time for the Party to Begin and End

Make sure that your invitations and announcements mention the time your party will begin, so that everybody will arrive within a reasonable period. If you all know each other very well, it's possible to have an "open house" kind of party that stretches over many hours without the risk of a dull party—but that kind of vague invitation is fatal to a party designed to help strangers become acquainted.

If there's a good reason to, mention the time the party will end. You might say something like, "Join us for coffee, cake, and a breakfast bag of tricks from 11:00 A.M. to 2:00 P.M. on Sunday" or "Jamboree Dance, 9:00 P.M. till Midnight, Friday."

10. Make One Person the Boss

It helps to have one person in charge of all the arrangements for the party, and preferably that person should be a jolly, energetic, outgoing type, well able to give orders pleasantly, and to make people obey them—strictly. Both adults and children quickly sense disorganization, and just as quickly rush to the breach, trying to run the party their way.

And now let's get down to the specifics of how to run a party for different age groups. Let's start with the youngest:

PARTIES FOR TOTS TO TEENS

It's harder to plan a children's party than it is to plan an adult gathering—but once the preparation is over, it's possible to have lots more fun! A circle of starry-eyed toddlers, sitting in fascination as they watch their first puppet show, or a gaggle of gangly nine-year-olds, seriously testing the doneness of their self-grilled hot dogs, the sound of deep-in-the-tummy giggles, the high-pitched excitement of shrill laughter, the off-key but moving strains of an old song, newly revived by thirteen-year-old voices . . . it's hard to match a children's party for fun and satisfaction.

On the other hand, you can't call up a group of seven-year-olds, invite them over, serve them Cokes and ice cream, and let them entertain themselves, without inviting disaster as well. And the larger the group of children, the harder your job is.

It helps if the children know each other, and have previously functioned as a group. A Brownie troop will be easier to entertain than a group of girls who have never seen each other before. But any group of children needs stimulation, direction, discipline, and encouragement in order to achieve even a semblance of "spontaneous" glee. This is true whether the children are toddlers or teen-agers, except that with toddlers the control can be out in the open and direct ("Let's all sit in these chairs, and I'll tell you a story!"), while with teen-agers, the control must be subtle and nondirect ("Let's vote on the party break-up time, shall we?").

Have Lots of Help

Don't try to give a large party for children without lots of adults on hand to help—not onlookers, but active participants who know exactly what their jobs are. *Three adults for every twenty-five children* is a good average. Take advantage of members of the sponsoring group who have special skills—nurse, actor, musician, teacher. If you're asking, "What in the world would they do?"—you've never given a children's party. They unbuckle galoshes, they blow up balloons, they serve ice cream, they help with pants buttons, they soothe hurt feelings, they twirl children and point them toward the donkey, they start the record for musical chairs, and in general give a great imitation of a perpetual-motion machine.

Limit the Party

Make sure the party lasts only a few hours at most, and for small children, only about an hour or an hour and a half. Better to have your guests going home eager for more fun than tired, drooping, and fretful—a burden to their parents and a bad advertisement for your association, church group, or club.

Allow Plenty of Time for Planning

Older groups will want to be in on the party planning. Allow plenty of time for endless discussions of theme, decorations, menu and committee assignments, but always with the adult in charge in pretty firm control of the discussion to keep it from wandering, becoming too ambitious, or petering out in plans that are never followed through. Make sure each child knows what his duties are, and what his responsibility is. Don't say, "Gerald, will you help with the refreshments?" Say, "Gerald, I'd appreciate it if you would serve the ice cream. You'll need a big tray, paper plates, spoons, napkins, and a big scoop. Wait until everyone has finished the main course before starting to serve. Maybe Tom and Bill would distribute the dishes while you scoop the servings." Incidentally, you should be equally specific in giving directions to adult helpers. Many a willing homemaker is struck with mortal terror at the sight of twenty or thirty starving children, all howling for ice cream—and it helps if she has a plan of action, knows just what to do.

Whenever possible, let the children decide the details of the party. It really doesn't matter if the crepe-paper swags are blue or orange or pink—to you. But the children will enjoy the party more if they can nudge each other, and say, "We picked the colors, and aren't they beeyootiful!"

When you plan your party, don't forget the gruesome aftermath—the clean-up afterwards. If the children have participated in the planning and preparation, they should help with this, too. If, on the other hand, your group is giving a children's party without their help—then you should be ready to clean up on your own. Be sensibly fair in estimating how much help the children are capable of. Willingness is no guide to ability. Better let the adults wash the breakables, letting the children gather up paper plates, take down decorations, and (oh, joy!) release the balloons.

Stick to One Age Group

Don't expect to have a come-one-come-all party for all the children in your school, or church parish, or town, without difficulty. The smaller children will be overstimulated by the presence of the older children. The teens will be scornful, the nine-year-olds will show off, out of control—and nobody will have a very good time. If you must include all age groups, then make the best of a bad bargain by dividing the party area and activities into categories suitable for various ages. Have a dance floor and Coke bar for the teens, a story corner for the little ones. You might call it a "bazaar" or a "circus" to emphasize the separate activities.

Change the Pace from Time to Time

Variety is the spice of any party. Plan your entertainment to alternate quiet games with exciting ones. Have enough ideas for games on hand so that if you feel the party is dragging, you can switch to a lively game in a hurry. Make sure all your assistants know the rules of each game completely so there isn't that awful moment when a child claims he's won, only to be challenged by another, with the nearby adult looking vague and helpless. (In such a case, it may be better to say firmly, "Yes, you have," or "No, you haven't," in an authoritative voice and suggest a new game rather than to show any hesitation, which would prolong the argument.)

What About Prizes?

Older children can take competition in stride, but for pre-schoolers and children up to ten or so, it's far better to have prizes for everybody in the form of favors than to single out any child by awarding a prize. You can ask everybody to clap for the child who wins at musical chairs. But the less said about prizes and winning, the more relaxed and happy the children will be.

This is true even in cases where it's traditional to award prizes— for "The Best Costume" or whatever. Every child wants to win, and when only one can, there are bound to be hurt feelings. How much nicer to use the money you would have spent on a large prize, for dozens of small favors and have a costume parade all around the room with much applause from the adults—and, as each child passes a "grandstand," hand out a little toy or a lollipop.

Make the Entertainment Professional

No, you don't have to hire a magician, or pay a large fee for a clown. But if you plan entertainment for the children, do make it as professional and skilled as you possibly can. It isn't fair to ask three- and four-year-olds to listen in rapt admiration to a story that is droned by a disinterested reader who couldn't care less. Pick a reader who will take the project seriously, who is unself-conscious and who can ad-lib noises, read with expression, and get the children to participate in the story. Or, rent a movie projector and some gay cartoons. If you have a singer in your organization, enlist his or her help in leading the children in songs. But don't pick the girl with opera ambitions, choose the jolly mother who has a fairly good voice and a wonderful personality. The pianist shouldn't take his piano playing too seriously, must not mind interruptions, and should be willing to use the loud pedal for emphasis in every song from "Home on the Range" to "Rock-a-bye, Baby."

It isn't too officious to ask the entertainers exactly what they plan to do. Know what type of story will be read. Is it too scary for three-year-olds? Are the songs that will be sung too limited in scope? Are they singable, so the children will join in? Will the "jolly clown's" make-up frighten the wits out of the tiny tots? Maybe a dress rehearsal would be overdoing the caution, but a few questions should be asked before the day of the party.

Be particularly careful in choosing an entertainer for teen-agers. Folk singers are fine, if they are casual, good singers, and talk the teen's language. By this age, the teens like to entertain themselves, so be wary of planning too much entertainment.

Don't Be Too Sophisticated

Here you are, planning a party for thirty children and suddenly, you're scared. Will they like it? Chances are, they'll love it, just because it *is* a party, and children love parties. Don't get too ambitious. Keep the food, entertainment, and games simple and there won't be any strain on you, or the kids. Little children love bright, bright colors and balloons. So do junior children. And so do teens. You may find that your "sophisticated" thirteen- and fourteen-year-olds would love to crack a party cracker, don a party hat, and giggle just as they once did in their "childhood."

Do Be Gracious

The same general rules for making your guests feel at home that you know work for adults will work for children too. Greet each child individually and warmly. Say you're glad he or she could come. If the first arrivals look a little scared and lost, set them to work "helping"—they'll relax as they co-operate in setting out the last chairs or tacking up the donkey or selecting the records for the dance music. Introduce each child to the other children as he arrives, if possible. In a crowd, each adult should try to do this for his "circle" of children. Or, prepare large name tags for the children, if you know their names. If you don't, cut out the tags, give the child a crayon as he enters, and let him letter his own name. Circulate among your guests, as you do at grown-up cocktail parties. Listen for the sound of boredom or strife, and be ready with an activity to clear the air. Serve the hot foods hot and the cold foods cold, and have plenty of music. Join in the fun, and take accidents in stride—this is the time when your mettle will be tested and proved. You wouldn't say, "Clumsy!" to an honored guest in your own home—don't say it to an embarrassed teen-ager, who's just spilled the punch bowl. Get a mop, and keep smiling.

What Kind of Party Shall It Be?

If you love party giving, you hardly need an excuse for a party, but children dote on themes. It helps to limit the decorations, menus, and entertainment, too, keeping it all simple and all of a piece. Graduation, Easter, Christmas, the circus coming to town, reward for a job well done, are all reason enough for giving a party. How you treat the theme will vary with the age group you are working with—but almost any theme is suitable for any age. Take a clown party, for instance. Preschool children will love dressing up in old clothes, smearing make-up on their faces, eating peanut-butter sandwiches from a bandanna, and performing "tricks." Junior children will elaborate on the costumes—may extend them to include the whole circus. They'll want popcorn, jelly apples, and will love throwing balls at stacked milk bottles, jumping through hoops, and lots of gay circus music. Teen-agers may have a clown party that includes charades and pantomime, or may even vote for a bus ride to a real circus, with a buffet supper after the matinee performance.

Holidays, the seasons, can be springboards for parties. A Halloween party can be wonderful fun—and may keep the trick-or-treaters off the street late in the evening. A Latin class might give a toga-wrapped, sofa-served Roman feast.

Don't Ask for Volunteers

If the game or activity you plan calls for one child to perform, don't ask, "Does anyone want to start?" Instead, put names in a hat (perhaps use the children's name tags) and draw out one name. In another hat, you might have slips of paper with the

23. Tiny cheese balls rolled in nuts, a cheese dip with pretzel sticks, or a molded cheese ball to cut and spread on crackers are all suitable appetizers to dinner or supper menus—always a friendly way of starting conversation at a table.

24. Caramel-frosted chocolate cake, topped with freshly popped popcorn, is fun for a Lincoln's Day party.

25. Happiness Cake has two golden layers flecked through with bits of colored coconut. It is lavishly frosted with meringue frosting and sprinkled with more colored coconut.

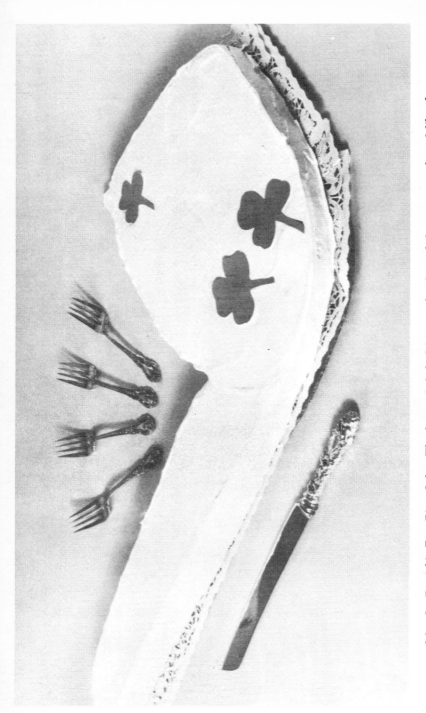

26. St. Patrick's Day Pipe Cake: The batter is baked in two aluminum-foil pans—one shaped like the pipe stem and the other like the bowl of the pipe. If the pans are carefully greased and floured, they may be used several times before being discarded. Turn cakes out of foil pans onto racks to cool, then stick

27. Easter Bunny Cake intrigues both young and adult, and doubles as a table centerpiece. For directions, see Chapter III.

28. Posy Cake makes a colorful dessert for a May Day party. Serve it with ice cream. For directions, see Chapter III.

29 and 30.   Two dessert ideas for May or springtime luncheons are the individual Flowerpot Cakes (*above*), or the Strawberry Cake (*below*). Both are as delicious to eat as they are charming to see. For directions, see Chapter III.

31. Laughing Pumpkin Cake or Trick-or-Treat Cookies are amusing desserts for a Halloween Party. For directions, see Chapter III.

32.   Carousel Cake carries out a Circus Party theme, always sheer delight
for the little tots. For directions, see Chapter III.

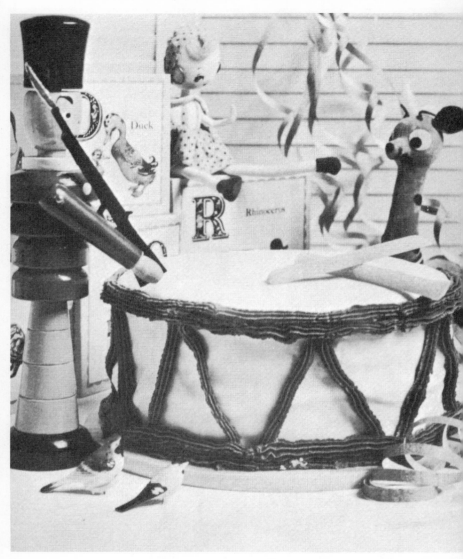

33. Drum Cake has special appeal for little boys. For directions, see Chapter III.

34. Space Party or Trip to the Moon is an imaginative theme for junior children. Menu consists of salmon loaf, scalloped potatoes, milk punch, and four-tiered Missile Cake. For directions, see Chapter III.

35. Waffles topped with scoo of ice cream and homema brownies are "the most" at preteen Pajama Party. For dir tions, see Chapter III.

36. A Bowling Party for teen-agers features a Bowling Ball Cake. Behind it, soft-drink bottles are disguised as ten pins. For directions, see Chapter III.

37. Pineapple-topped cake, artificial flowers, and paper *leis* set the stage for a Hawaiian Party.

38. Butter-Cream Frosting is easy to fashion with spatula into "waves" around base of this three-layer Bon Voyage Cake. Three small frosted cupcakes, halved, are arranged in formation on top, and tiny flags are inserted into each section.

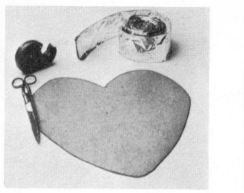

39.

40.

41.

42.

Foil heart pan can be any size desired or as large as the oven available in which to bake it. It's an ideal way to make cake to serve a crowd. Cardboard cutout is covered with heavy-duty aluminum foil, a long folded strip is taped around outline for sides of pan. Finished pan may be used several times, or it makes a convenient container in which to carry cake to its destination. For directions, see Chapter III.

43 and 44. Rabbit pan is as easy to make out of foil as the heart pan. See children's coloring books for other ideas. Just be sure to keep outline of the pan simple.

activity you want started (Sing a song; Tell a story; Bob for the first apple).

SPECIAL TIPS FOR SPECIAL AGES

The Little Tots (Three to Five or Six)

Children this age don't play too well with each other. They respond better to the directions of the adult who's leading the party, and will be quite content to follow suggestions. They respond even better if the adult joins in the fun.

They'd like to do something like this: Each child lies down on a huge piece of paper. The adult draws the child's outline with a big black crayon. Then each child colors his own outline "doll" and takes home the paper doll as a souvenir. The coloring will take awhile, and a fairly quiet while at that. The crayons, too, are a fine favor to take home.

Or, each child might draw a picture on a large piece of paper, to use as a place mat. The theme of the party will suggest the subject of the drawing. But don't be too specific—art should be creative!

For active games, beanbags are good. The children try to pitch them into a circle (if the theme is a circus, it's the circus ring; if it's a fairy party, the ring is the fairy ring).

The menu should be very simple and served so as not to interfere with regular meals, if possible (or, tell the mothers what and when you fed the children). The important element here is serving, rather than cooking. Remove the lid of each ice cream cup, or there will be lids all over the floor. Do pick ice-cream cups, not popsicles, which drip. Keep choices to a minimum—little children really can't make up their minds. If one child says, "But I don't LIKE vanilla," smile sweetly and say, "That's too bad, dear. Maybe at our next party, we'll have a flavor you'll like." Under no circumstances scrounge around for a cup of chocolate ice cream; every last child will switch his allegiance to chocolate!

Try to limit the menu to finger foods—crisp carrot sticks, raisins, small sandwiches, milk in paper cartons, cookies in interesting shapes.

Go slow. Give the children time to concentrate on what you're saying and to absorb what you want them to do. Be patient and relaxed, but don't be afraid to give directions when necessary: "Only one ice cream cup, please, Mary." "Wouldn't you like to help put the crayons away neatly, children?" "We don't climb on chairs here."

Don't forget the possibilities of the outdoors, in season. You might make it a tricycle party, where each toddler brings his wheeled vehicle to ride in an open court (a manageable number of toddlers, a large court). Set up traffic signs, and let the grown-ups give tickets, hold up stop-and-go signs, and blow whistles. Or, if your party is held in a school playground or a church play area, you might have a sandbox party. Active play outdoors lets off steam, is easy to supervise if the area is limited, and needs only a little trimming to make it partyish in feeling.

The Junior Children (Six to Nine)

These dedicated party-goers love all the traditional party joys. Don't go too far afield for ideas; you'll disappoint them. They love the party package of balloons, musical chairs, donkey game, and a basket of candy to take home—no matter how the package is wrapped. Younger children in this group, the six- and seven-year-olds, will droop quicker, and the menu might be a little simpler than for the eight- and nine-year-olds, but not much. There should be more emphasis on peanut butter than on the hot dogs the eight- and nine-year-olds love. For all these ages, try to avoid the self-service trap, but still maintain the fiction that they are grownups. Offer a choice of hot dogs and hamburgers with trimmings; or without, if you don't want them to smear the trimmings all over the party room. When it is possible, outdoors, or in a room where messes aren't a problem, let them go to it. Children this age love treasure hunts. Six-year-olds should have a smaller list to hunt for than the nine-year-olds, but they'll both enjoy the game.

Grammar school-age children love to dress up. Whether they are space-age cadets, pirates, or tramps, it adds to the party atmosphere. If you don't want to have them come in elaborate costumes, you can always have them make their costumes at the party, such as great big paper hats that they staple together—with lots of feathers, sequins, ribbons, and buttons on hand for trimming.

Outdoor cook-outs are great fun, and easy with enough grown-up help. The girls can tear apart lettuce and greens for the salad; the boys can roast the potatoes; and everybody can pitch in for the hamburgers. Marshmallows-on-sticks for dessert, and a mellow songfest around a campfire will send them all home in a glow.

Dagwood or hero sandwiches are another do-it-yourself idea that boys particularly will enjoy. Girls might favor a doll's tea party, with dainty sandwiches and hot-chocolate "tea" in tiny cups. But don't try to mix the two themes at one party . . . in a large group of both boys and girls, it's safer to stick to the kind of theme both boys and girls will enjoy.

The Preteens (Ten to Twelve)

These prickly children are hard to please. They're too young for teen-age dancing, and too old for "kid stuff." Yet, they love to get together, love the excitement of a party, and they're the age that benefits most from group activity. Perhaps one way to solve the problem is to plan an activity you know the group likes, and make the "party" with the refreshments an extra. Bowling, roller or ice skating, an afternoon swim, a hike are all reasons for getting together. Girls love pajama parties; boys would love an outdoor barbecue. A progressive party, with each course served at a different home, will keep the group busy all afternoon. Table tennis, darts, shuffleboard are active fun games.

One mistake you can make is to submit to the children's (and some parents') pressure to treat this group like older teens—with Cokes, dancing, pairing off, and much pressure to behave like grownups. It's worth the time and effort to plan a party that keeps them too busy for such "sophistication" and helps them to look forward to the fun of a party, without any worry about their maturity or lack of it.

The Teens

By the time children reach their teens, they want to plan and run their own party. Your guidance comes in suggesting themes, in chaperoning, and in controlling their enthusiasm and exuberance. If you're relaxed and easygoing about minor points, you're most likely to win the major points of behavior, closing time, and "rules" that must be obeyed.

It is at this age that it becomes necessary to plan for the possibility of dangerous "party crashing." Hire an off-duty policeman to serve for the evening. Don't be an ostrich about the possibility of alcohol being introduced, unasked, to the menu. Do treat your teen-age guests with respect, but with resources on hand for emergencies. Part of your duty as host or hostess is to chaperone, as well as entertain. This needn't be a "drag" on the party, if you welcome the guests warmly, serve them unobtrusively, and have a good time yourself, without taking over. Try to keep legitimately busy—serving food, greeting newcomers, changing records, so that you won't seem to be standing around, just watching. But do stick around; most teen-agers may grumble, but they like the security of your presence.

Teen-agers won't stand still for the traditional party games, unless they're tricked up to be unrecognizable or unless they know grownups play the games, too. You might get away with charades, in a group that loves dramatics. An old-fashioned hayride might turn out to be the party of the year. But don't plan every minute of the time, or the children will chafe under the control. Expect the teens to pair off, but be alert to the loner who's being neglected—manufacture an excuse to provide him or her with a companion in some necessary project like getting more ice or passing the popcorn.

Teens are (finally) more imaginative and daring in their food choices than young children are—the girls more so than the boys. Chinese food, an Italian dinner, chili, anything exotic, will please them. But be sure there's lots!

One idea you might want to try is a combined teens'-and-parents' party—well worth the effort it takes.

Teen-ager's Supper Party for Parents

Let each teen-ager participate. For every six guests expected, let one bring a casserole to serve six; elect one to make the salad for six, another to bake and bring cookies for six. Others can be responsible for setting tables, decorations, making coffee, supervising the service of the hot rolls—and, of course, the clean-up. Better let them draw straws for this!

Give the children elected to bring the casseroles the recipe well in advance (they might like to try it out once before making it for the party), and explain anything in it to them that they do not understand. An easy casserole that everybody enjoys is the following one for Chili Corn Pie.

CHILI CORN PIE CASSEROLE
(Serves 6)

1 *can chili con carne*	*Corn-muffin mix*
1 *pound hamburger*	*Egg and milk*
½ *teaspoon chili powder*	

1. Mix chili con carne, hamburger, and chili powder and put into a greased or oiled 1½-quart casserole dish.
2. Mix corn-muffin mix with egg and milk according to directions on package and spread over top of chili.

3. Bake in a preheated 400° F. oven for 30 minutes, or until corn-muffin mix is golden brown.

Reheat in a 350° F. oven for 15 to 20 minutes, before serving.

The Menu

CHILI CORN PIE

TOSSED SALAD *or* COLESLAW

HOT ROLLS

COOKIES

(Ice Cream, optional)

COFFEE, COCOA

The Grownups

Giving a party for adults is often easier than planning a children's party because grownups are able to co-operate in providing enthusiasm for the party, and will help you out by behaving in fairly civilized patterns. They won't criticize the food audibly, or cheat at the games, or spill their ice cream. On the other hand, because they are more inhibited it may be harder to get the party started than it is when you merely tell a group of toddlers to "form a circle and make faces at each other and whoever laughs first is out." Perhaps the most important part of your planning is the plan for the first thirty or forty minutes of the party—the period when there are new arrivals every minute, when conversation lags, and strangers eye each other warily. You'll want to have several "ice-breaker" games on hand to start the fun.

Don't push grownups around. Lead, but don't direct the games. If you've planned to follow a guessing game with an active game—and suddenly find that the guessing game has become absolutely fascinating to the guests and nobody wants to stop, submit graciously and just skip the active game until the time when the party drags and there's a lull in the conversation.

Allow time for talk. One of the joys of a good party is the chance it provides for making acquaintances, renewing old friendships, getting to know the other guests. Make sure there's a period during the party when there's a chance to circulate, an opportunity for guests to seek out each other. Perhaps you'll have dancing, or a buffet supper, with guests free to select their eating spot.

Be specific if a certain costume is expected. Newcomers to your group will be dismayed if they arrive at a formal party in informal attire. If you think it will add to the fun to have everyone in costume, be sure to have some simple props on hand to transform a "civilian" guest who isn't wearing a costume.

Don't embarrass your guests. If you don't know your guests well, don't suggest stunts they may not want to perform. Not every man likes to try on women's hats, as a matter of fact, few do. Don't ostentatiously drag a young pretty girl by the hand toward an embarrassed unattached man—they'll hate each other on sight. Instead, find indirect means of getting them acquainted, and less strenuous ways for them to relax.

Family Parties

A party designed to please Papa, Mama, and the little ones, has to be a daytime party, a party that has a simple menu so everyone can enjoy the same food, and one that provides plenty of chance for active games that both grownups and children enjoy.

Make a big point of identifying each family. If the group is small enough, you might make name tags with an identifying color, or a special shape. If the group includes strangers, make a game of matching children and parents. Have a child stand, and then let everyone guess which adult he "belongs" to.

Early in the day, have a game that mixes up adults and children, so the families don't cling in little clusters, without exchanging conversation or fun. Team the children against their daddies, with the mothers gathered in the "cheering section," waving paper flags.

If the children are old enough, it's nice to ask them to help serve, turning about the usual family practice of Mother serving, children sitting. Even small children can distribute paper plates, napkins, and cups.

Adults and children have so many enthusiasms in common, that it isn't as difficult as you might think to plan the entertainment. Fireworks, ice cream, hot dogs, gay music, bright decorations are all things oldsters and youngsters enjoy.

The smaller the children, the more desirable it is that adults and children be served their refreshments separately. Give Mother a break, and let her enjoy her cake and ice cream without having to worry about mopping up Junior. And give the children the extra treat of unsupervised enjoyment of their meal. If you have plenty of volunteers on hand, there'll be a minimum of accidents—and a happier party.

Older children will enjoy sharing their meal with their parents, and they can be expected to be on their best behavior.

A VARIETY OF PARTY IDEAS FOR INDOORS AND OUT

Every age and every kind of person can participate in parties that celebrate holidays. They make wonderful pegs on which to hang a good party—your theme, menu, decorations, and so forth, can follow tradition, or be brought up-to-date with interesting variations.

Let's take every month of the year:

JANUARY

New Year's Day Breakfast

Open House

Come as Your Resolution Party

Guests come dressed in costumes that depict their resolutions: an angel, a housekeeper, in an exercise suit with barbells, as a big clock to indicate they're trying to be prompt. Other guests must guess the resolution.

FEBRUARY

St. Valentine's Day Heart Party

Guests are given half a heart. They match the torn half with the other guests' to find their partner for the first game. Candy hearts are prizes; sandwiches and cookies are in heart shapes. A good game for a Valentine party is to offer a prize for the best Valentine assembled by a guest from a pile of clipped advertisements, magazine illustrations, bits of colored paper, ribbon, and paper lace. Provide paste, stapler, and a time limit, so the activity won't drag. Little children enjoy this. So do grownups, if part of the requirement is a poem or funny saying on the Valentine.

George Washington's Birthday Cherry-Pie Festival

The pies must be pierced in the shape of an axe. Decorations are red and white. If you want to add to the menu, make it Virginia ham and corn bread!

I Cannot Tell a Lie Party

Games to play might be Truth or Consequences or conduct your own version of the TV panel show, *To Tell the Truth*.

Lincoln's Birthday Popcorn Party

Try to capture the flavor of a pioneer party with a taffy pull, popcorn, and apple ducking. Square dancing, Indian wrestling, and spelling bees make fine traditional pastimes.

Popcorn Threading Game: Give each player a needle and thread. See who can string the greatest number of popcorn kernels, using only one hand, within a certain time limit. A popcorn-topped cake makes an appropriate dessert. A quick, easy frosting is made by melting caramels. (*See photo 24.*)

MARCH

First Day of Spring Party

Even if it's as cold as it can be, you can celebrate spring by planning a party that has a flowery theme. Decorate with cutout birds (including a great big robin, which you can use for a Pin-the-Worm-on-the-Robin Game), flowers and yellow balloons and crepe paper.

A good game to play is, "What Flower Am I?" The person who is "it" thinks of a flower. The other players must guess by asking questions about it: what color is it? how tall is it? et cetera.

Serve a Happiness Cake with ice cream. It's a yellow cake with bits of colored coconut mixed into the batter and sprinkled lavishly over the meringue frosting. (*See photo 25.*)

St. Patrick's Day Party

Leprechauns, potatoes, shillelaghs, and shamrocks make decorating easy and, of course, you must choose green as your dominant decorating color. Irish-American songs like "Mother Machree" and "Sweet Molly Malone" are fun for all to sing. For the children, provide white-clay pipes and lots of bubble liquid—they'll have fun blowing bubbles. Potato races would be fun. Older guests might welcome a St. Paddy's Day Corned Beef and Cabbage Supper, with lots of mustard, and a boiled potato. A St. Patrick's Day Pipe Cake is great for serving a crowd. (*See photo 26.*)

APRIL

April Fool Backward Party

Guests wear their clothes backward, have dessert first, say good-by as they enter and hello as they leave, and are prepared for easygoing, nonmalicious jokes and tricks.

An Easter Party

Pastel-paper streamers, daffodils, and tulips all spell Easter. Add some fluffy yellow chicks, chocolate Easter eggs, and let the children occupy themselves with an Easter-egg hunt. A charming table centerpiece might be a Bunny Cake. The cake is baked in a Pyrex bowl, frosted with meringue frosting, and sprinkled with shredded coconut. Set the bunny head on a cardboard collar and attach a ribbon bow and paper ears. Artificial or real flowers for eyes, pipe-cleaner whiskers, and a gumdrop nose make the Easter Bunny Cake so pixilated that no one will want to eat him. (*See photo 27.*)

MAY

May Day Outing or Lawn Party

Have a Maypole, May baskets containing picnic lunches, and gambol on the "green"—which may be someone's garden. Serve Posy Cakes and ice cream for dessert: To make a Posy Cake, bake batter in a ring mold and some reserved batter in tiny cupcake pans. Frost the little cakes gaily with pastel-colored frosting, insert wooden sticks, and let them radiate from the center of the ring-mold cake. (*See photo 28.*)

May Day Luncheon

"Ho! the merrie first of Maie," is a romantic and sentimental day to celebrate. Decorate the tables with Maypole centerpieces with streamers of real or artificial flowers strung on stout thread. Serve Flowerpot Cakes: Bake cake batter in real little flowerpots, lined with aluminum foil. Unmold, cool, and frost with a double band of frosting around the top. Sprinkle top with chocolate shot or shaved chocolate to resemble earth and insert a real or artificial spring flower. Another attractive May or springtime dessert, which doubles for centerpiece, is a lemon cake baked in an angel-food cake pan. Decorate attractively with strawberries and serve with strawberry sauce and ice cream. (*See photos 29 and 30.*)

JUNE

Graduation Parties

Proms, pre-prom parties, class nights, and all the other traditional events are all excuses for parties.

Shower and Wedding Parties

There will be lots of these in June. The Ladies' Aid Societies of many churches make a specialty of catering wedding breakfasts after the ceremony.

JULY

Fourth of July Picnic Party

This is a good idea, especially if you sell it to your group as a good way to avoid the dangers of Fourth-of-July traffic and the worry about firecrackers. It can be as simple or elaborate as your finances and resources permit, but it should include the elements of fun and patriotism in a nice friendly, informal blend.

Each family comes to the area (indoors or out) to find it arranged like an old-fashioned picnic grounds—trestle tables, covered with paper cloths or red-checked cotton ones, if your members have them. Canvass your members to find who have old-fashioned ice-cream freezers. Build a little wooden stand for the "speeches," and if possible, make it large enough to include room for a band— perhaps two or three instruments, played by talented members of your group. String up lanterns, alternating with bright balloons in red, white, and blue. Have flags everywhere, up high where the little children can't reach them, until the end of the party.

Have the menu as representative of good American cooking as you can—hot dogs and hamburgers or lobsters, fried chicken, potato salad, golden ears of corn—all the things you can't imagine the Fourth of July without. For dessert, choose watermelon, or apple pie with cheese.

Be sure to include the playing of the national anthem, and the recitation of the pledge of allegiance to the flag as part of your entertainment—but perhaps you *could* omit the traditional hour-long oration. For games, if there is a field, choose traditional ones like sack races, peanut-pushing races, relay races, baseball, or a watermelon-eating contest; if you are confined to inside, you could still have a freckle contest, a marble-shooting championship match —even a leapfrog—contest, if enough children can corral a "frog."

AUGUST

This is the month for ice-cream socials, hayrides, picnic outings of all kinds. The "dog days" might be an excuse for a dog show. August is a good time for a carnival, a water-sport festival, a beach party for young and old, or a hot-dog hullabaloo.

SEPTEMBER

Back-to-School Party

This might be a good way to "break the ice" if a class is small enough to entertain as a group.

Labor Day Party

Include activities that will produce a worthwhile result—everybody pitching in to paint the meeting hall, or spruce up the grounds.

OCTOBER

Halloween Party

A wonderful reason for a party. Ghosts and goblins and skeletons and scary witches should abound, and of course you'll want to duck for apples, tell ghost stories, and pin the tail on a black cat instead of a donkey. You'll need lots of "trick or treat" cookies and candies and you might enjoy a laughing pumpkin cake. To make the cookies, cut out cardboard shapes, place them on rolled-out cooky dough and cut around them with a knife. Frost and decorate as desired. The Pumpkin Cake is made by baking a cake batter in a Pyrex bowl. (*See photo* 31.)

Bones Roll is a game played with alphabet blocks. Players roll them as if they were dice. Any letter in the word Halloween counts 10 points for the players' team.

Get the Ghost. Make a ghost of a broom, sheet, and ghost mask. Players throw light sponges, and must hit the face to score 10 points for their team.

Columbus Day Discovery Party might include a treasure hunt, ending up with big steaming plates of spaghetti and meat sauce.

NOVEMBER

Harvest Parties and Football Parties are fun.

Thanksgiving Parties

These are usually family affairs, but your group might want to have a pre-Thanksgiving party to raise funds for Thanksgiving donations to an institution or charity. A game to play might be:

Get the Gobbler. The guests form two lines. All join hands, including the guests at the ends of the lines, forming a circle. One person left on the outside of the ring is the turkey. He runs around the circle, touches one player on the back, and continues on his way. The player touched, instantly starts running in the opposite direction. When the two "turkeys" meet, they stop, face each other, and say, "gobble, gobble." Then they pass, and continue racing around the circle to see which will reach the vacant place. The one who loses becomes the next turkey.

DECEMBER

A Tree-Ornament Party

Each guest brings an ornament, which may be donated to a hospital or charity, or they may be used to decorate the meeting-room Christmas tree. A pretty and edible idea is to decorate small Christmas trees, either real or artificial, with cooky ornaments for distribution to children's wards of hospitals or other needy institutions. (*See photo 106.*)

A Fix-Toys Party

Each guest brings a collection of old toys and games, and all fix them up for donation to a charity. Provide paint, needles and threads, tools.

PARTY IDEAS FOR VARIOUS AGE GROUPS

The Little Tots (Three to Five or Six)

Mother Goose Party

Circus Party
Cake and ice cream combine to make this gay Carousel Cake. Mold ice cream in the same size pan as the two layers are baked in and sandwich the layers together with the ice-cream layer in between. The carousel canopy and ponies can be purchased at five-and-dime stores, or you can cut the canopy out of paper, balance it with straws, and use animal crackers for the ponies. (*See photo 32.*)

Toyland Party
Drum Cake is made by putting two or three layers of cake together with lots of frosting between, then frosting top and sides with white frosting and piping chocolate frosting around edges and side triangles with a small fluted tube. Use long gumdrops for the sticks. (*See photo 33.*)

Farmer-in-the-Dell Party

Cowboys and Indians Roundup

Doll's Tea Party (for little girls)

Clown Party

Rhythm Band Party

Take a Trip Party

Bubble Party

The Junior Children (Six to Nine)

Balloon Party

Pinata Party or Mexican Fiesta

Treasure Hunt Party

Pirate Party or Peter Pan Party

Hobo Party

United Nations Party

Space Party or Trip to the Moon
Missile Cake is made by baking cake batter in different-size cans. An ice-cream cone forms the nose.
Salmon loaf, baked in a round layer-cake pan, is popular with children. Serve with a frothy milk punch. (*See photo 34.*)

Campfire Party

The Preteens (Ten to Twelve)

Skating, Swimming, Skiing Parties

Pajama Party for Girls
Waffles, topped with scoops of ice cream, and homemade chocolate brownies are "the most." (*See photo 35.*)

Cook-Outs for Boys

Progressive Party for Mixed Group
Guests go from house to house for games and refreshments.

An Arty Party
Finger painting, clay modeling, mural painting.

The Teens

Ice-Cream Social

Bowling Party
Bowling Ball and Tenpins form the centerpiece on the refreshment table. Cake batter, baked in a Pyrex bowl and frosted, makes the ball; soft-drink bottles with paper cutouts are set in formation for the tenpins. (*See photo 36.*)

Hawaiian Luau
Pineapple-topped cake, artificial flowers, and paper *leis* set the stage for a Hawaiian party. (*See photo 37.*)

Cook-It-Yourself Party
Teens make a batch of spaghetti with sauce, or pancakes and sausages or crisp bacon.

Come-As-You-Are Party

Let's-Read-a-Play Party
Teen guests read a three-act play, stopping for refreshments between acts. Play is chosen to provide a part for each guest, and duplicate scripts must be secured.

Beach Picnic Party

Family Parties

Mother's Day and Father's Day Parties

Watermelon Festival

Strawberry Festival

Turn-About Party (Children serve their parents)

Stunts and Tricks Party

Old-Fashioned Songfest

Bon Voyage Party

PARTY CAKES FOR ALL OCCASIONS

When most people, and all children, think of parties, they immediately think of cake and ice cream! The mere mention of such delights, to the young in years, means a wonderful fun-time celebration.

Cakes can set the stage for the theme of any party and, by means of cake pans, made from heavy-duty aluminum foil, cakes can be baked in almost any shape and size desired. These pans are easy to make, sturdy, and, with care, can be used several times. Use children's coloring or nursery-rhyme books for ideas and for designs. Almost anyone can make a simple outline of an animal, flower, or a toy on heavy cardboard. The only caution is to keep the design simple, with no part of the design too thin or complicated, or the cake batter in the thin part of the pan will bake to crispness before the rest of the batter is baked.

FOIL CAKE PANS

A heart-shaped pan is one of the easiest of all to make from foil, because of the simple lines of the heart. While heart-shaped cake pans are readily available in stores, the advantage of making your own is that the size can be adapted to suit large parties and one cake can serve many. The only limitations on size is the size of the baking oven.

Foil-Heart Pan

1. Cut a large heart out of heavy cardboard. Put a couple of shirt cardboards together with Scotch Tape. Cover the cutout on both sides with heavy-duty aluminum foil.
2. Tear off a long strip of foil, approximately the length of the entire outline of your cutout. Fold it lengthwise to within ½

inch of the other edge. Fold this again in half, and then a third time, always folding it lengthwise so that you end up with a strip about 2 inches wide and long enough to fit around the pattern. This strip serves as the sides of your homemade foil pan. (*See photo 39.*)

3. Place the strip around the outline of the heart and fold the ½-inch single layer under, taping as you go with Scotch Tape. (*See photo 40.*)
4. When completely around, let ends of strip overlap about 1 inch and tape. Finished pan is surprisingly sturdy. (*See photo 41.*)
5. Grease your foil pan thoroughly or brush generously with a mixture of half soft shortening and half flour.
6. Fill the foil pan half full of cake batter and bake in a preheated 350° F. oven until cake tests done. For very large cakes, bake at 325° F.
7. Cool cake for 5 minutes, then carefully remove from pan to cakerack to cool thoroughly. Then frost. Or leave in the pan to cool, and frost the top only. The foil pan makes a convenient way to carry the cake to another destination. (*See photo 42.*)

Other Shapes

Almost any shape you can think of is suitable to be made into a foil pan in exactly the same way as the Heart Pan above. Try a rabbit, man-in-the-moon, lamb, Rudolph the Red-Nosed Reindeer, umbrella, pumpkin, turkey, Christmas tree, doll with hoop skirt. . . . Be sure to keep the outline simple, with no very thin sections. (*See photos 43 and 44.*)

CHAPTER 4

Games for Tots to Teens

GAMES ARE INSTANT FUN

What you need at group socials is instant fun—a magic ingredient that will force acquaintances or even strangers to start conversations, smile at one another, laugh a little, and relax enough to add to the fun on their own. There's no better magic than a good game, carefully planned to include everybody in some harmless foolishness.

What kind of games are good for parties? Many different kinds are suitable, but they shouldn't be too complex, intricate, or difficult to "get" the first time you play them. Choose games that are easy to describe and easy to understand, and choose games designed to mix the maximum people in the maximum time. In this chapter you'll find several "mixer" games described—games designed just for the purpose of introducing the party guests to one another. Choose games that will create the mood you need at the moment—a quiet, thoughtful pen-and-pencil game just before serving dinner, or immediately after a hearty feast; an active, racing relay that has everyone laughing just before you ask guests to choose partners for dancing; a game that lets you choose the participants when you want to coax some shy guests out of their shell; a cheerful singing game that includes everyone, just before it's time for the party to end.

Keep the announcements about the games as brief as possible, and don't apologize—just assume everybody wants to play and even those who are reluctant will join in. Have the equipment so organized and the announcement so clear that there's no delay or hesitation.

If you are the chairman of the entertainment committee, and will be responsible for the games, rehearse them with your family or friends before the day of the party, so you are confident that the games are playable, enjoyable, and they don't present any problems as far as the equipment or space needed, and amount of skill required (considered in relation to the ages of your guests) or the time it takes to play the game.

Be sure to have enough ideas for games on hand to fill the time available. You can consult books on games at your local library, pick up ideas from magazines and television shows that use stunts or games, or just dig back into your childhood for games you particularly like. Almost any game can be adapted in some way to suit a theme. The Peanut Safari, for instance, listed under games for The Little Tots, can be switched to a hunt for Easter eggs, shamrocks for St. Patrick's Day, candy corn for Halloween, or any other small object your theme might suggest. Most games fit the following classifications: round-table games (like making Valentines); active, running games; relay races; musical games, guessing games, and pencil-and-paper games. Try to include one from each of these classifications during an evening or afternoon, so that you have a well-balanced program.

Small groups might like an evening of "boxed" games, such as jackstraws, checkers, parcheesi—a large assortment, from which they select their favorite game.

It seems hardly necessary to caution that stunts or tricks that subject your guests to ridicule are always a mistake. But you may find that in the course of an evening, the games that are the most fun may make some of the guests hard to control. Just switch the pace, suggesting a quiet game that will calm down the boisterous players.

Most good games present no age problem at family affairs.

Parents and children can join in any game that is simple and easy to explain, and get an extra thrill from playing together. It's fun to pair mothers and daughters or fathers and sons for relay teams or to let the children laugh at the spectacle of their parents balancing peanuts on the ends of their noses.

TEN TIPS FOR CONDUCTING CHILDREN'S GAMES

1. Children love praise. Find something nice to say about each player, especially the shy ones.

2. Alternate active games and quiet games, and make sure that the children aren't competing so hard that they are playing too strenuously for their age and strength.

3. Play a game often enough so that the children become familiar with the rules.

4. Let the children suggest a game once in a while.

5. The younger the child, the shorter the game should be.

6. Know the rules thoroughly, and assemble any supplies you need ahead of time. If markings are needed, as in races or circle games, draw them before the game starts.

7. Use a definite signal, like a whistle or a bell, to attract attention, rather than a shout.

8. Ask the children to help, when you can.

9. Make sure each child gets a turn, and select "teams" yourself, if necessary, to guarantee each child a chance to play.

10. Play will proceed more smoothly if you decide on teams early during the party and keep the same teams throughout, so that there isn't a repetition of the process each time you play a team game.

A REMINDER LIST OF OLD FAVORITES

In addition to the games explained in this chapter, such favorites should not be forgotten: Pin the Tail on the Donkey; Musical

Chairs; Hide-and-Seek; Red Light; Blindman's Buff; Animal, Vegetable, or Mineral; Button, Button, Who's Got the Button?; Twenty Questions; Truth or Consequences; Red Rover; Simon Says; Statues; Follow-the-Leader; London Bridge; I Spy; and The Farmer in the Dell.

GETTING-TO-KNOW-YOU GAMES
(For all ages)

Mixer games are designed to get your guests talking so the party will be off to a quick start, without the awful period of self-conscious silence that ensues when the guests don't know each other very well. Mixer games are variations on a main theme. Here are several to give you the idea:

Tots:

Give each child half of something with instructions to find the other half. You can tear playing cards in half, or mottos, or paper dolls.

Junior Children:

Label each child with the name of a famous person, and put the label on his back. The children must find out who they are by asking questions of the other guests. Be sure the person is famous to children as well as to grownups.

Preteens and Teens:

Tell each child he is half of a famous couple, such as, Romeo and Juliet, Mr. and Mrs. Jiggs, or The Owl and the Pussycat. Once the children have all found their partners, they assemble and each couple acts out their identities and the other guests must guess who they are. This means that during the identifying period, they must not reveal their names if they can help it, except to their partners when they have succeeded in finding them. Identity is established by asking a question to which only the partner would know the answer. For instance, Mrs. Jiggs might ask every boy, "Do you like corned beef and cabbage?", rather than directly, "Are you Mr. Jiggs?" This mixer works best with older children and teens, and serves to pair off girls with boys.

GAMES FOR LITTLE TOTS

Peanut Safari

This peanut hunt is a good icebreaker. Before the party, conceal peanuts in their shells throughout the party room. As each child enters, tell him that he must find a certain number of peanuts in order to qualify for the next game. Be sure to limit the number of peanuts for each guest so that the first children to arrive don't capture them all. Hide enough extra so that there's no danger that a child will not find them, and select the hiding places with the age of the children in mind. Toddlers will fail to see a peanut dangled in front of their nose, and get extremely impatient if they don't find a peanut right away! You can elaborate on the "safari" idea by providing butterfly nets, paper guns, or magnifying glasses. When the child has found his peanuts, he reports to the party hostess, who ties on his name tag, and if possible hands him a "prize"—maybe just a pretty box or basket to hold his peanuts, and any other "loot" the party will provide.

Who's Barking?

All the players stand in a circle except one, who stands in the center, with a handkerchief shielding his eyes. The circle moves slowly clockwise, very quietly, so it is hard for the blindfolded player to tell how far it has traveled. At a signal, all players stop and the blindfolded player must walk to one of the players, touch him with just one hand and say, "Nice doggie." The "doggie" must bark like a dog, and the blindfolded player then guesses which player it is. If he guesses correctly, the "doggie" takes his place in the center of the circle.

Only Birds Can Fly

The players stand at attention, with their hands at their sides. A leader is chosen who calls out the names of animals, birds, and objects. As he does, the children must flap their "wings" (their arms) ONLY when he mentions the name of a bird. As they get used to the game, the names are called out faster and faster. A child who flaps his wings for anything except a bird leaves the game, until all but one are eliminated. He becomes the next leader.

Variations on this game are obvious: Only Wheels Can Go; Only Fish Can Swim; and so forth.

Do As I Do

This game is very like Follow the Leader, except that it is played standing in one place, and is therefore quieter. The leader, in turn, pats her tummy, nods her head, clasps a hand on one knee, and wiggles a foot, and the children must do what she does—but performing all the actions at once. If they miss one of the motions, they are out of the game. The leader might do well to practice the motions in private before starting the game, to make sure she, too, can perform them all simultaneously.

Watch Out for the Wolf

The players are divided into two parallel lines six to twelve feet apart, facing each other. The leader, or an extra player if there is an uneven number of players, is The Wolf, and stands halfway between the opposing lines. The players, who can be sheep, or Red Ridinghoods, or lambs, or whatever your imagination dreams up, try to trade opposing places. The Wolf tries to gain a place by racing to an empty spot before another player can reach it. If he does, the player who has lost his place becomes The Wolf.

Toy Box

Each child is given a slip of paper on which is written (or drawn, if the children cannot read) the name of a toy. Each in turn must act out the actions of that toy, and the other players try to guess what toy it is. The child who guesses first acts out his toy next. Suggestions for toys: jack-in-the-box, bounding ball, skates, jump rope, train.

An alternate for this game might be to have each child act out an animal. Hand a child an animal cracker. Without showing the cracker to the other guests, he must imitate the animal. Of course, he gets to eat the cracker once he has performed.

Fish Pond

This game requires lots of preparation before your party, but it is well worth it. Prepare a fish pond by wrapping a huge packing box (or an up-ended card table) with blue crepe paper, pasting fish-shaped cutouts on it, to help create the effect of a pond. Then get fishpoles—just sticks with strings and hooks tied on will do—enough for three or four children to fish with at a time. Next, prepare the "fish"—little paper bags holding fortunes, or small favors, or instructions for a trick. A long-suffering volunteer, one who doesn't mind sitting crosslegged for a while, is concealed in the fishpond. The children take turns "fishing" in the pond. The volunteer hooks the paper bags onto the dangling hooks. You can make this game a simple handing out of favors, or stretch it by having the bags contain tricks that the children must perform to earn their "fish." The smaller the child, the simpler the game should be. If the children are old enough to take the suspense, once in a while have them pull jokes out of the pond—like rubber boots or plastic fish; but make sure each child has a turn for a real prize. Possible prizes might be small artificial turtles, little plastic boats, bags of marbles, balloons, or bubble pipes.

Ring the Bell for the Pussy

The children stand in a circle with the player who is "it" in the center holding his hands over his eyes. The children pass a small bell from hand to hand until the leader says, "Stop, Pussy." As soon as she says this, the child who has the bell must hide it behind his back. All the children place their hands behind their backs, too. The child in the center must guess where the "pussy" is. The child holding the bell may tinkle it very softly . . . little children will not be concerned about how easy it is to guess who has the bell, but will love the excitement of pointing out the "pussy." The child who is pussy becomes the next one to be "it." It's easy to control the game by saying, "Stop, Pussy" for each child in turn.

Hot Potato

All the players sit in a circle. A potato is handed to one child, who gives it to his next-right neighbor, who passes it on in turn. At a signal, play stops and the child left holding the "hot" potato is out of the game. You can play music while the potato is being passed, or simply blow a whistle when it's time to stop.

Dive-Bomb

This game requires a little skill, but not so much that it will discourage young children. Two milk bottles are placed next to a chair. Each child is given 3 or 4 clothespins and told he must dive-bomb the milk bottles. He climbs on the chair, kneeling backward, and drops the clothespins. If he gets one into the bottle, he's scored a hit. The child with the most hits wins the game.

GAMES FOR JUNIOR CHILDREN

Supermarket

This is a very quiet guessing game. The first player says, "I sent my son to the supermarket to buy B——, and the other players try to guess what it is that the son bought. Very little children will stick to simple products, such as, apples, milk, bread; older children will like complicated ones, such as, DFM for Devil's Food Mix.

Hot and Cold

The leader sends all the other players out of the room and while they are gone, hides an agreed-upon object somewhere in the room in a visible, but out-of-the-way place. He calls the players back in and they all try to find the object. The player who finds it first is the next leader. The player who hid the object is allowed to hint by saying "hot," when one of the players is near the object, or "cold," when he is going off in the wrong direction.

Squat Tag

This is played just like ordinary tag, except that a player can escape being tagged if he can assume squatting position before the player who is "it" can touch him. You can vary this: a player can escape being tagged if he can kneel, or raise his hands over his head, or place hands on knees, or whatever.

Another way to play tag is to play Link Tag. In this game, the player who is tagged joins hands with the player who tags him, and then they proceed to tag the next player and so on, until all hands are joined. The last person tagged becomes "it" for the next game.

Bean Basket

Prepare enough beanbags for all of the players, but half in red and half in blue. Divide players into the red team and the blue team. Have them stand in line at opposite sides of the room, and place a large bushel basket halfway between the teams. Make sure the throwing lines are drawn carefully. The player on each team throws toward the basket in turn. Each hit in the basket counts 5 points, and the team with the most points at the end of each round wins.

Pony Polo

Secure enough stick horses to mount two teams of about four children each. Line the teams up at opposite ends of the room, with a large bushel basket placed halfway between, as the "goal." The object of the game is to kick a large rubber ball into the basket, meanwhile riding the stick horses. If they are fairly young, the players may use their hands to swat the ball, but are not allowed to throw it. Older players should try to get the ball into the goal by kicking it with their feet.

Don't Break the Balloon

This is a relay game. Divide the players into two teams, lined up one in back of the other. Each player in turn runs down a track (you can use chalk lines), swatting a balloon with a fan or cardboard to make it go straight down the track to the goal at the opposite end of the room. If the balloon breaks, the player must secure a new one from the goal, blow it up and then start again from the point where the balloon broke. You can speed up the game, when there are lots of players, by having more teams, by blowing up the balloons ahead of time so the players need only run to get another when their balloons break, and by shortening the track.

Inner-Tube Race

Divide the players into two teams. The first two players on each team together don an inner tube and race toward the goal and back to their team. They remove the inner tube, and the next two players put it on, and race to the goal and back, and so on. The first team to have all its players complete the race wins. You can specify that one player must face front and one back, or you can let them race "free style." Keep the size of your players in mind when you schedule this game. It won't do for a parents-and-children picnic, if the mamas and papas are plump!

Candy Relay

Divide children into two or more equal teams. Place chairs, one for each team, at opposite ends of room; on each chair place a plate and on the plate place a number of jelly beans, one for each child on the team. Give the first child on each team a small basket. On signal the first person runs to the chair, picks up one jelly bean, drops it in his basket, runs back and gives the basket to the next child in line, and goes to the end of the line. Next person does the same. The first team with all the candy in the basket wins.

Button Relay

Divide children into teams. For each team select one young man wearing a coat with 2 or 3 buttons on it—all must have the same number of buttons. On signal the first child on each team runs up and buttons the coat and runs back. Next in line runs up and unbuttons the coat, and so on, to see which team wins.

Hop Toad

Arrange squares of paper on the floor, keeping them a reasonable distance apart. Make them not more than one foot in size, remembering that children have small feet. Make a pathway or circle with the squares and let the children hop to music, resting both feet on the floor only when the music stops. See how far the children can hop on one foot. Anyone who puts his foot down when the music is playing is out of the game. Don't make the pauses in the music too far apart.

GAMES FOR PRETEENS

Pack the Pocketbook

Fill two huge handbags with an assortment of strange objects —a book, comb, box, doll, dish, pencil—the odder the assortment the better.

Have players divide into two teams and stand, one behind the other, in parallel lines, with the players facing the front of the room. Draw a line across the front of the room and place the pocketbooks behind it. The teams' players, each in turn, must race toward their pocketbook, remove the contents, repack it, and then race back to the end of their line. The next team's player does the same thing, and this is continued until each player has packed the pocketbook. The first team to finish wins the game. You can shorten the game by letting the first person on each team unpack the bag, and the second person on each team repack it, and so on.

Toss the Plate

Each player is given five or six paper plates. He throws them, one at a time, at a bushel basket placed about ten feet away from the tossing line. The player who lands the most plates in the basket wins. The target can be a wire hoop, hanging from the ceiling, with the object to toss the paper plates through the hoop. It's almost as hard, usually harder, to throw a balloon at such a target as it is to throw the paper plates. If you don't have paper plates or balloons, try a handkerchief.

Word List

This is a nice quiet game to use as "breathing space" between two more active games. You need a watch with a minute hand. Divide the players into two teams. Alternating the teams, have them name as many words as they can, beginning with a letter you call out. Try to keep the difficulty level the same for each two letters. There are lots of words beginning with B, not so many beginning with Y. Time the period carefully, allowing one minute for each letter.

Untie the Knots

Two teams sit in relay position, one in back of another. Each team is handed a shoestring, or long piece of string, in which knots are tied—one knot for each team member. The first player on each team unties the first knot, hands the string to the next player, and so on, until every knot is untied. The first team to untie its knots is the winner.

A variation of this is to pass a shoe down the line. Each player must untie the tied shoelace, then tie it up again and pass it on to the next player.

Spell a Word

This is a good team game. Before the party, prepare cardboards on which you have printed the letters of simple words. Choose words that have the right number of letters to fit your teams—

about five or six is a good number. Shuffle the boards so that the letters are mixed up. At a given signal, the letters of a word are handed to each team (it's fairer if you use duplicate sets) and the team must arrange themselves in the correct order, holding up their cardboards to spell the word. You can use words which carry out the theme of your party—SANTA, TREES, CAROLS, for Christmas, for instance.

Fan-Fan

Get tissue paper in pretty colors, and crumple the sheets into large balls. Then cut out fans from cardboard, or buy inexpensive ones. The players, divided into teams, try to be the first to bat the tissue balls into a cardboard box or basket placed across the room from the team line. The first team that has all its players complete the task wins.

GAMES FOR TEENS

Divide the players into two teams, who sit facing each other. The first players each place an orange on their feet, then each passes it to the next player, without using his hands. He in turn must pass it to the next player and so on. The team that passes the orange to the last player first wins. If the orange rolls off a player's feet, as indeed it will, the player must get up, and get it back to his place and onto his feet again by using only his feet.

Necktie

Now that the boys are old enough to be wearing ties at a party, line them up in a row and ask them to untie their ties. Then have each of the girls select a partner, and stand facing him. At a signal, the girls must tie the boys' ties. The boys are allowed to help by giving verbal instructions, but they must keep their hands clasped behind their backs. The first couple to have a correctly tied tie wins. Older children and teens may like the more difficult version of this game, in which each boy must thread a needle at the same time that the girl is tying the necktie.

Where Am I?

A variation of Twenty Questions, in this game the object is to name the geographic location decided upon by the person who is "it." You can play this simply, with one person thinking of the spot, and everybody else asking the questions in turn. Or, you can divide the players into teams, letting each team ask a question in turn. You can speed up the game, if you want a short, quiet game, by limiting the game to rivers, or cities, or countries.

Guess the Record

Play just enough bars of a record to supply a fair clue, then ask the guests to name the song, or the vocalist, or the band. Start with obvious ones like Sinatra or Nat King Cole, then get progressively harder. The guest who guesses the most records might win a record or a record album as a prize.

People Ticktacktoe

Arrange nine chairs in ticktacktoe position—3 rows of 3 chairs each, and let the girls be the Xs and the boys the Os. The object, as in the paper-and-pencil game, is to get three in a row. The teams' players take turns in choosing seats.

CHAPTER 5

Themes and Decorations

CHOOSING AND USING A THEME

Just as the theme of a musical composition sets a mood, tells the story, and recurs just often enough to provide unity without monotony, the theme of your organization's affair should be the point of departure for all your planning.

Before selecting a theme, you should have a very clear idea of the kind of event you want to have and the purpose you hope to achieve. Why are you giving the party? Is it to raise funds, to attract new members and publicize your group, to celebrate a holiday, to honor someone, or is it just for fun? Is there a special date or event connected with the affair? Is a national holiday near the date of the party? Will it be held in spring, summer, fall, or winter? Will it be conducted indoors or out?

Who will be your audience? Do you want to appeal to young married couples, entire families, teen-agers, children? Will the average age be the twenties, the forties, the sixties? Will there be as many men as women? Will the majority know one another?

What will be the time of day of the party? Will it be a casual morning party? A luncheon? An elaborate evening affair?

Where will you hold the party and how many people do you plan to entertain? What type of activities will the space allow?

Will any other parties be given at the same time by organizations that will be competing for your audience?

What events, conducted in the past, have been successful—which have been flops and why?

Is the affair within the scope of your organization, and do you have enough members to absorb the work and responsibility without overtaxing the few? Better to lower your sights to a less-ambitious undertaking and do it well than to attempt an affair beyond your capabilities.

By the time you've finished answering these questions, your event will begin to assume definite proportions. You will know, for example, that you want to give an evening party for about a hundred people, that you are anxious to attract new members, both men and women, that the affair will be held in the spring in the new recreation room, and that most of the people you are inviting will need help in getting acquainted. Already a Spring Dance has been scheduled by another organization in your community, which will appeal to the same audience. So you decide to give a kind of Mardi Gras: it sounds friendly and fun, and it offers great possibilities for decorations, refreshments, and costumes.

Now it is time to settle down to the serious business of choosing a theme. It's something like finding a name for a baby. You can discuss and plan and almost settle on one, then another possibility is suggested, and it starts all over again. Yet, finally, there is one perfect theme, one that everyone agrees on.

Perhaps the best way to start the discussion of a theme is by elimination. Listed on the following pages are whole groups of theme possibilities. Go through the listing and rule out entire groups that are not appropriate to your affair, or that are beyond the scope of your organization at the moment. Write down a list of "possibilities," and keep on eliminating until you narrow down the potentials to a small list of ones that would be completely suitable.

THE SEASONS

Obviously:

Spring, Summer, Autumn, Winter

Less obviously:

Indian Summer

Showers and Flowers (April)

Dog Days (August)

Doldrums (January–February, when there's a winter letdown)
You'll get lots of enthusiasm for a gay party to break up the
dull winter months.

Suit Weather (October, in the East) A good time to run a
fashion luncheon, conduct a hike, or an "open house" tour.

Holiday Time (Thanksgiving through Epiphany, January 6)

DAYS AND DATES

Days of the Week

Blue-Monday Breakfast

Friday Fish-Chowder Supper

Lazy Sunday Brunch

Weekend Bazaar

Legal Holidays

New Year's (January 1)

Washington's Birthday (February 22)

Memorial or Decoration Day (May 30)

Independence Day (July 4)

Labor Day (First Monday in September)

Veterans' Day (November 11)

Thanksgiving (Fourth Thursday in November)

Christmas (December 25)

Other Public Holidays

Inauguration Day (January 20)

Lincoln's Birthday (February 12)

Columbus Day (October 12)

Election Day (First Tuesday after first Monday in November)

Holidays Celebrated in One or More States

Feast of the Three Kings (January 6, in Puerto Rico)

Battle of New Orleans (January 8, in Louisiana)

Robert E. Lee's Birthday (January 19, in some southern states; called Lee-Jackson day, in Virginia)

General Douglas MacArthur Day (January 26)

Franklin D. Roosevelt Day (January 30)

Texas Independence Day (March 2)

Mardi Gras (variable)

Andrew Jackson's Birthday (March 15)

Thomas Jefferson's Birthday (April 13)

Kamehameha Day (June 11, in Hawaii, but a *luau* is good anytime)

Bunker Hill Day (June 17)

Pioneer Day (July 24)

Will Roger's Day (November 4, in Oklahoma)

Other Days (not legal or public)

National Freedom Day (February 1)

Groundhog Day (February 2)

St. Valentine's Day (February 14)

Susan B. Anthony Day (February 15)

St. Patrick's Day (March 17)

Pan American Day (April 14)

Arbor Day (variable according to States)

May Day (May 1)

Mother's Day (second Sunday in May)

National Maritime Day (May 22)

Air or Armed Forces Day (Third Saturday in May)

Flag Day (June 14)

Father's Day (Third Sunday in June)

Citizenship Day (September 17)

American Indian Day (Fourth Friday in September)

Child Health Day (First Monday in October)

United Nations Day (October 24)

Sadie Hawkins' Day (First Saturday after November 11)

Bill of Rights Day (December 15)

Wright Brothers' Day (December 17)

Forefathers' Day (December 21)

GEOGRAPHY

The Universe

Many fantasy ideas present themselves when you consider this subject as a possible theme: A few suggestions might be: A *Space Age Party*, A *Martian Funfest*, A *Trip to the Moon*, A *Star Dance*.

The World

Here, too, theme ideas are limitless. You might decide to give a United Nations Party or a Round the World in 80 Days' Bazaar, with one booth for each different country en route. A Latin Festival might include France, Italy, Portugal, and Spain, yet interesting party themes can be developed around each individual country, with lots of color and authentic decorations and costumes.

The United States

Your own state is a fine idea for a party theme, especially appropriate for Statehood Day, the day that your state was admitted into the Union, or on the birthday of a famous citizen of your state. You might decide to give a New England Dinner, an Old West Jamboree, a Southern Hospitality Night, a Gold-Rush Bazaar, or a State of the Union Fair. Here the fair grounds could be divided into several or more logical geographical areas but, for an extremely ambitious affair, it's conceivable that you could have as many as fifty booths, one for each state. Both the decoration of the booth and the merchandise for sale would reflect the industry, history, and climate of the state.

HISTORY

The many thousands of ages, eras, civilizations, empires, dynasties, and memorable events in history are filled with color, costume ideas, decorative ideas, and fascinating customs and traditions. From the pages of history can be found themes for almost any kind of gathering, from the serious, the educational, the artistic, to those that are just plain fun.

A Gay Nineties' Night, for instance, is noisy and colorful and appealing to all ages; A Victorian Evening might appeal to an older, more serious group. The Twenties, complete with Gramophones, the Charleston, and raccoon coats, never fails to charm the college crowd, and boys would be highly intrigued by an Age of Chivalry Afternoon of tournaments, relay games, games of skill, and chivalrous deeds. The teen-agers would delight in a Paleolithic Age Ado, once this unwieldy name is explained as nothing more than a Caveman Party. You can suggest they arrive in "skin" costumes, provide clubs for the men, and use plenty of imagination in décor and the menu—dinosaur hamburgers, Stone-Age bread, and pre-Caesar salads, are a few suggestions.

The World Almanac contains thirty-two pages of historical data entitled Memorable Dates, beginning with 3000 B.C., when the pyramids were built by the kings of Egypt.

COLORS, FLOWERS, JEWELS

Individually, these subjects do not lend themselves to very flexible themes, but together or in combination, or combined with the seasons can be most useful in inspiring some exquisitely beautiful themes with imaginative fantasy décor.

Fairyland might be all white and silver, scattered with diamond dust and pearls, with large white flowers resembling fantasy roses or gardenias. Another interpretation of the land of make-believe might be rosy-pink with gold and rubies and sapphires. The Emerald Ball immediately connotes an elegant evening and the color scheme would logically be green. Combined with seasons, certain flowers become traditional, such as a Holly Fair at Christmas or a Rose Festival in June.

A list of the Flowers of the Month will be found in the chapter, *Church Flowers and Gardens*. Herewith are the Jewels of the Month:

January	Garnet
February	Amethyst
March	Bloodstone or Aquamarine
April	Diamond
May	Emerald
June	Pearl or Moonstone
July	Ruby
August	Sardonyx or Peridot
September	Sapphire
October	Opal or Tourmaline
November	Topaz
December	Turquoise or Zircon

ANNIVERSARIES

Your organization's anniversary, the wedding anniversary of your president or minister, or the fiftieth wedding anniversary of the elder citizens of your group are reason enough for a party, large or intimate, but still built around a theme. The symbols for social anniversaries are, in some cases, the same as the traditional wedding symbols, but in others are different. You would not be remiss in using whichever gives you the most flexibility or imagination for your décor.

	Wedding	*Social*
1st	Clocks	Paper
2nd	China	Cotton
3rd	Crystal, glass	Leather
4th	Electrical appliances	Fruit and flowers, silk
5th	Silverware	Wood
6th	Wood	Sugar, candy, iron

7th	Desks, pen and pencils	Wool or copper
8th	Linens, laces	Bronze or pottery
9th	Leather	Willow or pottery
10th	Diamond jewelry	Tin or aluminum
11th	Fashion jewelry	Steel
12th	Pearls or colored gems	Silk or linen
13th	Textiles, furs	Lace
14th	Gold jewelry	Ivory
15th	Watches	Crystal
16th	Silver hollowware	
17th	Furniture	
18th	Porcelain	
19th	Bronze	
20th	Platinum	China
25th	Sterling silver jubilee	Silver
30th	Diamond	Pearl
35th	Jade	Coral
40th	Ruby	Ruby
45th	Sapphire	Sapphire
50th	Golden jubilee	Gold
55th	Emerald	Emerald
60th	Diamond jubilee	Diamond

LITERARY CHARACTERS

A few obvious themes present themselves, such as: A *Peter Pan or Mother Goose Party for Children*, A *Charles Dickens Christmas Party*, An *Alice in Wonderland Fair*, A *Treasure Island Pirate Party*, A *Come As Your Favorite Book Costume Party*, A *Shakespeare Festival*, A *Tom Sawyer Painting Party* (your meeting room or kitchen needs painting!) There are of course, hundreds more such literary themes.

HOBBIES AND OCCUPATIONS

These may provide further ideas, as for instance, A *Photographer's Ball*, A *Fisherman's Supper*, A *Garden Show*, An *Art Show*, A *Games Night*, or A *"What's My Line" Party*.

At this point, it must be fairly obvious that almost any subject under the sun is "meat" for a theme. Now, how do you turn a theme into a successful affair? Let's follow the course of such a theme, as it was developed.

A woman's club, numbering about fifty members, decided to have a fund-raising affair in August. Because most of the members were from commuter families they selected a weekend rather than an evening during the week to stage the party. They were anxious to introduce the husbands of the club members to each other, and some members felt that the whole family should be invited. This was voted on, and it was decided to make it a family affair. The party therefore must be held during the day so that the small children could be included. Now the choice was narrowed down to something for a hot day in August that all members of the family could enjoy. After much discussion and eliminating, the members narrowed their list down to three ideas: a Country Fair, a Beach Picnic, and a Watermelon Festival.

The Country Fair was voted down as being too ambitious a project for a small club and the Beach Picnic was ruled out because the local beach was usually crowded on weekends, and there were no facilities for storing and serving refreshments convenient to the beach. This left the Watermelon Festival. It was a happy choice for it was the type of party that could be moved indoors, if necessary; and it was sure to appeal to both parents and children. No sooner was the final decision made than ideas for decorations were popping thick and fast.

The Decorations Committee designed everything for the party. They made tickets from colored paper, cut in the shape of watermelons, with string tags for tying or pinning to each guest's lapel. They fashioned red-and-green oval place mats. Paper plates, cups, and napkins were all decorated with watermelon designs. Two huge watermelons were made into jack-o'-lanterns to flank the entrance. The menu was kept simple and hand edible: fried chicken, potato chips and pickles, carrot sticks, rolls and, of course, watermelon. Several husbands were recruited to slice the melons.

For them, one talented seamstress made red-and-green-striped aprons, each with a big pocket in the shape of a watermelon. The women who served wore red-and-green aprons and hairbands to match.

For entertainment, there was a watermelon-eating contest, and a watermelon-roll relay. Prizes followed the theme.

Publicity was fairly easy to arrange. The local newspaper accepted a picture submitted by the publicity chairman. She had perched her small son on a pile of watermelons and given him a slice to eat. His toothless grin was appealing, and the paper ran it in the middle of a hot spell, with plenty of credit to the coming festival.

The party was a huge success because it was a unified affair, easy to plan and execute, and one that filled all the needs of the particular organization.

PARISIAN PARTY

Paris is a theme that can be developed in many different directions. You can use it to form the nucleus for an artists' ball, a fashion luncheon, a gay bazaar, or a celebration for the graduation class. For decorations use travel posters, the gay French tricolor, or the more delicate fleur-de-lis. Long loaves of French bread, red-checked tablecloths, café tables and chairs, and bright kiosks all add to a Parisian background. You might block off special sections and title the "streets" with French names: Place de l'Étoile, Champs Élysées, and so forth. Wagons filled with flowers, real or artificial, and paintings hung around the room, help create the look of Paris.

Costumes need not be exactly authentic, but can reflect the stereotyped Parisian characters: apache dancers, artists in smocks and berets and big flowing ties, chefs in high white hats, modistes with hatboxes, gendarmes, and cancan dancers.

At a fair the booths might reflect various aspects of the city: for example, a fashion section. In it, include a knitware booth.

Decorate the booth with giant balls of wool—actually, wadded up newspapers, rolled into a ball and thinly covered with a layer of thick yarn. Insert knitting needles made of wooden dowels. A local department store or dress shop might co-operate in a fashion show with "straight from Paris" designs. Another area might stress French cuisine: a *cordon bleu* booth could sell French kitchen equipment such as omelet pans, chopping boards, knives, peelers, slicers, soufflé dishes, and so forth. If your organization includes several good cooks, have them demonstrate some of the items to draw crowds. Have a "recipe of the night" promotion, offering tiny samples of a special dish made with one of the kitchen items. You might offer collections of recipes for sale, neatly typed cards with some of your members' favorites, the more French the better. THE FLEA MARKET booth would be just that—a bazaar in miniature offering everything under the sun for sale. Display antiques, white elephants, and other merchandise on simple wooden planks set in tiers around a kiosk. THE LEFT BANK would stress art. Combine attractive prints with originals by your club's best artists. CAFÉ PATISSERIE might not only sell fine cakes and pastries to take home but serve ice cream with a variety of toppings and sauces, and slices of cake at small café tables. Another booth might sell all kinds of bread and rolls, brioches, croissants, and sweet breads. A slice of sweet bread and a cup of hot chocolate could be served on the spot.

Luncheon or supper could be a simple stew, salad, French bread, and dessert—but do make it a typically French meal. There are many excellent, yet easy-to-make French recipes, from appetizers to desserts, in the recipe section at the back of the book.

PENNSYLVANIA DUTCH

Here's the makings of a "wonderful good" party in a Pennsylvania-Dutch theme. Hex signs make quaint and colorful posters and decorations, and the colors are appropriately bright red and blue, vivid yellow and strong green—all gay and easy to combine.

You can use hearts and tulips, scrolled vines, little Amish boys and girls. Or, you can research in the library for authentic Pennsylvania-Dutch themes for everything from costumes to wall hangings.

If you are planning a bazaar, you might design each booth as a Pennsylvania-Dutch barn, with a stylized motif giving some indication of the booth's wares. A gingerbread boy for baked goods, and hearts and flowers for "hope-chest" items, such as linens or decorated wood chests. Dress your "staff" in Amish costumes, with cardboard hats and calico jackets, and borrow the idea of little red wagons from the Amish children and use them around the grounds to sell small items. Toys, such as hoops and wooden jumping jacks, when decorated, make good items for sale to children.

A Pennsylvania-Dutch theme is particularly appropriate for clubs or organizations specializing in handcraft items like quilts, knit goods, woven materials, or wood carvings. Woodenware, such as salad bowls and bread boards, decorated with hearts and flowers, roosters, or hex signs are popular.

For children, be sure to include pony or donkey rides, and perhaps, a junior farm, where they may pet the little rabbits, ducks, and chickens. Older children and teen-agers will enjoy a hayride. And all ages will love buying the great big pretzels that are part of the Pennsylvania-Dutch tradition.

THE GAY NINETIES

Gaslight and floor-length tablecloths, trimmed with fringe; ornate mirrors, stuffed birds, and artificial flowers; candelabra, velvet settees, and lots and lots of pillows. You know the look of the Victorian era, and, whether you're planning merely a Victorian Tea or a larger party, you'll find the preparation more than half the fun when you choose a Gay Nineties theme.

Velvet bows might be your main decorative motif—from hair ribbons for your hostesses to trim on the ball-fringe swags you hang from the ceiling. Handle-bar mustaches are a must for the men, and don't forget the bicycle clips on the sleeves of their peppermint-striped shirts! Costumes will include feathered hats, bouffant or hobble skirts, striped blazers, Eton caps, and canes. Props might be borrowed from a local antique shop or attics, or cut out of pasteboard—shaving mugs, rococo knickknacks, hitching posts, gaslights, and fringe and more fringe. Old white lace curtains can soften the whole effect, and don't forget that lighting should be dim.

You'll want to have ice-cream-parlor chairs, set at cloth-covered tables. A player-piano's rinky-tink sound will be the perfect accompaniment—and you can get that sound on records, if your research doesn't uncover a real player piano. All the old heartthrob songs like "Sweet Adeline" will be more fun if everybody joins in, led by a barber-shop quartet dressed as Victorian beaux.

A "mellerdrama" might be part of the fun, complete with a villain to hiss and a heroine to applaud. Sell popcorn, and encourage the audience to participate!

If you are holding a Gay Nineties bazaar out of doors, you might line up station wagons and sell merchandise from the tail gates—just as patent medicine used to be sold from the tail gates of horse-drawn wagons. Sell bottled preserves and pickles, homemade jams and jellies, baked goods and candies. Other items for sale might be velvet pincushions; hand mirrors covered with cherubs, velvet, and bows; antique picture frames (or new ones, treated to look antique); old prints framed in unusual ways; cut-glass, decorative candles; and velvet-covered photo albums. You might schedule a puppet or peep show and rope off a section of the grounds for a "Midway."

For the occasion, you might bring back the old-fashioned free-lunch counter and the corner "saloon." Sell soft drinks in mugs and provide the makings of sandwiches on a buffet table, with hard-cooked eggs, pickles, pretzels, and chunks of cheese. Lunch or dinner might feature corned beef and cabbage.

In warm weather months, the Gay Nineties theme can be applied to a picnic, complete with basket or box lunches, ice-cold lemonade, a raft of ukuleles, and an old-fashioned ice-cream freezer. If you can find a site by a lake, round up lots of rowboats and charge a fee for a ride. Dress up the boats with velvet cushions and provide parasols for the ladies.

IRELAND

It's long been a matter of record that everybody is Irish on St. Patrick's Day—so whether or not your group boasts members of Irish descent, feel confident in scheduling an Irish Night if you want an evening of fun with a strong, definite theme. Green and white, with the brown of Irish potatoes and bogs to highlight it —what better color scheme could you ask? You can fasten shamrocks on walls, ceiling, and tablecloths; cut out giant clay pipes from white cardboard; and even spot a few large field stones around the room, labeling them "Blarney Stones" so there'll be no confusion about their purpose. Tuck flowers around them, to make them less forbidding, and charge a fee for the privilege of kissing the largest, most impressive stone.

Scrubbed potatoes in baskets, with shamrocks tucked in and around them, make suitable table decorations, and don't forget to hide some leprechauns in a few unusual places.

Make the guests all Irish as they assemble; tag them with their names preceded by a Mc or Fitz or an O'; green neckties, made of paper and elastic, for the men; carnations or paper shamrocks for the ladies.

You'll have Irish jigs and reels, and the sentimental ballads like "Mother Machree" and "I'll Take You Home Again, Kathleen." Perhaps a group of children from the high school or a local dancing school could entertain with an Irish jig. Even if only one person knows the jig, have him or her give an Irish-jig lesson.

If children are among your guests, be sure to schedule potato races and bubble-blowing contests with Irish clay pipes. Relay races can be built around a Paddy's Pig theme—the contestants having to capture a cardboard pig (green, of course) and pass it along to the next runner.

Special fair booths might range from items as elaborate as Irish knits, linens, and tweeds and leprechaun dolls and beanbags to simple sugar cookies in shamrock shapes. (See *Directory* for source of Irish merchandise.) Lucky shamrocks in pots make a nice item for sale. Oatmeal bread, shortbreads, and cookies can be packed in containers that stress the green-and-white theme. You might set up an "Irish Coffeehouse" and serve coffee milk shakes or hot coffee mixed with hot chocolate and topped with whipped cream. If you plan a raffle, you'll call it the Irish Sweepstakes, of course.

Irish food for your refreshments would be Irish stew, corned beef and cabbage, bowls of potato salad made green with lots of chopped parsley, green peppers, and green onions; Irish hams, green sage cheese, and coleslaw; Irish bacon.

SOUTH SEAS OR ISLAND *LUAU*

Soft balmy breezes, palms, flowers tucked behind ears, soft guitars—the mood of a South Seas party is one of relaxed friendliness, as informal as a family gathering. You can plan it for a beach party in summer, or you can save it for a wintry day, when it will be a welcome treat to transform an indoor room into an island paradise for a few hours.

If this is an outdoor affair, you can have surfboard floats for the swimmers, sand castle contests for both young and old, and sailboat cruises for a small fee. At such an outdoor affair, you might set up little beach cabanas as booths where appropriate merchandise would be offered for sale.

Indoors, lots of green plants and palms will help create a tropic mood. Tuck a few birds of paradise and some orchids among the green leaves. Costume your helpers in tropical muumuus, tattered jeans with straw hats and paper *leis*; sarongs or hula skirts for the pretty girls. Distribute paper *leis* to the guests (see *Directory of Sources*).

Soft Hawaiian music is available on records, and real ukuleles are even better. Tropic fruits make colorful decorations, and can be used for the feast, as well. Serve the meal on a grass mat decorated with large "ti" leaves cut from paper or aluminum foil. Ti leaves are about 14 inches long, 3 inches wide, with rounded tips, decreasing to small stems at the opposite ends. Layer them to cover the table in authentic *luau* style, and pile colorful fruit directly on the table's center. Barbecued pork or spareribs might be your main dish, or baked ham and sweet potatoes; serve it with a salad, a punch, and a coconut dessert.

Bazaar items would include merchandise made of shells, coconuts, and pineapples.

THEMES IN DETAIL

NEW ORLEANS MARDI GRAS

The Mardi Gras theme is especially appropriate when you want to conduct an all-day-and-on-into-the-night affair. The very words, Mardi Gras, lend an air of festivity to posters and invitations, and there are innumerable colorful elements to combine for decorations.

To achieve a truly carnival effect, there should be emphasis on costumes. Supply "jeweled" or spangled masks for the ladies, more tailored ones for the men.

The decorations should be as bright and gay as you can make them. Paper confetti, crepe-paper strips, clusters of balloons, and huge masks cut from colored cardboard, create a festive air. Paper lanterns, artificial flowers, all the noisemakers used for New Year's Eve parties, should be on hand to add to the carnival atmosphere.

Dancing is in order at a Mardi Gras celebration, so hire a small orchestra, or set up a "library" of lively dance tunes. Start the fun going with a conga line to get your guests into the spirit of the occasion. Of course, you'll want a pageant, too—a parade of all the costumes, perhaps even choosing a King and Queen of the Mardi Gras. Have the Queen demand stunts of her "subjects" to add to the fun.

Colorfully dressed "street vendors" might wander through the crowd, selling miniature French pastries, or pralines, or hot crullers, fresh from the frying pan. An ice-cream vendor might dispense paper cups of tutti-frutti.

In England and France, Mardi Gras time, or Shrove Tuesday is celebrated by eating innumerable pancakes, so you might set up a booth where pancakes are cooked and served, with steaming cups of hot coffee.

DIXIELAND CARNIVAL, PLANTATION PARTY, SOUTHERN-HOSPITALITY NIGHT, OR JULEP JAMBOREE

The atmosphere should be romantic. Moonlight and roses, Spanish moss, white columns, magnolias and rhododendrons, fake or real. Keep the colors delicate and use pastel lanterns and soft candlelight for illumination. Don't hesitate to add a garden swing, a little garden house, a fake "balcony." Hang flowers in baskets from the ceiling and spread artificial grass around the borders of the hall.

The ladies will bless you for the chance to wear becoming hoop skirts, organdy, lace, and long curls. Lace mitts, fans, and leghorn hats with ribbons are appropriate, too. Dress some of the men as Kentucky colonels, with white mustaches and goatees, and planters' coats. Or, if you prefer, dress the children in pretty crinolines and ask women to wear colorful cotton dresses.

Cotton is king in the south, so a bazaar booth can feature items made of cotton. The booth might be decorated with tremendous wads of cotton. Sell cotton candy and include a watermelon booth. A peanut booth will specialize in peanut butter, freshly roasted peanuts, and even tiny peanut dolls. The pie booth will, naturally, sell yam and pecan pie, either whole or by the slice. Pralines are southern and delicious. A fish-fry booth might sell fish sticks, fish-wiches, or deep-fried shrimp. Other foods might be: hot baking-powder biscuits, honey, sliced ham, hominy grits, fried hominy pancakes, Southern-fried chicken, johnnycake, black-eyed peas, and chicken gumbo.

For dinner, serve chicken-in-the-basket, hot biscuits, and a green salad.

COWBOY JAMBOREE

A Jamboree can be held indoors or out. Split-rail fences, real or cardboard, will set the limits of your "ranch," and can be used to divide the area into sections for booths, games, or eating. Ten-gallon hats, ropes, lariats, rugged high boots, guns and holsters help set the stage, and cactus plants add a touch of authenticity. Good colors to use are yellows, browns, burnt orange, and yellow-red. If Texas is your state, use real or artificial yellow roses or Texas bluebonnets.

Cowboy costumes are obvious. You can have elaborate ones with chaps, holsters, bright shirts, and cowboy hats, or simple ones, just the guns and neckerchiefs in bright colors. Distribute lots of shiny sheriff stars, and dress the children as Indians, for what are cowboys without Indians? And you don't want to forget Buffalo Bill, Annie Oakley, or The Lone Ranger.

Music will render "Home on the Range," "Tumbling Tumble-weed," "The Streets of Laredo," "Git Along Little Dogie" and "The Eyes of Texas Are Upon You." You might stage an old-fashioned campfire sing, with guitars, soft lights, and marshmallows to toast. Earlier in the evening you might schedule a barn dance. Let a cowboy quartet stroll the range strumming guitars and yodeling "Don't Fence Me In."

Bazaar booths might be decorated as a dance hall, an old-fashioned "saloon," a poker palace. Arrange pony rides and an Indian village for the children. Serve flapjacks, hot off the griddle, with gobs of butter and pitchers of maple syrup; mugs of hot coffee, too. Chuck-wagon duds for sale might include barbecue aprons and potholders with cowboy motif. Little Dogies' booth would dispense hot dogs, of course.

Dinner tables could be long narrow planks covered with bandannas or horse blankets. Use harnesses or cowboy boots for the centerpiece. Serve beefsteak or hamburgers and let waiters in white cooks' aprons and cowboy hats, or waitresses with gingham aprons, roll around a series of "chuck wagons" containing casseroles of chili and beans. Salad, apple pie, and mugs of hot coffee round out the meal. Other appropriate food would be barbecued spareribs, chuck-wagon stew, homemade bread, and apple cider.

A BARN DANCE OR A HOEDOWN

This is an especially good theme when you want an easy, relaxed evening, with a minimum of fuss. The whole atmosphere should be a happy blend of casual costumes, good music, and simple refreshments.

It's great if you have a real barn, but lacking this, you can convert almost any large hall into a barn, by the use of corn husks, pumpkins, bales of hay, rakes, hoes, and other barn tools. Gourds, Indian corn, and shiny red apples make good table decorations, and so do great bunches of autumn leaves, if your barn dance is scheduled in the fall.

Let the feminine helpers dress in gingham with aprons and sunbonnets; dress the men in overalls or blue jeans, bright cotton shirts, and straw hats. For music, use a trusty phonograph or hire a small group of fiddlers, a pianist, or an accordionist.

The most important element of your Barn Dance is your square-dance "caller," and it is worth investing in the price of a professional to insure a successful evening. He must be able to start the dances, keep them moving, and keep everybody in good spirits. If the dances are properly directed, even novice square dancers will have a good time. In addition, there is lots of mixing up of the couples, so that wallflowers are avoided.

You'll want to have plenty of cold soft drinks on hand for thirsty dancers. Cold apple cider is especially good. You might serve doughnuts, small individual pumpkin tarts, popcorn, and old-fashioned taffy. Refreshments should be kept as simple as possible, but at intermission, you might stage an old-fashioned taffy pull.

ITALY

Italy's food, music, and color make an excellent starting point for several kinds of parties. You can plan a spaghetti supper for a small crowd, or an elaborate fair with many booths; a street carnival, like the fiestas of Italian villages, or a simple pizza-and-Coke party for the teen-agers. Keep colors bright, mixing with abandon, orange, pink, blue, red, and purple. String onions from the ceiling, and alternate the strings with hanging cheeses and salamis.

Italy means music and dancing, so be sure there's plenty of both on hand. You can select almost anything—from gay tarantellas to operatic scores—depending on your audience.

If you are staging an Italian Fair, you have a host of foods to offer. A fruit and vegetable market might sell fresh garden produce in attractive baskets. A pasta booth would sell homemade noodles and special casserole dishes. A meat and cheese booth would offer Italian cheese and sausage, and salami and pastrami sandwiches. A sauce and dressing booth would display homemade Italian salad dressings and spaghetti sauces. You might buy olive oil in gallons and repackage it in attractive bottles, selling it at a good profit. A pizza booth could sell miniature pizzas, using a base of toasted English muffins. Spoon a good spicy tomato sauce over the muffin and garnish with pepperone, anchovies, herbs, black olives, chopped green pepper, chopped onion. Top with a slice of Mozzarella cheese and brown in a portable oven.

THE SILENT SCREEN

Old still photographs, movie posters, cartoon figures, and clippings from old movie magazines can cover the walls of your party room. You'll want big bowls of buttered popcorn and peanuts in the shells. Directors' chairs, searchlights, and old-fashioned megaphones can be arranged strategically to help create the effect of a movie studio. You'll want some of your members dressed as old-time directors with backwards-caps, puttees, and riding crops. As your guests arrive, give them each a big pair of sunglasses, exaggerated cigarette holders and, just for fun, have a few prop wigs. For a costume party, you might ask the guests to come as their favorite movie stars—everybody from Rudolph Valentino to Charlie Chaplin will show up and it's harder to guess if you don't limit the stars to the old-time ones, but let newcomers in, too.

The selection of music is almost unlimited—from Judy Garland's "Over the Rainbow," any Bing Crosby record, all the Jeanette MacDonald-Nelson Eddy nostalgic numbers, to some of the newer crooner records.

For entertainment you couldn't do better than rent a projector and show some old-time silent movies.

A WEST-COAST WHINGDING
OR A SEAPORT FIESTA

This theme is too complex for small parties or suppers; it is a better choice for a fair. However, some aspects of it can be used as themes for smaller gatherings: Fisherman's Wharf or Farmer's Market might provide a springboard for a smaller party.

The fiesta is divided into three areas: (1) Fisherman's Wharf; (2) Farmer's Market; and (3) The Pike.

The section called Fisherman's Wharf can be decorated with fish nets, shells, buoys, rowboat oars, and abstract-fish shapes, brightly colored, perhaps hanging in a mobile from the ceiling.

Dress your "staff" as fishermen, with blue jeans, striped jerseys, and gay bandannas. Set up booths in a row, with rough planks to serve as a common counter. From booths, you might sell hot chowder; lobsters boiled in big pails over open fires; shrimp cocktails; a variety of canned and smoked fish. An oyster and clam bar would dispense oysters, either raw or in stew, clams on the half shell or steamed. Other booths would have such merchandise as turtles, goldfish, small decorative objects trimmed with shells, floating fish toys, cooking utensils and serving dishes for fish, fishnet shopping bags, and aprons with fish-shaped pockets. Let wandering fishmongers peddle their wares of fish'n'chips or fried shrimp.

The Farmer's Market would include everything of interest for gardeners as well as farmers. You might take orders for bulbs, pack garden tools in flowerpots tied with bright cellophane, have flower and plant stalls. In country-fair style, have a contest for the best or biggest home-grown fruits and vegetables. If you buy food products in bulk, and repackage in smaller containers, you can reap a neat profit with little work. Offer peanuts, peanut butter, cheese, meat, and sausages. You might have a *tacos* bar; another might serve hot chocolate flavored with cinnamon; still another might specialize in tortillas and tamales. Dress the men who man the booths in bright *serapes* and Mexican hats.

The third section, called The Pike, is the amusement section, where guests play games of chance and skill. Sell jewelry, small gadgets, ceramics, salt-water taffy, beads and bangles for the girls, pirate hats for the boys. Boothkeepers should be dressed as sailors.

EASY TABLE DECORATIONS FOR VARIOUS OCCASIONS

CHRISTMAS

For a long table: Arrange several wreaths of holly on wire frames, at intervals down center of table. Set a large dark-green candle in center of each wreath. This is very striking on a medium-blue tablecloth. Or fill glass bowls with colorful Christmas baubles interspersed with holly. Use red and gold balls on a green table-cloth; green and silver on a red tablecloth. If desired, cloth may be lightly sprayed with gold or silver paint.

For a round table: Cover tables with white cloth. Cut large circles of red oilcloth for center of table, and circles, a little larger than a dinner plate, for place mats. In center of table on top of large red circle put a white flowerpot filled with sand and insert cedar branches to make a small tree. Surround tree with white candles stuck onto small wooden bases covered with a white cutout star.

For children's table: Fill a large glass bowl with tinted water and carefully lower a piece of dry ice into the water. Cover surface of water with Christmas balls. The dry ice will keep "smoking" for quite a long time.

EASTER

Secure good-sized bare branches to a block of wood. Hang brightly colored empty eggshells on the tree with ribbon or gold cord. Dime-store gems may be stuck onto the eggs with glue.

Arrange doughnuts on a bed of shredded colored paper and fill the holes with colored jelly beans. A few artificial birds might be set around the arrangement. Nice for a breakfast.

SPRING

Arrange branches of forced forsythia or azalea in large contain-ers or bottles. Tie them together with multicolored ribbons and let the ribbons fall over and around the bases of the containers. Hang wire lettuce baskets filled with flowers around room; tie matching ribbons to handles.

Decorate table with white pots holding different spring flowers;

hyacinths, narcissuses, daffodils, primroses, jonquils, tulips. The tablecloth should carry out the colors of the flowers.

JUNE

A few garden roses or other flowers, pulled through a paper doily, might be placed in front of each place setting, or could be made into a large centerpiece which includes enough for one per guest.

SUMMER

A basket of fresh fruit could be the first course of a breakfast menu. Tuck green leaves and flower heads between the fruit. Arrange rocks in an interesting design and insert candles for a focal point. Tuck a few flowers and greens among the rocks, which are lovely painted in pretty colors or sprayed gold.

FALL PARTY

Use green-and-yellow striped tablecloths. Make center decoration of decoys set on greens in an arrangement of bulrushes or pampas grass. Surround with stones and large green chunky candles. Or, glue fall leaves onto a rough-textured tablecloth and decorate with driftwood onto which are cemented sprays of ivy and artificial-flower heads.

HARVEST TABLE

Use a dark-green tablecloth and yellow-brown napkins. Decorate with handsome cabbages, green acorn squash, yellow crooknecks, yellow onions, and corn. Or use shades of purple and red; red cabbages, red peppers, radishes, green peppers, eggplants, zucchinis, cucumbers, and peas.

MIDWINTER PARTY

If possible, set up small tables to seat six or eight. Use table-cloths of different colors: orange, brown, yellow. In center of each table arrange a circle of lemon leaves and in the center pyramid a stack of lemons on one table, tangerines on the next.

WINTER GARDEN PARTY

Decorate tables with white wrought-iron plant holders holding potted plants and fruit. If available, let wrought-iron tables hold the punch and cake. Decorate room with pastel balloons and paper lanterns.

WINTER INDOOR PICNIC

Create an outdoor atmosphere by the use of plants. Set up picnic tables around the room and provide picnic baskets or box lunches contributed by your members.

WINTER

Fill large bowls with glacéed apples on sticks—an apple for each guest. Add green leaves for color.

BON VOYAGE

Cover tables with natural-burlap tablecloths decorated with seals and stickers from steamships and airlines. Set a small boat or airplane in center of each table and use baggage tags for place cards.

GOLDEN ANNIVERSARY

Fill a garden basket with artificial fruit and flowers, and spray it gold. This is lovely on a soft moss-green tablecloth with gold-paper doilies at each place, secured to the cloth with rubber cement.

TEEN PARTY FOR GIRLS

Use pink gingham tablecloths, caught up at intervals with bunches of flowers or bows. Decorate table with old-fashioned bouquets of real or artificial rosebuds with lace-doily frills around them.

TEEN FOOTBALL PARTY

Use rough-textured cloths on tables with pennants lined up and down center. Decorate table with a football in middle surrounded by masses of mums or mum corsages. At either end of the table put two large yellow candles each on a base of wood, and run yellow ribbon from one to the other for goal posts. Or use real or cardboard megaphones for centerpiece, filled with flowers, or popcorn, or pretzels.

TEEN PARTY FOR BOYS

Stack dominoes in centers of tables covered with blue denim, and arrange a few geraniums in between for a gay color.

CHILDREN'S PARTY

Use dark-red tablecloth and in center put a large bowl of greens mixed with varicolored lollipops. Or use pastel-colored cloths and decorate with white-painted flowerpots filled with candied almonds and marshmallows stuck on wooden sticks.

MUSICAL PARTY

Glue black cutout notes with bars and staff on a white table-cloth. Make centerpieces of metronomes surrounded by ivy and genaniums. Use sheet music for place mats.

GYPSY TABLE

Put two long runners down each side of table—one of orange and one of red. Make centerpieces of dime-store tambourines, strings of colored beads, and gold candy money spilling out of the tambourines. A few gay flower heads may also be used.

SEASHORE PARTY

Use fish net over a sea-blue tablecloth and decorate with sea fans, shells, and sand. Set candles into green-glass bottles.

WESTERN BARBECUE PARTY

Make the table out of old boards laid across wooden horses. In center place a wagon wheel engineered so it will turn. Place all the "fixin's" for the barbecue on dishes on the spokes and let the wheel serve as a Lazy Susan.

SCOTCH PARTY

Arrange roadside thistles, dried or fresh, in pewter mugs set into tam-o'-shanters.

MEXICAN PARTY

Make table centerpieces out of cactus and fresh limes.

For photographs of decorative ideas for centerpieces or bazaar booths, see photos 1–22.

CHAPTER 6

Bazaars and Fairs

Bazaars and fairs have been a popular means of gathering a group of people together for barter and amusement since before the birth of Christ. They originated in ancient Egypt. Each year, when the Nile overflowed its banks, the population gave thanks by feasting and joy making in the great temples of the principal towns, where produce and merchandise found a ready market. People crowded into tremendous barges, which transported them from one temple to another, and merrymaking and mingling continued until the Nile finally subsided, converting the former parched lands into fertile valleys.

In the Middle Ages, fairs sprang up wherever pilgrims gathered to worship. Tradesmen flocked to the sacred places to dispose of their wares, and various amusements were introduced to attract the attention of the public; jugglers juggled, minstrels strummed, and knights and ladies gathered around storytellers to listen to their tales. Three important aspects of life—religion, barter, and pleasure—combined to popularize fairs throughout Europe and the British Isles. Fairs—such as the Bartholomew fair held at Smithfield, London, from 1133 to 1840; the London Frost fair; the Llandaff fair in Wales; and the Donnybrook fair in Ireland—became celebrated and historic events.

Today, fairs and bazaars continue to be a popular means of obtaining needed funds beyond the regular channels of revenue, and are an excellent means of uniting a group or congregation in a common cause.

ORGANIZING A FAIR OR A BAZAAR

WHY A FAIR?

Perhaps your community needs a new parish house or Sunday-school room, the church carpet is worn and should be replaced, or a favorite charity is behind in much-needed funds. A fair or bazaar is one of the best ways of supplying these needs, and most members of an organization feel that contributing time to a worthwhile cause is a rewarding experience.

HOW TO BEGIN

A Fair Director must be appointed. She must be a capable executive, a hard worker, willing and able to devote a great deal of time to the project and, above all, she must be a diplomat! It is her job to co-ordinate all facets of activities and inspire enthusiasm and co-operation among the members. The magnitude of the task the Fair Director is assuming should not be underestimated.

The size of the organization and the number of active members, the anticipated scope of the event, will determine how many officers should be appointed to work under the inspiration and direction of the Fair Director. There should be a Chairman and Cochairman and, for very large affairs, it is wise to have both a Secretary and a Treasurer. The responsibilities that these officers must undertake should be explained in detail, so that, if they do not feel equipped or cannot devote the necessary time to do a good job, they should offer to function in a lesser capacity and pass along the honor of the larger job to someone else.

THE FIRST MEETING

At the first meeting, the Fair Directors and key officers should decide on the over-all plan: the place, date, hour, what the fair will consist of, the theme, and so forth. They should decide how any funds appropriated for the fair's expenses are to be spent and must use these funds wisely.

Make a budget with estimated costs and anticipated revenue for each separate project of the fair. Be as detailed and specific about costs as possible, allotting funds for materials, supplies, rentals, mailings, printing, posters, telephone, publicity, decorations, etc. If it is your first affair, you might be able to enlist the co-operation of someone in your community or neighboring community, who has had experience as a Fair Director, to help.

At this meeting or at subsequent meetings, Committee Chairmen should be elected. Again, the size of the event will determine how many Chairmen will be needed to head committees to assure that the fair will run smoothly and efficiently. In general, you will need a Committee Chairman for each separate activity of the fair: *Grounds or Hall; Decorations and Display; Publicity and Advertising; Refreshments; Dinner; Food for Sale; Games; Handicrafts.*

In addition to these general categories, you will need a Committee Chairman for each lesser activity of the fair. If you plan to have attractions such as antiques, books, toys, "white elephants," and so on, you will need a Chairman to head up each of these activities.

The Chairman of some of the large activities may feel she needs a Cochairman to share some of the work and responsibility, and the first job of each Chairman is to enlist as many committee members as she feels she needs to make sure that no one person is overburdened either financially or physically.

ENLIST HELP IN PERSON

Setting up committees requires considerable telephoning to enlist help. For large affairs it is a good idea to organize a telephone squad of people, well known in the community with persuasive ways and voices, to make the initial contacts and to follow through. Some women in your organization, who are confined and not able to participate in more active duties, are willing and cheerful candidates for such an assignment.

But whether your fair is large or small, try to make a telephone call to every member of your organization, or contact personally as many as possible. Find out what they like to do best and ask for their help. Remember that there are many shy people who won't come forward or, perhaps, don't think they could contribute in any way. People like to be ASKED and everybody has some talent that they perform better than anyone else. Encourage them to donate that talent to the forthcoming event.

WHAT CAN MEN DO

Plenty! They're practically indispensable. Every bazaar needs men with strong arms and backs, equipped with hammers and saws. They can help with construction ideas. Some men have hobby shops or workshops which they are glad to make available to others. Never try to do anything with one saw where six will help. Encourage members of your organization, both men and women, to share their facilities with others.

Boys can help their fathers. Perhaps one father is an art director: he can make posters. Maybe another is head of the lumberyard and can give invaluable advice on how many two-by-fours you're going to need. Others can contribute ideas for publicity and advertising. There are a hundred other ways where men can help. For some reason, men are more fun than women behind a counter, flipping flapjacks or dousing hot dogs with mustard.

LINES OF COMMUNICATION

It is important that the Fair Director keeps abreast of the progress being made by the various committees. She cannot personally supervise every activity, that is why she has her Chairmen, but, unless she is kept informed of problems as well as progress, she cannot function efficiently. The Fair Director may assume the responsibility of making decisions on various points that will arise as the fair's plans progress, or she may delegate all or part of this responsibility to her Chairmen. The Chairmen should work closely with their Director and channels of communication should be clearly defined and unconfused, with each group working as a team and reporting to the one in charge.

THE SECRETARY should keep a detailed logbook for future reference, recording the weekly or monthly progress of each committee and noting suggestions for future improvement or errors to be avoided. Don't forget, you can always do something better the second time than the first and, even though some members will retire from future fair activities, accurate records can help new officers from making the same mistakes that might have been made before.

THE TREASURER should open a fair bank account. Her bank manager can advise which is the best kind. Careful record should be kept of all deposits and withdrawals, and any cash expenditures should be conscientiously recorded in the form of vouchers or petty-cash slips so that—at the end of the fair—there will be an accurate account of how much money was spent on food, games, display, handicrafts, publicity, etc. At the actual time of the fair, the Treasurer should be set up in a separate room to handle money and tickets. All personal money should be kept strictly apart from that of the fair.

ANNOUNCE THE FAIR IMMEDIATELY

If you have a monthly bulletin, announce your fair the moment you are organized. If it is a church fair, ask your minister if he will discuss it from the pulpit, endorsing the event with approval and enthusiasm. Post notices in the parish house, Sunday-school rooms, and club rooms. Ask for help and volunteers. Let your members know that everyone is needed, that whole families can participate, that functions have been planned where children can help. In other words, try to make your fair a "family project."

ANNOUNCE THE FAIR OFTEN

Refer constantly to the event in bulletins or house organs. Pass along amusing anecdotes, keep members informed as to the fair's progress. Remember, it is the enthusiasm of the people in your organization that is going to make your fair a success.

HOW FAR AHEAD TO WORK

Give yourselves plenty of time to prepare for your fair. The more time the better. Many organizations, which have successfully conducted annual bazaars, begin working for the next event the moment the Secretary turns in her final report on the current fair and the Treasurer has totaled and presented the profit to the proper person. The presentation of the check can be made into a noteworthy moment or event in itself, which will immediately inspire enthusiasm for another fair, whether it is scheduled to take place in six months or two years.

WHAT MAKES A FAIR A SUCCESS

Plenty of space, either inside or out. If out, plenty of shade and protection from heat, sun, wind or rain . . . order in the space, with prominent signs pointing the way to the various attractions . . . color and gaiety . . . as many different and varied attractions as possible . . . amusements for children . . . pony rides . . . magic . . . puppets . . . music, such as strolling musicians . . . costumes . . . fortunetellers and games . . . special homemade pies and cakes, preserves, and jellies . . . pink lemonade . . . popcorn . . . pretzels . . . spun sugar and candied apples on sticks . . . eye-catching displays of merchandise, reasonably priced . . . quality handicrafts.

SPRING, SUMMER, OR FALL?

The best time of the year to hold a fair is dictated partly by the community itself and partly by the physical layout of the church, clubhouse, or other building that will house the event. If yours is a summer-resort colony, naturally, you will want to have your bazaar in the summertime, selecting one of the loveliest spots in the area to hold it. If, on the other hand, your community is deserted in summer months, then you would plan your fair in spring or fall.

September is never a good fair month. There are too many personal chores that consume the time and energy of young and old. Children must be readied for school, leaves must be raked, and the garden prepared for winter; houses need refreshening or redecorating. So, if you plan your fair for the fall months, it is better to schedule it for mid-October or even November, the month of highest buying activity in preparation for the onset of the holiday season.

Spring is, also, a delightful time to have a major bazaar, tying it in, perhaps, with the garden club. It's a season of the year when people are starting to get outdoors, so a spring fair has an entirely different atmosphere from a fall fair. It is gayer, lighter in spirit, the concentration is on gardening, outdoor living, new ideas and accessories for porch and patio, novel barbecue equipment, and beach accessories.

Summer is the only time for a fair *for* children *by* children. It's a wonderful way to inspire children to contribute to a worthwhile plan, to teach them co-operation and organization, and to keep idle hands at work during vacation months. You may not make much money, but you can have a lot of fun. But no matter when you hold your fair, plan activities where children can help. Fairs are family affairs, so make it a family project.

INDOORS OR OUT?

Considerable thought should be given as to where you will hold your fair. If it is to be an outdoor event, plans must be made for bad weather and all displays and booths should be designed to be adaptable for setting up outside, or inside in case of rain. You can have bad weather as well as good, and nothing dampens the spirit of a fair more than if it has to be postponed to another day. Sufficient protection against the elements must be planned, such as canvas covering, yet nothing except complete coverage can save a fair in a downpour. So, it is better not to plan an outside bazaar, unless it is adjacent to some building capable of housing it in case of rain.

Also, in choosing the location for the fair, indoors or out, traffic hazards should be considered. Are there plenty of facilities for parking cars? For big events, arrange for parking attendants. If the parking lot is some distance from the fair, organize a jitney service; ask members to donate the use of their station wagons to take people from the parking lot to the entrance to the fair. Teenagers love being chauffeurs. If the fair is to be held in a very congested area, it is better to plan a two-day affair than to concentrate all activity on one day.

MAKE VISITORS COMFORTABLE

Arrange for cloakrooms and free checking service in cold weather. See that chairs or benches are set up for "rest centers" at strategic points. Be sure that restrooms are clean and clearly marked. Free shopping bags are a great incentive for people to buy more. You may want to have a playground or nursery for children, which must be tended by competent helpers. You can charge a small fee to adults for leaving their children in the special area but, usually the fact that parents have the opportunity to wander, unburdened by small fry, is sufficient recompense for this extra service. Appoint clean-up teams (boys are good at this) to keep the grounds or hall free of litter.

TO SOLICIT OR NOT TO SOLICIT

This is a decision to be made by the Fair Director, consulting with the Minister or President. It can never hurt to announce that all contributions of merchandise or food products will be gratefully received, but it is another thing to actively solicit donations in the form of merchandise. Remember that the merchants in your neighborhood are vulnerable to every fund-raising activity in the community—they get it from all ends. If your fair is the only such activity in your area, then you might ask for a specific number of this or that, but do it without pressure. Otherwise, it is better to enlist the co-operation and help of the merchants and ask their advice on specific problems, for there are many areas where the merchants can be of tremendous help. Some will offer donations, others will back away, but all are likely to graciously co-operate by selling their merchandise at a reduced rate, allowing you to make a small profit, but without loss to their stores or factories.

Prove to the merchants that you are not competing with them. Make a plan of the help you want and present it briefly. Point out what benefits, such as program credit, you will give the merchants in return for their help and confirm any agreement in writing. When you offer credit, make sure you follow through to even a greater degree than promised . . . arrange credit in the form of thanks to be prominently displayed on bulletin boards or large blackboards posted on the fair grounds or printed in the program in bold letters, "We want to thank so and so for their contributions in helping make this fair a success." Sincere credit will do much to assure further contributions another year. Then, write a personal thank-you note to each and every contributor, no matter how small, including your own members who gave so willingly and generously of their time and talents.

ADMISSION OR NO ADMISSION

Another decision to be made by the Fair Chairman, is the question of charging admission. Some organizations believe, and strongly so, that guests should be allowed to enter the grounds free of charge. On the other hand a certain percentage of visitors to the fair might find nothing that really intrigues them enough to buy, have a good time wandering about and socializing with friends whom they meet there, and leave the fair grounds empty-handed. They would have been delighted to contribute an entry fee, and the amount of that fee is something for the Fair Committee to decide. Perhaps, a happy solution to the admission question is to charge a nominal entry fee and, in return, pin a tiny boutonniere on each visitor, or supply each one with a shopping bag. These can be simply and inexpensively decorated with a decal or a tissue-paper flower, to make them look festive and gay, and provide an incentive for visitors to leave with a bagful of goodies, which they purchased at the fair. Local supermarkets might donate bags, or you can buy them wholesale from a supplier, which you will find in the yellow pages of the telephone directory under "paper bags."

CASH OR TOKENS?

Certainly the large booths at a fair must handle cash, be prepared to make change, and be responsible for the revenue. But, if the bazaar is a fairly comprehensive one, you don't want all the small spot booths, game directors, or children handling money. It is far better to sell script money or tokens at the admission booth and at various other locations throughout the grounds. Such items as washers, which can be bought from a local hardware store, make excellent tokens, or wooden beads or marbles. These would be priced at ten or twenty for one dollar. In this day and age, it is likely that a dime will be the lowest common denominator, but every community knows what the traffic will bear. Usually tokens are not redeemable for cash and must be spent on food, games, or other merchandise for sale at the fair.

At booths where cash must be handled, appoint one person as cashier to be responsible for the cashbox, and supply him or her with plenty of change. Keep incoming money in closed boxes, out of sight. It is sad to report that petty thievery is a common source of irritation at many large bazaars and fairs.

KEEP WITHIN THE LAW

Check with the police department and chamber of commerce on building, fire, and safety regulations, and tax laws. Raffles and games of chance are subject to strict local and state regulations. When food is involved, contact health authorities for local and state rules.

ADVERTISING AND PUBLICITY

Most community newspapers will give freely of editorial space in announcing your forthcoming event or referring to specific incidents in so-called "gossip" or social columns. It's up to you to feed material into the proper channels. Make a publicity schedule and stick to it. Make personal calls and send a variety of information about all stages of the fair to the appropriate editors of local newspaper, radio, and TV. Send food news to food editors, fashion news to fashion editors, social news to social editors, etc. Include photographs, when possible. A local photographer may be willing to take candid shots for the cost of his film and developing.

Advertising must be paid for, but you may be able to get a special rate from your local advertising media. Advertise well in advance and increase the insertions as the date of the event approaches. Small "reminder" ads inserted often are sometimes more effective than one large ad.

When the fair is imminent, send out reminders to all publicity avenues, about the date, hour, location, and purpose of the event. Hand out flyers on street corners, put up posters in prominent places, and ask the store merchants to display window banners or cards.

BE CONSCIENTIOUS IN CONCLUDING THE FAIR

Leave the fair grounds as clean, after your event, as it was before you set up.

If any merchandise is left over, don't give it back. Either auction it off at the close of the fair, or load it in the back of a station wagon and drive the wagon to some well-trafficked area, such as in front of the library or supermarket or gas station. Sell the items at a discount directly from the wagon. Try to sell everything possible to get every last penny that you can, or pack it away for the next fair.

Save every bit of decoration and props from one year to another. They can all be dusted off and adapted to a new theme.

Make all necessary reports, both financial and editorial, and be as detailed as possible. What was good about the fair? What items proved to be the best sellers? What was not good? Where can you improve next time? Where did confusion set in? Don't gloss over the rough spots; report them honestly and factually to the Fair Director. Send a success story to the editors of your local newspaper, radio, and TV, and mail or phone thank-yous to everyone who contributed to the event. Follow up on all or any pledges that were made from the conception of the fair to its well-organized conclusion.

ATMOSPHERE, DECORATIONS, AND WARES

ATMOSPHERE

It is important to create an atmosphere that is colorful, gay, and slightly noisy! There should be music and costumes, and a great deal of hustle-bustle activity. Put everyone working at the fair in costumes. If this is not practical or feasible, make the most of colorful scarves, caps, aprons, or corsages.

If any of your members are good at pulling rabbits out of hats or doing card tricks, playing the accordion or guitar, enlist their talents for the fair. The entertainment need not be earth-shattering to win applause. If you feel you need additional attractions, consult your local chamber of commerce, the Rotary, Elks, or Lions clubs as to where to find talent. Also see your classified directory under "entertainers." Most entertainers have special rates for charitable functions, but don't resort to professional entertainers before you have exhausted the possible talents of members within your organization.

EVERY FAIR NEEDS A THEME

Decide on an imaginative theme and follow through down to the smallest detail. Plan the over-all picture first, then discuss each separate event on the program and see how you can tie your theme in with them all.

Many bazaars and fairs, although successful from the fund-raising standpoint, leave much to be desired. They seem to have been thrown together with little thought as to continuity and detail.

Decide on a symbol representing your theme, and have an artistic member make a simple drawing that will reproduce easily. Use this symbol every place possible; stress it in all activities, in public announcements, booth decorations, on costumes, aprons, hats, etc.

The more intriguing you can make your theme, the larger turn-out you'll have. Call the fair a Carnival or Festival or something that suggests fun and has appeal to children as well as to grown-ups.

In the chapter, *Themes and Decorations,* you will find many ideas for themes, some only suggestions, which can easily be am-plified according to your concept; others have been detailed, but all can serve as springboards for your own originality. All can be used in part or in their entirety. All can be adapted to the par-ticular physical layout and scope of your event, from a small one-room fair to a comprehensive bazaar which might encompass an entire building or several acres of land.

Every fair is bound to have characteristics in common and it is only by imagination that you can make yours unusual and differ-ent. Every fair has food, wares, hot dogs, and balloons, but you can give these items a new twist to make your affair something special. They all should, in color and presentation, complement your theme.

DECORATIONS

All decorations in general should amplify your theme, but spe-cific decorations depend to a great extent on the physical aspects of the room, hall, hotel, or building in which the fair will be held, or of the grounds, if your fair is going to be held out of doors.

If, for example, your church or clubhouse has an attractive façade with gracious steps leading to an unusual entrance, make the most of it. Use the entrance as a means of leading your visi-tors inside, by banking potted plants, flowers, and a few suitable, attractive displays on the steps. If your fair is an outdoor occasion, the steps can make a wonderful background for entertainment, with tables and booths fanning out on either side.

If your fair is indoors, inspect the hall or room and write down the essential measurements—the length and width, number and size of windows, doors, balconies or stages, if any, or any nooks or alcoves that you plan to trim and decorate. Then begin to adapt the physical layout to your theme, motif, and colors selected by the Fair Committee. Many large decorative units can be wholly or partially prepared in advance, all ready to simply assemble and set into place.

Materials for decorations are numerous. Cheesecloth, mosquito netting, fish netting, burlap, and tissue paper are the most popular because they are easy to cut and drape and are relatively inexpensive. A little skill in the use of crepe paper, in combination with other materials, produces marvelously effective results. For excellent books on decorating with flameproof crepe paper, costumes, flower-making, write to Dennison Manufacturing Company, Framingham, Mass.

Aluminum foil, gold-spray paint, spangles, stars, sequins, shells can turn most commonplace items into dazzling décor. Gay balloons, colorful lanterns, paper streamers fit into almost any theme. Large, sturdy tree branches make marvelous racks from which to hang and display your fair wares. These can either be stuck into the ground or anchored to a wooden base. Smaller branches may be inserted in a three-pound shortening can filled with plaster. When the plaster sets, paint both can and tree branch gold or any color that fits your selected color scheme and decorate with tiny artificial leaves. The more twigs on your branch, the more merchandise you can display. Clothespins will clip items onto the smaller branches; use thumbtacks on the main branch.

Another simple display idea is to wind poles with ribbon or paper, or paint in gay colors. Set them up at intervals with a clothesline strung between. Fair wares such as knit goods, needlework, or embroidery can be hung from the line by clothespins or clip-board clamps. Stickpins can display wares from large painted or cloth-covered sheets of cardboard fastened to the walls or set on easels.

PACKAGING

Plan every detail of your fair, right down to the packaging. Don't leave anything to chance. Nothing should be brought to the fair that doesn't have a suitable box or bag to put it in, and this holds equally true for cookies to potholders, aprons, cakes, jewelry and so on.

So, right from the beginning, ask your members to save and contribute to a central depot, miscellaneous boxes, jars, baby-food containers, coffee cans, etc.

Some organizations set up a Box COMMITTEE, and it is the sole responsibility of this committee to solicit, gather, and attractively decorate sufficient packaging to house the wares for sale. Mrs. Candy-Maker, then, can call the Box Committee in advance and notify them that she is going to need twelve containers of an approximate dimension for her special chocolate fudge, and Mrs. Potholder calls and reserves six bags or boxes, each to hold two potholders.

ASK FOR BITS AND PIECES

Announce or print in the monthly bulletin, or stick a notice on the bulletin board, requesting scraps of ribbon, pretty paper, and material. Right before Christmas is the perfect time to ask members to save their Christmas cards and any whole or good pieces of wrapping paper and ribbon. Also ask them to save their magazines for scrapping; such cut-outs as pretty flower and food prints from the magazines can be inexpensively but tastefully framed to sell at a nice profit. Christmas cards can be divided into categories: figures can be silhouetted and appliquéd on cans and pencil holders; others can be cut into tags, holes punched, string inserted, and packaged at a bargain. You may want to announce, with frequent reminders, the place to which the donated material should be delivered and the date, or when it will be collected from individual homes.

DO SOMETHING TO EVERYTHING

It's surprising what a small piece of brocade can do to a cigar box, or how many place mats can be cut from a half yard of left-over printed cotton. A bit of ribbon and some gold paint can transform baby-food jars into attractive canisters for herbs and spices; scraps of wallpaper pasted around store match folders make attractive gift matches and so on; just make it a point of pride to "do something to everything. . . ."

AND DO IT WELL

Don't try to pawn off on gullible fair guests, in the name of sweet charity, wares that are sloppily or amateurishly made. Set a standard of quality, equal to that found in the local gift shop, and stick to it—discard any items that look unprofessional. This may take a little diplomacy, especially if members are allowed to work at home unsupervised. It's far better to have most of your fair wares constructed at group meetings with a capable person directing and instructing. There are, however, exceptions to every rule, and some members of your organization, who are expert in one particular hobby, can best perform this craft in their own home. You may be sure that any wares they donate will be well made.

FAIR WARES

There are innumerable how-to books with instructions to make almost everything from baby sweaters to muumuus. Such companies as Singer Sewing Machine, and pattern, wool, and yarn companies, issue booklets each year of functional and imaginative items that can be made for sale at fairs and bazaars. The monthly women's magazines also do a comprehensive job, explaining how to make gifts and household items to please father, mother, children, and babies; how to gift-wrap and make seasonal decorations, in their Christmas issues. And, in this book, in the chapter on *Handicrafts to Make and Sell*, will be found over fifty items that can be made without patterns.

In general, try to plan to make items that take little time, yet look expensive. A highly overrated and discounted rule of thumb is that, if materials put into an item cost fifty cents, then it must sell for a dollar. However, if you can make something quickly from a few cents of material that is attractive and looks as if it is worth a dollar, it should be priced at a dollar.

Fair items should not be sold at a ridiculously high price, just because the fair is given for charity. Each suggested item should be submitted to a committee for appraisal: first, if it's worth spending money on and, second, how much it could sell for, before time and money goes into its making.

Nor should items be purchased at local stores and sold at a premium, unless you add something to them. If, for example, you buy a pair of wool gloves, appliqué a pretty flower on each of them, trim them with braid, or add a simple tailored bow—do something extra to them that is imaginative and makes them more attractive. You can then sell them for two or three times the cost.

The more creative and inventive you can be with cutouts, paint, wallpaper, bits of ribbon, pebbles and stones from the beach, old jewelry, brilliants, sequins, etc., the more profit your organization will net. Remember, THE LESS MONEY SPENT, THE MORE PROFIT!

And no matter how many fine articles of apparel, housewares, paintings, gifts there may be for sale at your bazaar, let there be hundreds and hundreds of small items to sell for a dollar and under. In this category, everybody can find something to buy, and this is from where the really big fair revenue is derived.

PRICING FAIR WARES

Give the best price possible. It's better to give your visitors a bargain, providing the fair makes some profit, than to overprice. In pricing the wares, take into consideration the cost of materials and add a percentage for overhead, an item that must not be forgotten. Remember all the funds that went into printing, general decorations and construction, advertising, etc., that are helping to make your fair a success. Your treasurer should have a last-minute tally of exactly what the entire overhead costs of the fair are; each booth should be responsible for a certain percentage of that total cost.

DISPLAYING FAIR WARES

Not all merchandise should be displayed at one time. Some of everything should be held back so that items are available throughout the duration of the fair, and late-comers are not faced with bare booths containing only leftovers. This means that items must be carefully scheduled throughout the day, with a larger percentage displayed during rush hours.

An announcement should be made to the effect that merchandise will be equally distributed throughout the fair hours and that no favoritism will be allowed. Under no circumstances permit committee members to speak in advance for special "luxury" items known by them to be in the making.

GOOD ITEMS TO MAKE

Here is a partial list of items that find a ready market at club and church bazaars and fairs. They have weathered the test of time, but their success as sales items depends entirely on the imaginative and expert way in which they are constructed:

Aprons, pouch "carryall" bags, clothespin bags and aprons,

stuffed animals, beanbags, Raggedy Anns, potholders, decorative baskets, firewood slings, gilded pine cones, sachets, table mats and napkins, hot-plate tiles, dried flowers, gourds, potted ivy and house plants, barbecue mitts, pajama bags, eyeglass cases, throw pillows, teen-age skirts, petticoats, toys, head scarves, guest towels, cocktail napkins, decorative candles, and homemade candy.

BAZAAR BOOTHS

HOW MANY AND WHAT KIND

The number of booths at any given fair depends on the scope of the fair, the physical accommodations, and the number of people in the community working together on its execution. It also depends, to a certain extent, on the particular talents of the participants. For example, one food booth might be sufficient to accommodate all the food items for sale at one fair. Or, if yours is a community where people love to make and donate homemade cakes, pies, breads, casseroles, candies, and preserves, you may need several booths to display the items in the food category alone, with no concern about a lack of appreciative customers for this homemade bounty.

The type of any and all merchandise for which you will find a ready market depends on your kind of community. If it is a cultural center, emphasis might be put on art and music; if a young people's center, with loads of children, then you will want to concentrate on more than the average attractions for children; if a very sophisticated suburban town, you may decide to eliminate the "white-elephant" booth and stress the boutique. In another community the "white-elephant" booth might steal the show.

SPOT STANDS

In addition to the large booths which will be the major attractions at your fair, you will want to have "spot" booths or stands located at every turn, or have them on wheels so they can be moving constantly through the fair grounds. This is an excellent method of distributing wares over a large area and of eliminating a great deal of confusion at the major booths. Many people like to just wander and never go near the large display booths. You want to catch them as they stroll.

Wheelbarrows are excellent for spot displays. These can be painted or decorated according to the theme of your fair. Pile one with cracker "sandwiches," with cheese or peanut butter between, packaging two or more together in transparent bags, tied shut with ribbons and bows. Fill another with packages of hard candy or with soft drinks bedded in cracked ice. Fill another with real or artificial nosegays.

Empty barrels also make fine display units for spot booths. Right-side up they may be filled with merchandise; bottom-side up they make sturdy surfaces on which to display a big wheel of cheese. Sell thin wedges of the cheese on crackers to passers-by. It's hard for anyone to resist the lure of a slice of good honest Cheddar. You may only charge a couple of pennies per cracker, but pennies add up at the end of the day to money in the till.

Other merchandise ideas for spot booths are popcorn balls, big bags filled with fresh popcorn, sprinkled with salt and melted butter; watermelon slices; caramelized apples; fortune cookies; treasure cakes (small cupcakes, each containing a "treasure").

If you can arrange for charcoal-burning hibachis, you might have a roasted-chestnut stand. Or insert wooden sticks into marshmallows and let the children toast their own over the burning charcoal.

Girls' and boys' bicycles, their wheels and handle bars decorated with flowers or tissue paper, again make attractive spot booths. Attach decorative handle baskets, and fill them with grab bags, pretzels, balloons, licorice sticks, or assorted candy. Teen-agers will flock around a bicycle devoted to selling gay handkerchiefs and colorful scarves. Attach a mirror to the rear of the bike, so that the girls can judge how the color of the scarf complements their own coloring of skin and hair. Let there be a prize for the best-decorated bicycle.

The small children love to be a part of whatever the grownups are doing, so let them participate at your bazaar or fair. One idea might be to let the children paint and fix up their wagons, and fill each wagon with various merchandise. Such a plan needs supervision, so concentrate the wagons in one section, perhaps in a circle, row, or semicircle. Let one or two children be responsible for selling the wares from their wagon, but all under the supervision of a teen-ager who would head the children's wagon committee. Make the wagon wares appealing to other children, and keep the cost to pennies or no more than a nickel. One wagon might be converted into a punch or lemonade stand. Award a prize for the best-decorated wagon.

Following are suggestions for a variety of major booths from which a Bazaar Committee can select those they feel would appeal most to their particular audience:

TOYTOWN

One of the most successful booths at any fair consists of toys, games, and sporting goods. Everyone has an attic or closet filled with items that their children have tired of or outgrown, which they are happy to donate to a worthwhile cause. Children seem to love toys that belonged to other children.

Enlist the help of the men and teen-agers in the community, to repair the toys and put them in good condition. Nothing should be offered for sale that looks in poor state. It's amazing what a little paint and repairing can do to give a new look to old toys. Collect and repair, in addition to toys and games, such items as footballs, soccer-balls, baseball mitts, golf clubs, skates, hockey sticks, boxing gloves.

THE ALMOST-NEW BOOTH

Miscellaneous household items can be donated to a specific workshop to be repaired and scrubbed, polished or painted. You might be able to arrange for several "fix-it" depots in various spots in the community where members can deposit their donations. Many women, as well as men, enjoy scraping, painting, and decorating or antiquing small tables, chairs, outdoor furniture, etc., which can eventually go on sale at the fair. Small items such as lamps, ashtrays, vases, throw pillows, table linens, also go into this category, but all must be in good condition before being displayed at the fair. A small section of this booth might be devoted to costume jewelry. Many women are happy to donate good costume jewelry that they have tired of, or jewelry given them at various times, which no longer seems to complement any particular costume. Clean and polish it, put it into a small box, and it will look like new.

THE MERCHANDISE MART

Here are offered for sale, large household items, usually of too great value to be casually donated by the owner, and also too large to be transported to the fair grounds. Many people have antique furniture, a vacuum cleaner, lawn mower, or refrigerator, even cars and boats, paintings, radios and TVs that they would like to dispose of, but would welcome a buyer for them, rather than give them away. They are more than willing, however, to donate a percentage of the sale price to swell the gross profits of the fair. Some people will put their own price on the item, and others will appreciate expert help on how much the item would be worth on the open market. Original paintings and antiques should be appraised by reliable dealers.

A small table and chair, beneath a colorful umbrella, is all the booth that is needed for this department. At the table will sit the "broker," with a well-indexed card file at hand. Surround him with easels or blackboards, on which are listed the various items being offered for sale. The "broker" supplies his customers with as much information as possible from his card file about the item in which they are interested, such as condition, model number, manufacturer, age, etc., and where the items can be viewed. Later, an agreed percentage of any sales consummated as a result of the fair, is immediately turned over to the Director of the Fair.

THE FAIR EXCHANGE

This booth should in no way compete with a local Woman's Exchange. Should your community, however, have no Woman's Exchange, your bazaar can be a means of exposing an art or craft to the community, be a source of income to women who need additional household funds, and provide a steady income for your church or organization.

Items that require many tedious hours of handwork, such as men's needlepoint vests, hooked rugs, afghans, needlepoint bags and chair covers, bulky mohair sweaters, hand-painted Christmas cards, etc., can be displayed and orders can be taken at the fair. Various available patterns, sizes, and choice of colors for each item should be on view, and careful notation of these details should be made on each order. When the item is completed and delivered, an agreed percentage of the sale price is turned over to the Fair Director.

PET BOOTH

Pets have unquestionable appeal for children of all ages. But, here again, your type of community must dictate the variety and kinds of pets you wish to sell. Perhaps, you'll settle for just turtles, or you may decide to sell white mice, hamsters, rabbits, chickens, Bantam roosters, goldfish, snails, seahorses, marmosets, parakeets, cockateels, love birds, budgerigars, and so on. . . . If so, add birdhouses, chicken coops, and other suitable accommodations for the small pets, which the men and boys in the community can build. Aquariums of various types and sizes, pretty fish bowls, colorful shells and stones, colored sand, and seaweed are fine additions when goldfish are offered for sale.

Your local Bide-a-Wee or ASPCA might be glad to co-operate by supplying kittens and puppies who need homes, with the provision that you could return any that you were unable to dispose of. If so, plan to show the animals to their best advantage in protective cages or screened boxes and sell other allied items, such as dog leashes and collars, baskets and carrying cases, books on animals—and even coloring books of animals with sets of crayons. Perhaps, a child, whose parents do not feel up to absorbing the additional responsibility of an animal in the home, might dry his tears and settle for a coloring book.

PORTRAIT CENTER

Someone in every community has a Polaroid camera and tripod. Have this set up in the fair grounds to take amusing pictures of guests at the fair. When selling the pictures, be sure to take into consideration the cost of the film, which is not cheap. Your local camera store may be willing to sell you film at a good quantity discount and allow you to return any unopened boxes that are not used. If so, be sure to give the camera store a credit.

Ask some artistic person in your organization to paint an amusing backdrop with holes through which heads can protrude. You can limit it to a single-head hole, or have several—a boat, for example, with two headless people rowing it and a large faceless seagull perched on the prow. For family portraits, forgo the backdrop, have some prop mustaches, hats, shawls, etc., on hand, and arrange Mother, Father, and children in the manner of an old tintype. Before the fair doors open, ask several committee members to pose for their pictures and post these on a display board to intrigue customers.

FLEA MARKET

This type of project is often a fine source of revenue, either as a booth at a fair or when conducted independently of a fair. It is particularly good in spring and fall, when attics and cellars are house-cleaned and unused items are discarded.

Spread large rugs or blankets or colorful coverlets on the ground or floor, and on them stack all manner of old and used merchandise . . . books, furniture, bric-a-brac, knickknacks, utensils, toys, games . . . something for everybody. Sell at extremely low prices.

When run as a special project, other items can be sold, such as food, plants, books, and boutique articles. Members of an organization can gather donations in station wagons and set up shop at a local farmers' market or in the parking lot of a supermarket. Signs should notify shoppers as to the purpose of the sale and let them know what charity will benefit from their patronage. At such locations, home-baked goods and preserves sell like "hot cakes."

FORTUNES

Analyzing handwriting, reading palms or cards are always a lucrative source of revenue for a fair. All that is needed is a person in your community who has a flair for telling fortunes. The more people she knows in the community the better, for news of personal activities predicted for the children, will make your "gypsy" unusually clairvoyant! Put her in costume or disguise, such as a gypsy or witch, and let her gaze into an upturned fish bowl, covered at the base with fabric or gay beads. Give her a secluded corner in a well-trafficked spot. There are loads of books available on fortunetelling, as well as decks of fortunetelling cards that will give a highly imaginative novice enough information to bluff her way through. Nobody really takes their fortunes seriously. It's all in the spirit of fun and adventure.

THE MAKE-UP BOOTH

Did you ever know a child who didn't get great fun out of being made up? Little girls love to be "prettied" with lipstick and eyebrow pencil, powder, and rouge. Little boys adore to be smeared like a clown or Indian. Above the booth, hang drawings of two or three ways that the children can be made up. Let them select whether they wish to be a clown, a bride, an Indian, a little Dutch girl. . . . When possible, tie the ideas and costumes in with the fair theme.

Dutch Girl

Apply lots of lipstick, rouge, and blue eyeshadow. Give each girl a little Dutch cap to wear, made from a paper doily to which two long yellow-wool or -paper braids are attached.

Indian Boy

Make Indian headbands out of brown corrugated paper, cut about one inch wide. This can be stapled to fit the child's head. Stick a long goose feather down one of the corrugations and apply lots of "war paint" to the boy's face.

Bride

Apply a dainty make-up and put on a headband decorated with tulle, ribbon, or flowers.

Clown

Hats are easily constructed out of colored background paper. Stick crepe-paper streamers in the top. It's cheaper to make clown hats than to buy them from the dime store. Use red, white, and black make-up pencils for clown faces; make exaggerated mouths with the red and high, inverted V-shaped black eyebrows. Fill in between eyes and eyebrows with white.

DRESS-UP BOOTH

In addition to being made up, little girls adore to dress up in Mother's clothes and stagger around in a pair of much-too-large high-heeled shoes.

Ask mothers in the organization to donate a hatbox, covered with wallpaper, in which are packed an old hat, a scarf, a bunch of artificial flowers, a string of beads, a pocketbook, and a pair of high-heeled shoes.

Dress-up boxes should be reasonably priced, yet can sometimes bring in more money for an organization than if the old accessories were donated to a rummage sale.

FOR CHILDREN ONLY

Announce a Children's Table well in advance, so children can be prepared to open their piggy banks and do their shopping at the fair for birthday or other occasion gifts for family or friends. It's a highly successful table prior to Christmas, and children will get better value for their money and, usually, more practical gifts than if they are allowed to do unsupervised gift shopping at the local stores. Have plenty of "salesladies" to give individual attention, help, and advice to the children.

Rope off a small area, enclosing a table, topped with a pretty felt skirt. Here—for sale to children only, both boys and girls, up to twelve or thirteen years of age—are carefully selected gift items, costing no more than $1.50, with plenty for less. Some of the items on adult tables can be duplicated, such as aprons, barbecue mitts; but, the fussier, fancier, and more colorful, the better. Adults should not be permitted to go near the table.

ART GALLERY

There are many types of profitable art exhibits, that can add interest to a fair. If yours is an art-conscious community, advance publicity on the Art Gallery will entice many customers to view the art—who might not otherwise attend. Let the professional and amateur artists in the community exhibit their works. You can either charge an entry fee to the artists for exhibit space, or take a percentage of any sales the artist makes at the fair.

Should your organization conduct an art exhibit as a special project, admission can be charged and refreshments sold. (See *Index of Recipes.*)

Many children do fantastic work under the direction of a teacher. For an exhibit of children's art, discuss the project with the art teacher at the local school. See if the children wouldn't be proud to each contribute one picture to the Art Gallery.

Pretty prints, attractively framed, can bring in additional revenue.

A CHRISTMAS BOOTH

When fairs are held in late fall, a Christmas Booth is one of the most popular. Here, every decorative item for the holiday season can be profitably sold. A small list of suggested merchandise could be:

Christmas cards; tree ornaments; candy canes; Christmas stockings; gilded walnuts, pine cones, and decorated, empty egg shells; popcorn strings, packaged in cellophane; wrapping paper and ribbon (especially good when sample box-wrapping ideas are on display); tissue-paper flowers for trees or parcels; wreaths, mantel, and table-centerpiece arrangements; small Christmas trees, fully decorated; Christmas candles and holders; Christmas place mats, cloths, and napkins; Christmas napkin-ring holders; Christmas firecrackers; holly and mistletoe; Christmas hostess aprons; Christmas corsages.

PLANT, FLOWER, AND GARDEN BOOTHS

There are so many potentials for plant, flower, and various gardening booths, that it is not difficult to mushroom them into a Flower Festival. Individually, each category can become a booth at a fair; combined they can be developed into a special fund-raising event, particularly good for springtime, but also suitable for fall.

The grounds can be colorfully and beautifully decorated with plants, flowers, and shrubs. Bulbs can be sold or orders taken for bulbs, seedlings, and seeds. There can be booths for gardening fashions, garden implements and tools, garden books, flower-arranging accessories, and small, outdoor furniture. There can be flower-arranging contests and displays made by the local garden club. There can be other allied items for sale, such as potpourris, herbs—fresh and dried, pomander balls, herb and flower jellies and vinegars, and so on. Following are details for only a few garden booths:

Hall of Flowers

Try to work with your local florist rather than compete with him. Many florists are happy to co-operate with fair committees, selling flowers and plants at a discount price to resell at a profit. If so, don't forget a big credit line so they will want to contribute and work with you every year. If you wish, you can successfully combine flowers with vegetables; award prizes for the most beautiful exhibits of home-grown flowers and/or vegetables. Include a children's category for displays and prizes.

HERB AND SPICE BOOTH

With the renaissance of cooking with herbs and spices that has taken place during the past ten years, a booth devoted to herbs and spices has great possibilities. In addition to attractively bottled and labeled spices and dried herbs, herb racks and other allied items can be sold, such as potted herb butters, *pâtés*, herb mayonnaise, herb and wine vinegars, herb faggots (*bouquets garnis*), herb jellies, spiced fruits and butters, pickles, and other preserves.

If the season of the year is suitable, potted herbs can be displayed and slips sold in tiny pots for replanting. Put the green thumbs in your organization to work, making and tending miniature herb gardens for sale at the booth. The thin wooden boxes, that wheels of cheese are shipped in, make charming miniature herb gardens and can be collected from local markets in sizes varying from six inches in diameter, suitable for accommodating a single clump of chives, to about sixteen inches in diameter and six and one-half inches deep.

To transform the box into a container for herbs, drill a circle of holes, about half an inch in diameter, in the bottom of the box for drainage, keeping them two inches from the outer edges. The boxes can be painted with Bondex or Curpinol, according to package directions, or can be decorated with decals, wallpaper, decorative wrapping paper, etc. Shellac the decorations well, as protection against dampness and rain. Scatter stones or rubble over bottom of box, spread with a layer of sand, and fill with a good potting soil.

In the larger boxes a variety of herbs can be planted, such as rosemary, garden thyme, sweet marjoram, sweet basil, winter savory, and chives. Plant the one that grows tallest in the center, leaving plenty of room between the plants for the herbs to grow.

Attach a small tag to each plant to identify it and include an instruction sheet for the buyer. Instructions for the care of the herb garden should read:

"With loving care, these newly potted plants will have established good roots in about a month. Set your miniature herb garden on small cleats, to allow proper drainage, in full sun, but against a wall or under the edge of an awning, where it will have shade part of the time. Water each day; more often if the weather is extremely hot and dry. After one month, feed the plants once a week with a liquid plant food, carefully following manufacturer's directions for use."

Tuzzie-Muzzies

Tuzzie-muzzies are small old-fashioned herb bouquets. They are meant to be held in the hand, for the warmth increases their fragrance. Each flower in the nosegay has a sentimental meaning, such as violets in the center for loyalty, surrounded by heliotropes for eternal love, surrounded by marjoram for happiness or rosemary for remembrance.

Bath Herbs

A bouquet of aromatic herbs to drop into the bath is a delightful custom, dating back over a hundred years. They are supposed to relax tired muscles, relieve nervous tension, and aid poor circulation. A three-inch square of cheesecloth is used to hold the herbs. They can be single herbs or combinations of equal parts of pennyroyal and angelica; sage and rosemary; lemon balm and peppermint—or equal parts of the flower heads of camomile, thyme, and elder flowers. Tie the bags with colored embroidery cotton and package several together in a gift box.

Herb-Rubbing Lotion and Skin Freshener

Rubbing alcohol, infused with herbs, can be a fine addition to the herb booth. Package it in decorative bottles and label attractively. To make the infusion, fill jars one quarter full of crushed herbs, such as lemon balm, verbena, rosemary, lavender or mint, or any combination of fragrant herbs. Fill jars with rubbing alcohol, cover tightly, and let the herbs steep in the alcohol for two weeks; shake the jars occasionally. Strain through several thicknesses of cheesecloth and, if desired, tint with a few drops of food coloring.

Hair Rinse

Camomile rinse gives a wonderful high light to hair. Simply simmer the flower heads of camomile in rain water for thirty minutes. Strain and bottle.

Moth Bags

More pleasant than moth balls, but just as disliked by the moths, are small muslin or cheesecloth bags holding about one tablespoon each of crushed, dried thyme, tansy, southernwood, and crushed cloves. Another combination is dried lavender flowers, rosemary, crushed cloves, and a piece of dried lemon peel.

Sachets

Many beautiful sachets in a variety of colors and sizes may be made from silk, satin, or velvet. Either squares or bags drawn together at the top with ribbon are easy to make. Fill the bags with mixtures of lavender, lemon verbena, sweet geranium, rose petals, and mint leaves. For lasting power, a fixative should be included. For fixatives, see Potpourri.

Potpourri

The word potpourri comes from the French verb *pourrir*, to rot, which is the way our great grandmothers preserved rose petals. The petals were put into a crock in layers alternately with layers of salt until the crock was full and the petals were then allowed to cure or rot. The color was lost by this method and eventually the fragrance was dissipated. The drying method is now considered the best for retaining both the color and the fragrance of the petals.

Collect the roses in the early morning, before the sun is high, and after two or three days of dry weather. Select the freshest of flowers and ones that have not been open for more than a day or two. Remove the petals and keep the colors separate if you wish to arrange the dried petals in a rainbowlike effect, or a combination of colors, with a whole flower such as a pansy or violet pressed against the inside of the glass container. Place petals in a thin layer on window screens or some kind of rack that will hold the petals and still let the air circulate. Window screens may be stacked one on top of the other with blocks between to separate them. Do not set the racks where the sun can strike them, and if there is too much breeze, cover the screens with cheesecloth. Leave the petals until they are very dry, stirring them gently from time to time so they will dry evenly and thoroughly. Store each color in a tight jar, away from the sun, until ready to use.

When ready to make your potpourri, put petals in a bowl and add a fixative, which may be purchased from a drugstore. (About one tablespoon to one quart of petals.) There are two kinds of fixatives, the animal fixatives, such as ambergris from whales, beavers, or civet cats, and vegetable fixatives, such as gum benzoin, storax, or the crushed roots of calamus or orris. The vegetable fixatives are better to use as they are not so expensive and are more readily available. They should be crushed, not powdered, or they will cloud the potpourri. If the potpourri is going to be put into decorative crocks or opaque jars, there is no need to separate the colors or to worry about the colors fading.

Any number of crushed spices may be added to a potpourri in the proportion of about one tablespoon to a quart of potpourri. Cinnamon, nutmeg, allspice, and mace are nice. So, too, are crushed seeds of anise, caraway, coriander, cardamom, or vanilla bean. The thin peels of orange, lemon, and tangerine, cut into small pieces and each studded with a clove is a delightful addition;

the peel should be allowed to dry for 24 hours before it is added to the potpourri. A few drops of fragrant oils may also be added and thoroughly mixed with the petals. Oils such as rose geranium, eucalyptus, rosemary, lemon verbena, or peppermint are good. Be careful not to let the oil overpower the petals and don't use more than a combination of three different oils. Oils may be bought at the drugstore. Experiment with oils and spices, added to small batches of petals, to see what combination is the most pleasing.

After the potpourri is well mixed put it in crocks, filling the crocks about two thirds full and leaving enough room to let you stir the petals from time to time. Cover tightly for six weeks to allow the mixture to blend. Stir once a week and, two or three times a week, turn and rock the jar. At the end of the six weeks' period, mix again thoroughly and fill decorated or glass jars. The potpourri will continue to age and improve in fragrance when repackaged.

Vinegars

Many herbs may be used to flavor and scent vinegar, and so may flowers, savory seeds, and spices. In the middle of the nineteenth century, vinegars flavored with roses, violets, lavender, and rosemary were popular, not only for greens and fruit salads, but were enjoyed as a cold beverage.

Whether you use flowers, herbs, seeds, or spices, the method is the same.

Herb Vinegar

To attain the best flavor, use fresh herbs. Pack the herbs in a crock, and bruise or mash with a wooden spoon or pestle. Bring white or cider vinegar to the boiling point and pour over the leaves to within two inches of the top of the crock. Cover crock and let the mixture steep for ten days, stirring daily. If the herb flavor is not strong enough, strain vinegar through a sieve and add more fresh, well-bruised herbs. Steep for ten days longer. Then strain off vinegar and filter it through filter paper or through moist flannel. Store in glass bottles. A sprig of herb may be added to each bottle.

Flower Vinegars

Measure 1 cup of petals and remove the white part at the base of each. Put them in a jar and add 2 cups boiling white vinegar and continue as for herb vinegar.

Seed or Spice Vinegar

Use 3 level tablespoons crushed seeds or spices to 1 quart boiling vinegar and proceed as for herb vinegar.

RECIPE AND COOKBOOK BOOTH

There is a ready market for favorite, tested recipes, and many ways of turning recipes into a profit. Inexpensive file boxes, attractively decorated with paper, felt, or decals, are in themselves a good fair item. Add index cards, broken into categories to be sold with the box or separately. Type recipes on plain or colored file cards, tie a group together with ribbon, and promote them as the best community recipes ever. Give credit to the homemaker who tested or developed the recipe, by naming them after the donor: "Mrs. Murphy's Favorite Shepherd's Pie" or "Mary Williams' Cream of Pumpkin Soup." Or you can ask noted cooks in your organization to type six or a dozen of their favorite recipes and sell or raffle each contributor's recipes as one unit.

At this same booth you might display and sell the current best-selling cookbooks. Publishers will usually allow a good discount to organizations on orders of six or more of the same cookbook. Write to the various publishing houses, such as Doubleday &

Company, Inc., 575 Madison Ave., New York 22, New York, for a list of cookbooks and their discount terms.

GOURMET'S KITCHEN BOOTH

A booth, specializing in unusual kitchen equipment, difficult to get in many localities, is becoming increasingly popular throughout the country. There are several large distributors of French kitchen equipment that will sell to charity organizations at a good discount and will even take back unsold merchandise, providing the organization is willing to pay the return charges. (See *Directory of Sources* and write for prices and catalogue.)

Don't tackle such a booth unless you live in a community interested in good food and have people in your organization, who are expert cooks, to man the booth and to either demonstrate or explain what the various gadgets are for. You might have a cookbook author in your community who would be willing to demonstrate how to make French omelets or crepes suzette or some other dish, using one or more of the utensils on sale at the booth. Or you might find someone who is adept at using a pastry bag, who will demonstrate simple decorative effects on cakes and cupcakes.

Utensils worthy of consideration for sale at this booth are: scallop shells, butter-ball makers, apple corers, *attelets*, tongs, *madeleine* pans, soufflé dishes, omelet pans, popover pans, truffle cutters, melon-ball cutters, cucumber slicers, potato peelers, wire whisks, wooden spoons, cheese graters, food mills, pastry bags and tubes, pepper mills, French lettuce baskets, corkscrews, egg slicers, trussing needles, pastry boards and covers, rolling pins and covers, pastry brushes, mortars and pestles, charcoal-burning hibachis, chopping blocks, pastry cutters, jelly-roll pans, spatulas, ceramic canisters, and glazed-pottery casseroles.

Be selective in the merchandise you order, trying to anticipate the type of utensils and gadgets that would appeal to the people in your community and varying them between the *haute cuisine* equipment and the everyday cooking needs with a good price range. Some of the items can be emphasized by attaching a suitable typed recipe and including with the item one of the ingredients in the recipe, as in the following suggestions:

A pretty copper mold filled with almonds and cranberries for a Steamed Cranberry Pudding. A cheese grater containing a chunk of Swiss cheese; wooden forks and a recipe for Swiss Cheese Fondue tied to the handle. Flexible steel spatula, a bag of dried mushrooms, and recipe for French Mushroom Omelet are tied to the handle of a small omelet or crepe pan. A bag of oatmeal and recipe for Grandma's Oatmeal Cookies, tied to a wooden spoon, will appeal to basic cooks. Something as simple as an egg in a wicker egg basket with recipe for a One-Egg Cake can sell for a small sum. A vanilla bean and a recipe for Vanilla Bavarian Cream, tied to a wire whisk, is bound to attract the gourmets. (*See photo* 117.)

FOOD BOOTHS

There can be one or many booths where homemade food specialties are offered for sale. Homemade cakes, pies, puddings, chocolate fudge, brownies, jams, jellies, and pickles head the list of best sellers, but many other homemade food items have special appeal in certain communities. It is up to the Food Committee to be able to wisely evaluate the types of food that will find ready customers. Pots of real home baked beans (not out of a can), and special casseroles can be sold directly in the containers in which they were made. If produced in any quantity, an attempt should be made to buy the pots or casseroles at a wholesale price. An additional buying incentive is to attach the recipe, typed on a file card and signed by the donor, onto each casserole. In any event be sure to attach correct reheating instructions when necessary.

Homemade breads and muffins, steamed Boston brown bread, baking-powder biscuits, sweet rolls, and sweet breads are items eagerly sought for by fair customers. Aluminum pie plates and baking dishes make inexpensive and suitable containers. These should be overwrapped with transparent film to keep the food fresh-looking. Aluminum dishes are also good containers to hold country baked ham, roast turkey, and other cold cuts, sliced and sold by the pound. Wedges of good, aged cheese, cut from a wheel, can be sold by the wedge or by the pound.

Potted cheese and *pâtés* are other good homemade special items worthy of consideration. In such cases, the packaging of these items can add tremendously to the sales appeal.

Don't put too much food out for sale at one time. An over-abundance of food can be repulsive rather than appetizing. If food is your specialty at a fair, it is better to have several tables, tastefully arranged, than too many different items on one. Keep the tables neat and surplus supplies tucked away in covered containers to protect them from dust and insects. Decorate the tables appropriately, either tying in the theme of the fair or the type of food on the particular table. Have signs announcing anything special, such as: REAL HOMEMADE COFFEECAKES or BEANS BAKED FROM AN OLD NEW ENGLAND RECIPE. Try to glamorize the food items as much as possible. And every item must have suitable bags or boxes in which to package them for travel.

All food need not be necessarily concentrated in one special area; often it is profitable to have many "spot" booths at strategic places around the entire hall or grounds, as detailed earlier in this chapter. Also, if a food item ties in with the merchandise in other categories, it can be sold at more than one table: herb jellies at the garden booth; casseroles at the Gourmet's Kitchen Booth; Christmas cakes and puddings at the Christmas booth.

Such food items as cookies, candies, and fruitcakes can be purchased in wholesale quantities—and often in bulk—to be repackaged; for instance, vinegar, honey, maple syrup, peanut butter can be bought by the tub or gallon and transferred to pretty, smaller containers. But, in general, the charm of a fair and the popularity of food at the fair is due to the fact that it is homemade. This doesn't mean it should not look professional; it should, indeed, and it will if you let women contribute those items which they specialize in and take pride in producing. Don't ask people to make pies who don't like pie baking, or a woman to make a batch of chowchow, when she'd much rather bake some pots of beans. Let each person contribute what she does best.

Stress quality in food, and imagination in the way it is packaged, displayed, and presented. Select pretty but inexpensive containers that can be used again by the buyer, such as, baskets, snifter glasses, trays, metal boxes, bread trays, and so on. The food in or on such containers should be covered with transparent film. Glass apothecary jars, empty baby-food and spice jars, glass bottles, all make perfect containers for colorful foods and need little further embellishment except a ribbon bow, bauble, a spray of greens, or an artificial flower. Any foods that must be refrigerated should be so labeled, and cooked foods to be reheated should be labeled with heating-and-serving instructions.

BAKE 'N' TAKE CAKES

Bake cake batter in glass mixing bowls lined with heavy-duty foil. Remove cakes from bowls to cool. When cool, frost, sprinkle with chopped nuts, and insert in attractive baskets with handles. The cake need not fit the basket exactly. When smaller, pack tissue paper around it. Cover cake with transparent film and decorate basket with greens and a ribbon bow. Cake batter may actually be baked right in shallow wicker baskets. Be sure the baskets have not been varnished. Soak them in water for a few minutes, then line with aluminum foil. Fill two thirds full of cake batter and bake at required temperature until cake tests done. Let cool, then frost or glaze and garnish. (*See photo 118.*)

CHINA RECEPTACLES

Pottery, ceramic, or china cups, mugs, cake plates, all make attractive receptacles in which to package food. (*See photo 119.*) Select food that is suitable, such as tiny fried cakes in the coffee mug, crisp sugar cookies in earthenware coffee cup, ladyfingers on earthenware cake plate, chocolate-coated raisins or nuts in demitasse, tea bags, each tagged with a tiny artificial rose, in a pretty china teacup, animal-cracker "sandwiches" in the baby mug, chocolate-covered mints in a chocolate cup. Cover all food with transparent film and decorate with seals, bows, baubles, or greens.

WOODENWARE

Wooden trays, cups, mortars, and other woodenware make fine, and generally inexpensive, receptacles for fair food (*see photo 120*), a highly polished, leaf-shaped tray filled with fresh fruit, nuts, and cheese; a straw-trimmed wooden board holding homemade baking-powder biscuits surrounding a container of honey butter; two ceramic-lined wooden receptacles filled with potted cheese; a lacquered Chinese wooden box topped with fondant-filled dates; a mortar filled with spiced nuts.

GLASSWARE

Almost any empty glass jar or bottle can be filled with such foods as oil, vinegar, salad dressings, jams, preserves, jellies, pickles. (*See photo 121.*) Label the jars attractively and decorate with decals, ribbons, gilded corks, baubles, and bows. Miscellaneous drinking glasses, relish dishes, and custard cups, can also be used. The foods within the glass containers should be as colorful as possible.

A CAKE BOOTH

Cakes of all kinds can be sold at the cake booth and this is usually one of the most popular food booths at a fair. In addition to cakes to buy and take home, have pieces of cut cake temptingly displayed and sold by the slice, pound, or dozen. When possible set up small tables and serve cake slices with ice cream and either coffee or hot chocolate. Here at this booth might be sold recipe books, file cards containing recipes for the cakes on display, or an inexpensive multigraphed booklet of recipes with decorative but simple cover, printed with the name and date of the fair.

At one fair, the cake booth specialized in Pennsylvania-Dutch cakes and tied in the means of presentation with Pennsylvania-Dutch motifs. A blackboard in the rear listed the regional specialties for sale to take home or eat on the spot.

FAIR REFRESHMENTS

In addition to the scheduled and advertised fair luncheon, tea, or supper, you will want to have one or more booths at which food is sold and eaten on the spot. Such items as hot freshly baked waffles and pancakes with maple syrup, hot corn muffins or baking-powder biscuits with honey or strawberry jam, are welcome foods at a fair. In using any electric cooking or heating units, make sure to check on the availability of electric outlets and the amount of power that you can load against the lines.

Hot dogs and hamburgers should be separated and not always served at the same location. And great care should be taken that any food served is protected from possible contamination. Hamburgers should be kept refrigerated or, preferably, frozen. They can be made up several weeks in advance; make them rather thin, with waxed paper between and freeze in stacks. Transport them to the fair grounds in the frozen state and keep them in insulated containers. Styrofoam carrying cases or buckets with small chunks of dry ice will keep them cold for many hours.

Have as many extras as possible to accompany hot dogs and hamburgers, such as pickles, sliced onions, sauerkraut, mustard (both hot and mild), scallions, piccalilli, chili sauce, catsup, and so on. Chili hamburgers are popular.

PANCAKES BAR

Such a refreshment booth might specialize in hot cakes and sausages during the morning hours, but do a switch to sweet pancakes, topped with strawberries and ice cream or whipped cream, during late afternoon. Try thin Swedish pancakes served with preserved cranberries or canned Lingonberries. Almost every country in the world has a special type of hot cake, which could amplify any theme based on a foreign land. From the blinis and blintzes of Russia to the delicate crepes of France, style your pancake bar to your theme. Fried-meal mush cakes and johnnycakes are a must at a New England fair.

Doughnuts and fried cakes are also easy to adapt to a theme. Arrange to fry them on the spot if possible and serve them hot with a cup of coffee or hot chocolate. Just plain American doughnuts are hard to beat but, if you wish, you can fry and serve Spanish *churros*, Swedish kelnater or "rosettes," Southern hush puppies, French crullers.

SANDWICH BAR

Almost every fair has a sandwich and beverage bar. The sandwiches will, of course, be made in advance and individually wrapped in protective paper. Do, however, make them appetizing, using a variety of breads rather than just plain white sandwich bread, and make the fillings appetizing. For meat and cheese sandwiches, don't include anything like lettuce which will wilt; better to make the sandwiches as plain as possible and equip the bar with pots of mustard, horse-radish, pickles, and containers of freshly sliced tomatoes, cucumbers, and a bowl of lettuce greens. Let each person add what he wants to his sandwich. Again, you might want to tie in to your theme the kind of sandwiches served. At a Mexican fiesta, for instance, you would want to serve a variety of *tacos*—Mexican sandwiches made of tortillas. Let each person add the shredded lettuce and minced onion to his *tacos*.

ICE-CREAM BAR

Ice cream in paper cups is easy to keep frozen in dry ice and easy to dispense. However, this bar can be as elaborate as your facilities permit. Ice-cream cones with various dishes of chopped nuts, crushed-peppermint candies, and chocolate shot in which to dip them are good. Or you might arrange to have bar stools and serve fancy banana splits and specially devised fair sundaes, sodas, milk shakes, and other soft drinks. Small tables set around the bar can augment the seating capacity but, in this case, you need "waitresses."

If members of your community have several Waring Blendors, and electrical outlets are no problem, you might have people behind the bar making frozen-fruit sherbets or serving "snowballs" topped with a concentrated fruit syrup. For this you'll need a quantity of crushed ice.

FAIR SUPPERS

Usually one or more meals are scheduled to be served at a fair. The number and kind of lunch or supper is entirely up to the Fair Committee. Should your fair be scheduled for two days, you should plan very different types of meals and have different women and committees in charge. For example, if you serve a smorgasbord featuring meatless casseroles and salads on Friday, you might change the pace and have an Italian spaghetti supper on Saturday.

Your community dictates what the best hours are for a fair dinner. The time factor may also be influenced by whether your fair is held on a weekday or a weekend.

Publicize the type of supper and the time it has been scheduled. If you sell as many supper tickets as possible in advance, you will have a slight idea of how many guests to plan for. You may need to have two or more sittings, depending on the number you can comfortably accommodate at one time.

When possible, let your fair meals reflect your fair theme. At an Early-American fair, you might serve luncheon or supper in "The Colonial Room." Hang cured hams and bunches of onions (later to be sold) from the rafters, dress the waitresses and hostesses as Puritan maidens, and serve baked beans, pumpkin pies, doughnuts, and sweet cider.

At a country fair, luncheon or supper might be served from "The Hayloft." Set bales of hay around the room; dried corn, rakes and other farm tools can add to the atmosphere. Dress helpers as milkmaids or farm hands and serve country-fried chicken, scalloped potatoes, succotash, apple pie, and homemade ice cream.

But whatever you serve and however closely you tie it in with your theme, be sure all dishes are easy to make and that you have the facilities to make them well. Serve real, honest food with a homemade flavor. Serve it at small or large tables or cafeteria-style, whichever suits your facilities best. Serve hot foods hot and cold foods cold; serve them in attractive dishes with a special touch of garnish. Keep the area spotless and free of trash or dirty dishes and put the "waitresses" in costume, when possible. At least give them pretty aprons and caps to wear.

Plan and organize the way the food will be served, and chart your spots of heaviest traffic to eliminate as much confusion as possible. Be sure to plan a place for dirty dishes to be piled, and have enough large garbage cans to take care of the refuse. In general you must count on one helper for every sixteen guests.

See Chapter 1 for supper menus, and select the one most appealing to your committee.

THE FAIR AMUSEMENT AREA

GAMES OF SKILL

At most fairs, a section is devoted to simple amusements and games of skill, which never fails to attract the children, and often amuses adults. Most of the games can be constructed at little cost by the men or boys in your organization or, there are carnival houses which sell games, ranging from those relatively inexpensive to very expensive. (See *Directory of Sources* at back of book.)

Each game set up or devised by your group should be tried beforehand by several people, of different ages, to determine how hard it is and what percentage of chances should be established to give the player a fair opportunity to win a prize, without letting the game go "broke." If you devise games that are impossible to win, people will soon lose interest. The price per chance and the prizes should be based on the amount of skill necessary to win. It's also great salesmanship if the game master has practiced his game sufficiently to be able to demonstrate to the spectators "how easy it is." Prizes should be kept simple, such as paper *leis*, clown hats, candy bars, gold-coin chocolates, gum, and trinkets. Or the prizes may be tokens, enabling the winner to go on to other games.

Poolball

This is a game that can be constructed from a child's plastic wading pool. Fill it with water and float plastic dishes in it. The object of the game is to throw Ping-pong balls into the pool and have them land and stay in one of the dishes. You might sell three balls for ten cents and award a prize if the person gets one or more balls in one of the dishes.

Tableball

Set a large, decorated box or carton on top of a card table and supply the player with a basketball. The object of the game is to bounce the ball on the side of the table at just the right angle to have the ball drop into the box. Sell three "tries" for ten cents and award a prize to the player who gets the ball in the box twice out of the three attempts.

Ring Toss

Nail canes or dowels into a baseboard and use embroidery hoops for rings. The object of the game is for the player to throw the rings over the canes or dowels. To make the game more difficult, cut the centers out of paper plates and use the rims for rings. Sell three rings for ten cents, and award a prize if the player places one, two, or all three rings, depending on how difficult the game has been devised.

Hammer the Nails

This is a ridiculous game, but one that appeals to the boys. Stud a two-by-four with large nails and let the player try his skill in sinking the nails into the wood. Test the game before setting the stakes, to determine the average number of hits it takes to sink the nail for boys of various ages.

Write the rules on a blackboard:

Under 9 years	12 hits
9 to 11 years	6 hits
12 years and over	4 hits

If you include the men in this game, set the number of hits so low that the men CAN'T WIN, but the boys can. The boys will enjoy beating their fathers.

MISCELLANEOUS AMUSEMENTS

Pig-in-a-Poke

Wrap used merchandise, white elephants, gifts, gags, and other items intriguingly; price them reasonably, and sell them sight unseen. Have some really worthwhile prizes among the items and list on a blackboard some of the choice items that can be won.

Fortune Peanuts

Remove peanuts from shells, place a fortune inside, glue them back together again and gild them. You need only one- or two-word fortunes such as: JOURNEY . . . WEALTH . . . A PRESENT . . . SUCCESS . . . NEW LOVE . . . HAPPINESS.

Fish Pond

Always intriguing for children. Stretch a blanket or sheet between posts or doorway and pile miscellaneous merchandise on a table behind it. Provide fishing rods and lines with harmless hooks on the ends, such as cup hooks. An attendant stands behind the sheet and attaches a "fish" to the lines as the children on the other side "go fishing."

Grab Garden

Plant a flower garden in a child's painted wagon. Paper blossoms, each with a "root," are arranged in rows. The roots might consist of a treasure or a fortune wrapped in tissue paper and tied to the paper blossom. Let a child, dressed as "Mary, Mary Quite Contrary," supervise while the customer plucks a blossom.

Fortune Tree

Use an ordinary pine tree or fashion a tree out of branches. Use one half for adults and the other for children. Hang decorated empty eggshells from the branches, each containing a fortune for the adults; a trinket, such as a small toy or a marble, for the children.

How Many Beans in the Pot?

Let guests at your fair buy the opportunity to guess how many beans, or other small item, is packed into a large fish bowl or apothecary jar or some other large glass container. Announce the time of the day that the prize will be awarded to the person who comes closest to the right estimate.

Weight-Guessing Booth

A simple bathroom scale and a person with a sense of humor and some ability to judge weight is all that is needed for this attraction. The ability to make fun out of the game is more important than judgment, for even if the "expert weight guesser" is wrong more often than he is right, the game can be a source of amusement and the cost of the trinkets won, when the guesser misses, can be less than the charge made to each person who climbs upon the scale.

Fun for the Children

Of tremendous help to mothers and fathers visiting the fair is a well-supervised children's play area, where children can be left while their parents tour the fair. Fence off a small area at an outdoor event or use a separate room, where games and hobbies can be set up for the children. Be sure that there are enough competent and responsible young men and women for thorough supervision.

If any parents in your organization have a hobbyhorse, ask if you may borrow it to give the children rides at the fair. At an outdoor event, pony rides or pony-and-cart rides are a great contribution. If live ponies are out, you might be able to borrow an electric golf wagon. Some electric lawn mowers are powerful enough to draw several carts or wagons, tied together to form a train. The sides of the wagons can be built up and amusingly decorated.

CHAPTER 7

Handicrafts to Make and Sell

A good slogan for organizations to remember is: "Do something to everything!" With a little imagination, little cost, and a lot of time and patience, many attractive items may be made by members of your group for sale for fund raising.

If you are planning a bazaar or fair, you should give yourself plenty of time for making various sale items and handicrafts. Many organizations work around the year. If your organization is a large one, it's a good idea to form various groups and let each group set aside one evening each week to devote to handicrafts. Request your members to save empty cans, old Christmas cards, scraps of felt, ribbon, and other material. It can all be put to good use.

The following chapter is devoted to sale items that require no particular talent and need no complicated directions or patterns. They represent only a small percentage of imaginative ideas that are possible for your organization. Your members will have many more. In addition, you will find hundreds of handicraft items in knitting books, magazines, and instruction booklets devoted to special crafts. During the year, keep your eyes open for attractive items that you see in gift shops, and at other fairs and bazaars that might be duplicated by your group. Either make a mental note, a sketch, or buy one to use for a model.

Don't make too many of any one item and do vary the colors and sizes when possible. Set a high standard of quality for yourselves and make every item look professional. Let each person do the things she does best. Let the sewers sew, the knitters knit, and the others can stick and paste. Keep track of the popular items, for they can be restyled and duplicated for another year.

Don't overprice and don't sell merchandise too cheaply. Try to hit the middle of the road. Ask many people how much they feel the item is worth and judge accordingly. Don't offer left-over items at a discount. This can be the ruination of the best-laid plans. Let it be known that nothing will be offered at reduced rates. It's better to carefully pack away the leftovers to be used at another occasion or another year. (*For pictures of the following items see photos 45–105.*)

COVERED WASTEBASKET

Material:

Metal wastebasket
Wallpaper
Clear shellac
Rubber cement

Directions:

Shellac wastebasket. Cut wallpaper to fit, allowing a small overlap on the sides. Working on a small area at a time, paste wallpaper on, smoothing as you work around basket. When paper is fully dry, shellac over surface.

WALL HANGING

Material:

1 piece of felt, 9 × 12 inches
Scraps of colored felt
Glue
Black yarn
9-inch piece of wood or dowel

Directions:

Cut background 9-×-12-inch felt with pinking shears. Using white felt, cut horse's body. With black felt, cut mane, halter, eye, and saddle strap. Using red felt, cut out saddle and rocker. Glue in place. With wool, bring one continuous piece of wool through felt (for tail), leaving loops on right side. Cut loops to form tail. On top of background piece, punch one hole on each about 1 inch from side and ½ inch from top. Braid 6 pieces of yarn and fasten through holes. Insert wood dowel and glue felt across center of dowel.

CHILD'S SKI HAT

Material:

4 ounces sports yarn, color A
2 ounces color B
½ ounce color C
1 pair No. 4 needles
1 button

Directions:

With B, cast on 136 sts. Work even in stockinette st. for ¾″ ending with a K row. K next 2 rows for hemline. P 1 row. Attach A. K 3B *2A 6B Repeat from * across, ending 2A 3B.

Row 2 * K 3B, 2A, 6B, 2A, 3B Repeat from * across row.

Row 3 *K 2B, 1A, 2B, 1A, 4B, 1A, 2B, 1A, 2B. Repeat from * across row.

Row 4 repeat row 3.

Row 5 repeat row 2.

Row 6 *K 3C, 2A, 6C, 2A, 3C. Repeat from * across row.

Row 7 * K 1B, 6A, 2B, 6A, 1B. Repeat from * across row.

Row 8 * K 1A, 1B, 4A, 1B, 2A, 1B, 4A, 1B, 1A. Repeat from * across row.

Row 9 repeat row 8.

Row 10 repeat row 7. Break off B.

Shape cap: P 27, place marker on needle, P 82, place marker on needle, P 27. Next row * K to 2 sts. before next marker, K 2 tog. K1, Sl 1, K1 Psso, repeat from * once more. K to end of row. Next row: P across. Repeat last 2 rows 26 times more (28 sts). Work even in stockinette st. until piece measures 21″ from hemline ending with K row. Next row: P7 place marker on needle. P 14 place marker on needle, P7. Dec in same manner as before every other row 6 times. Bind off remaining 4 sts.

Sew center back seam. Sew hem. For chin strap: with right side facing you, using B and starting in 27th st. from back, pick up and K 6 sts. across hemline. Work even in garter st. until strap measures 5¾″. Make buttonhole on next row: K2, bind off next 2 sts., K 2. On next row, cast on 2 sts. over bound off sts. Continue in garter st. and dec 1 st. at beg. and end of every other row twice. K 2 tog. Break off. Sew on button. Knot top of hat.

3 KNITTED GOLF-CLUB COVERS

Material:

> *4 ounces knitting worsted*
> *½ ounce contrasting color*
> *1 set each dp needles, Nos. 2 and 5*

Directions:

Using #5 needles cast on 48 sts. Join being careful not to twist sts. K2 P2 in ribbing for 3½″. Change to #2 needles and * K2 tog. P2 tog. Repeat from * around. K1 P1 in ribbing for ½″.

Change to #5 needles and inc 1 st. in each st. around. On the next round K2, P2, K6, P2, work in K2, P2 in ribbing on all sts. until piece measures 8½". *SHAPE TOP* * K2 tog. P2 tog. Repeat from * around. K1 round even. K2 sts. tog. around. Break off leaving an 8" end. Run end through all sts. and draw up tightly. With contrasting color embroider numbers on covers in the plain area (K6).

BOOK COVER

Material:

Felt to cover
Scraps of felt for trim

Directions:

Fold felt piece over closed book. Cut with pinking shears even with top and bottom edges and allowing 1½ inch extra on each end for overlap. Fold overlap back and stitch by hand on top and bottom edge. Cut oval of felt trim with straight top at one end to fit glasses. Stitch on center of front. Trim as desired. Pink a strip of felt 4 inches longer than book cover. Stitch on inside of center back, for bookmark.

TRADING-STAMP BOX

Material:

1 small file box
Assorted trading stamps
Shellac

Directions:

Beginning with top of box, stick stamps onto cover. Continue until box is completely covered. Shellac.

CHRISTMAS STOCKING

Material:

½ yard red felt
Scrap of green felt for Christmas tree
Ball fringe—½ yard

Directions:

Fold felt in half and cut out stocking. On front half, sew or glue on Christmas tree and sew or glue on ball-fringe decoration. Put sides together and stitch ¼ inch from side, including a small felt loop for hanging.

COVERED HANGERS

Material for each hanger:

1 plain wooden hanger
3 yards 1½-inch-wide satin ribbon cut into three equal lengths

Directions:

Fold 1 length of ribbon in half lengthwise with wrong sides together. Sew sides and one end in ¼-inch hem. Push on to end of hanger—repeat on other side. With remaining length of ribbon, wrap around center where sides meet. Continue wrapping over hook of hanger until covered. Fold under end of ribbon and stitch end and folded end.

KITCHEN HELPER

Material:

> 1 *dishtowel*
> 1 *dishcloth*
> 1 *plain colored potholder*
> *Ribbon*

Directions:

Roll dishcloth lengthwise and tie ends with ribbon. Fold dishtowel over cloth and baste just under cloth to hold. With marking pencil or crayon, draw face on potholder and baste to back of dishtowel. Sew ribbon bow to neck.

CHILD'S FELT BLOCK

Material for each block:

> 6 *pieces of colored felt, each* 4 × 4 *inches*
> *Scraps of contrasting felt for letters*
> *Shredded foam rubber or silk stockings*

Directions:

Cut six 4-×-4-inch squares of felt with pinking shears. With scraps of felt, cut out desired number of letters (one for each side or evenly spaced on three sides), and stitch to felt squares. Sew squares together at edges, leaving small opening for stuffing. Stuff and stitch opening.

YARDSTICK COVER

Material:

12 inches material, 36 inches wide
1 package narrow bias tape

Directions:

Cut strip of material 3 × 36 inches. Cut strips 3 × 33 inches, 3 × 24 inches and 3 × 16 inches. Sew bias tape over short end of last three strips cut. Turn top edge of longest strip over and stitch. Place longest strip right side up and with lower edges even, place remaining strips, longest first, on top of each other, forming pockets. Stitch across smallest pockets through all but longest strip (forming size pockets desired). Sew bias tape on all sides of yardstick cover allowing extra tape to form loop at top.

REVERSIBLE HOOD

Material:

1 yard wool flannel or desired material
1 yard velveteen, suede cloth, or desired lining

Directions:

With brown paper, or tissue paper, cut a pattern for half the hood making over-all length 31 inches and width of hood at widest point 14 inches. Cut head opening into half-moon shape measuring 8½ inches at widest point. Cut tie end into point. Using paper pattern, cut four pieces, two of main material and two of lining. Using main pieces and ⅝-inch seams, stitch only across center back of hood leaving 6 inches open on back of hood above tail piece. Repeat on lining piece. With right sides together, stitch lining to hood, leaving opening at tie end for turning. Turn right-side out and sew opening closed. Press.

DECORATED BUSHEL BASKET

Material:

> *Bushel basket*
> *Spray paint*
> *Glue*
> *Felt scraps*

Directions:

Spray-paint bushel basket. Cut felt scraps into desired design (flowers, birds, abstract design). Glue design to basket, and line with contrasting cotton material if desired.

WORK APRON

Material:

> 1 *yard mattress ticking*
> *Heavy-duty cotton thread*

Directions:

Cut out apron to desired size. Cut side ties twice the length and width desired. With right sides together folded lengthwise; stitch. Turn right-side out and cut in half, making two ties. Turn all four ends in and stitch. Cut desired-length strip for neck tie, double in width. Repeat as for side ties but do not cut in half. Make 1-inch hem across top and bottom of apron; stitch. Make ¼-inch seams on remaining sides; stitch. Cut desired-shape pockets, hem ¼ inch on all sides and stitch to apron. Make loop pockets same as for tie. Stitch ends to apron, allowing for loops, and stitch down in several places to allow for hanging tools. Stitch side and neck ties to apron.

TEA COZY

Material:

> 1 *yard unbleached muslin*
> *Cotton batting*
> ½ *yard satin*
> ½ *yard cotton lace*

Directions:

Allow ⅝-inch seams for muslin; ¼-inch seams for satin and lace. Cut four ovals of muslin, making straight edge 12½ inches long, and measuring 9½ inches from straight edge to top center; stitch two sides together over cotton batting cut to size. Repeat with remaining two sides. Put the two finished pieces together, matching bottom and sides. Stitch, leaving straight side open. Turn and finish off bottom seams by hand. Cut two ovals of satin, make hand hem on bottom. Put right sides together and stitch, leaving bottom open. Turn. Repeat with lace. Fit lace cover over satin cover and tack in several places on straight edge. Insert muslin.

MISTLETOE HANGER

Material:

Embroidery hoops
1 yard netting
6 yards main-color satin or velvet ribbon ½ inch wide
3 yards contrasting satin or velvet ribbon ½ inch wide

Directions:

Insert smaller hoop into larger hoop to form double circle. Beginning where circles meet, wind tightly with 3 yards of the main-color ribbon, completely covering all parts of hoops. For each side of hoop (4 sides), cut double piece of netting 4 inches wide, and 3 times length of side. Fold in half lengthwise and gather on the fold. Pull up to fit. Adjust gathers evenly and sew to ribbon that covers the side. Repeat for all sides. With remaining main-color ribbon and contrasting ribbon, cut four equal pieces and tie two to bottom of hoop, and two to the top forming loop inside to hang dried flowers or mistletoe.

CANDY WREATH

Material:

1 heavy metal hanger
3 pounds assorted wrapped candy
Red bow

Directions:

Cut off hanger hook and bend remaining wire into a circle. Using 12-inch lengths of fine wire (for ease of handling), twist

wire onto end of candy paper and twist onto hanger circle. Attach
two candies to each side and one to stand up in the center. Continue in this manner until wreath is full, filling in any remaining
spaces. Twist several pieces of fine wire together and attach to
top for hanging loop. Tie red bow to top.

BIRD STOCKING

Material:

⅛ yard red oilcloth
Wire for hanging

Directions:

Cut oilcloth stocking and stitch sides, leaving top open. Fold
over 1 inch on top. Letter the stocking with a marking pen, and
attach wire on the top for hanging. Fill with suet or birdseed and
hang on tree for the birds.

WASTEPAPER BASKET

Material:

Wastepaper basket
Spray paint
Wallpaper trim

Directions:

Spray basket with any colored paint desired and trim top and
bottom with wallpaper trim.

BATHROOM REMINDER

Material:

Small child's slate
Narrow velvet ribbon
Artificial flowers
Rubber cement or Elmer's glue
Chalk

Directions:

Paint wooden edge of slate and fasten a velvet border next to slate with rubber cement or glue. Tie chalk onto length of velvet ribbon, tie ribbon to spray of artificial flowers, and fasten in place with glue.

PLASTIC NAPKIN RINGS

Material:

Plastic shower-curtain hooks
Artificial flowers or velvet ribbon
Elmer's glue or waterproof cement

Directions:

Decorate plastic hooks with flowers or ribbon bows, sticking them securely in place with glue or cement. If desired, plastic rings may be sprayed with gold paint.

FELT NAPKIN RINGS

Material:

Piece of scrap felt
Artificial fruit
Mailing tubes
Glue or cement

Directions:

Cut mailing tubes into rings from 1½ to 2 inches wide. Cover with felt, cutting the felt with pinking shears about ⅛ inch larger than the tube and allowing ¼-inch overlap. Cover rings with the felt, gluing overlapping edges and glue on artificial fruit.

ROLLING-PIN POTHOLDERS

Material:

1 child's rolling pin
2 cup hooks
Embroidery thread
2 circles 4-inches-diameter cotton print
2 circles 4-inches-diameter plain cotton material
2 circles 4-inches-diameter quilting
Scrap of cotton print for binding

Directions:

Place circles of plain and print material, wrong sides together, with quilting between. Quilt through all thicknesses. Bind edges with cotton print. Repeat for second potholder. Sew loop of embroidery thread to plastic rings for hanging. Screw cup hooks to rolling pin and hang rings on hooks.

DECORATED FLY SWATTER

Material:

> 1 *metal fly swatter*
> *Yellow yarn*
> *Scraps of felt*
> *Red ribbon*

Directions:

With needle and wool, work binding stitch tightly over side edges of swatter. Work around top edge, leaving loop every other stitch for bangs. Sew on felt scraps to make face. Paste on felt collar and tie, covering fly-swatter base. Attach nine strands of yarn on each side for braids. Braid yarn and tie with red ribbon.

KEY RINGS

Material:

> *Leather luggage tags*
> *Decals or pack of round playing cards*
> *Gold marking paper*
> *Glue or cement*
> *Key rings and chains*

Directions:

With leather puncher, punch holes into luggage tags and fasten luggage tags to key chains. Decorate one side of tag with

For instructions on how to make all these items, see Chapter VII.

45. Covered Wastebasket

46. Wall Hanging

47. Child's Ski Hat

48. Golf Club Covers

49. Book Cover

50. Trading-Stamp Box

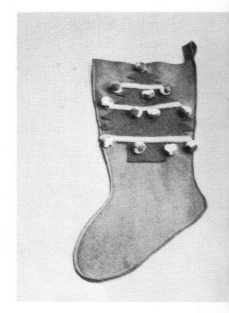

51. Christmas Stocking

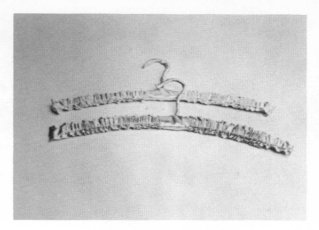

52. Covered Hangers

53. Kitchen Helper

54. Child's Felt Blocks

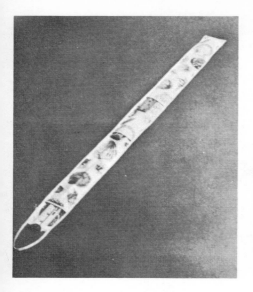

55. Yardstick Cover   56. Reversible Hood

57. Decorated Bushel Basket

58. Work Apron

59. Tea Cozy

60. Mistletoe Hanger

61. Candy Wreath

62. Bird Stocking

63. Wastepaper Basket

64. Bathroom Reminder

65. Plastic Napkin Rings

66. Felt Napkin Rings

67. Rolling Pin and Potholder

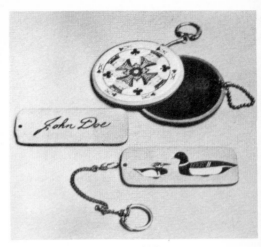

68.   Decorated Fly Swatter

69.   Key Rings

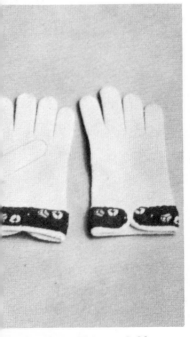

Children's Trimmed Gloves

71.   Desk Basket

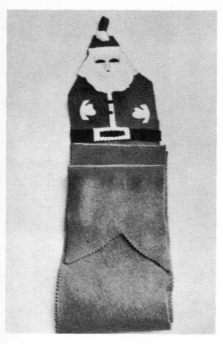

72. Christmas-Card Holder

73. Engineer Bib

74. Clothespin Bag

75. Felt Golf Club Covers

6. Framed Telephone Directory

77. Desk Set

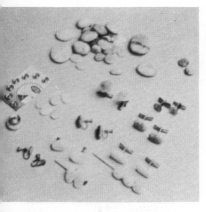

78. Stone Jewelry

79. Children's Dresser Set

80. Velvet-trimmed Accessories

81. Butt Pail

82. Children's Wall Blocks

83. Button Box

84. Nightcap and Roller Bag

85. Half Slip

86. Webbing Belt

87. Pocket Tissue Holder

88. Child's Ear Muffs

89. Clown Place Mat

90. Child's Doorstop

92. Piggy Bank

91. Doorstop

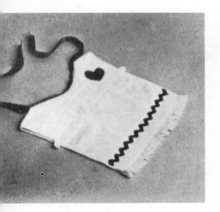

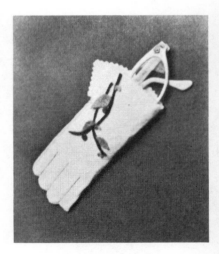

93. Child's Bib

94. Eyeglass Case

95.   One Yard Kitchen Set

96.   Octopus

97.   Decorative Basket

98.   Beach Bag

99 and 100.   Child's Dress-Apron

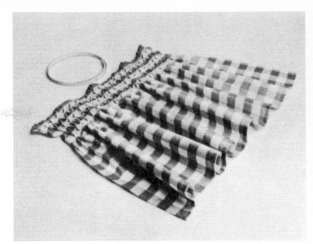

101. Smocked Apron

102. Woven Place Mat

103. Tray

104. Cheese Board

105. Pomander Ball

playing card or decals and write name of buyer on opposite side with gold marking paper or with marking pencil.

CHILDREN'S TRIMMED GLOVES

Material:

Inexpensive woolen stretch gloves
Decorative braid

Directions:

Sew braid around wrist opening on the gloves.

DESK BASKET

Material:

Christmas cards
Large needle and wool or heavy thread
Shellac and brush

Directions:

From largest Christmas card cut a circle 5 inches in diameter. Mark around circumference at 2½-inch intervals and cut a straight line between each two markings, making a six-sided base. Cut six other cards into side pieces, measuring 2½ inches at base and flaring out to 3 inches at top. Sides may be cut low or high. Leave top edges straight and curve them slightly. Sew sides together and bottoms to base with blanket stitch and heavy thread or wool. Overcast upper edge. Brush inside and out with shellac.

NOTE: Shape of these little baskets may be varied in any way you wish.

CHRISTMAS-CARD HOLDER

Material:

1 yard felt 5 inches wide
Pink, black, and white felt scraps

Directions:

Cut felt with pinking shears, making top come to flat point and cutting inverted V out of the bottom. Sew or glue on Santa face, belt, and hands as shown. Put small ribbon or felt piece on top for hanging.

ENGINEER BIB

Material:

½ yard blue denim
1 red print kerchief
Red thread

Directions:

Cut kerchief in half diagonally and hem with 1-inch hem on the two short sides. Machine hem ¼ inch on remaining long side. Cut denim 18 × 13 inches. Cut scoop for neck and make bottom come to slight point. Machine hem on all sides ¼ inch, stitching center of bias edge of kerchief to scoop of neck (right side of kerchief to wrong side of denim).

CLOTHESPIN BAG

Material:

½ yard cotton print material
½ yard plain cotton material
1 clothesline hook

Directions:

Cut cotton print into large square. Repeat with plain material. With right sides together, stitch two squares together allowing ¼-inch seam and leaving opening to turn. Turn, and sew opening closed. Bring each corner of material up to one corner of hook base, and sew with heavy thread or wool to holes in base plate.

FELT GOLF-CLUB COVERS

Material:

Eight 5-×-9-inch pieces felt
Scraps of felt for numbers, trim, and strip
4 curtain rings
1 yard elastic

Directions:

Cut 5-×-9-inch pieces of felt with pinking shears, rounding top corners. Pin ¼-inch strips diagonally across lower-right corner of four front pieces. Cut numerals from felt scraps and pin to front pieces. Stitch numerals and strips to fronts. On wrong side of back pieces mark a 2½-inch line crosswise 3½ inches above rounded edge. Cut 4 pieces of elastic 2½ inches long (when stretched.) Sew stretched elastic to marked line. Cut four strips of felt ½ × 2½ inches; fold each over curtain ring. Pin between front and back pieces of mitts. Stitch front and back together ¼ inch from outside edge. String 14-inch strip through rings; fold ends over rings 1 and 4; stitch.

FRAMED TELEPHONE DIRECTORY

Material:

1 *small picture frame*
1 *piece heavy paper to fit*
Marking pen
Colored pencils

Directions:

Decorate edges of paper with small design, being sure frame does not cover design. With marking pen, write list of important names, leaving space at bottom for any additions. Insert paper in frame.

DESK SET

Material:

Paper cement
Empty 1-pound fruit or vegetable cans (or soup cans)
Decorative wrapping paper
Paper pads
Velvet ribbon
Pencils
Spray paint

Directions:

Spray-paint cans both inside and out with paint. When dry, cover both can and first page of paper pad with attractive wrapping paper. Tie pencil onto length of velvet ribbon and glue ribbon onto back upper edge of pad.

STONE JEWELRY

Material:

Assorted small stones or pebbles
Earring backs, pin backs, cuff-link backs
Jeweler's cement
Dress snaps
Clear nail polish

Directions:

Select matching stones or pebbles and, with jeweler's cement fasten stones onto the backings, making attractive earrings, cuff links, pins, and sweater buttons. For a shiny effect, brush with clear nail polish.

CHILDREN'S DRESSER SET

Buy inexpensive sets of mirrors, combs, and brushes. Spray the frames with gold paint and decorate with colored velvet, velvet bows, rickrack braid or lace, and tiny velvet flowers. Stick decorations in place with upholsterers' glue or transparent cement.

VELVET-TRIMMED ACCESSORIES

Many other inexpensive items lend themselves to improvement by a touch of velvet, a velvet bow, or some artificial flowers. A dime-store picture frame is edged with velvet. An ordinary scallop shell, covered with velvet and given a spray of tiny flowers, makes a pretty pin tray. Velvet-covered paper clips for "the woman who has everything."

BUTT PAILS

Painted children's pails, filled with sand, make practical ashtrays for porch, patio, or garden.

CHILDREN'S WALL BLOCKS

Cut designs from wallpaper, gift-wrapping paper, or old picture books; glue onto wooden blocks cut to fit design, and shellac. Paste wall-hanging hook on back.

BUTTON BOX

Material:

Coffee can
Felt to cover
Buttons
Glue

Directions:

Cut felt strip slightly wider than sides of can. Apply glue to can and press felt on, leaving top strip of can uncovered. Let glue dry; trim to fit. Cut felt circle to fit top of can (not going over edge). Apply glue and stick. Cut strip to cover side of lid allowing ¼ inch to overhang. Cut overhang with pinking shears. Glue on. Glue flat buttons on felt to decorate. If preferred, buttons may be sewn on felt before covering can.

NIGHTCAP AND ROLLER BAG

Material:

Fine elastic
½ yard fine white cotton
6 yards lace
Small ribbon bow

Directions:

Cut circle 18 inches in diameter of cotton material. Hem finely around edge. Divide lace into 2-yard lengths and gather slightly. Stitch in overlapping rows, beginning with the first row which is attached to the hem. On inside sew fine elastic, cut to fit head size, just above last lace trim. Sew ribbon bow to center top.

NOTE: Simple draw-string pouches for hair rollers can be made of plain white cotton or gay chintz.

HALF SLIP

Material:
(for size 12)

1 yard 39-inch silk (for larger sizes, 2 yards)
Elastic for waist

Directions:

Stitch 2-inch seam along selvages, leaving 11 inches open for back slit. From top edge to within 1 inch of slit, trim seam to ¾ inch. Turn right-side out. Turn up 5¼ inches at lower edge. With pencil draw saw teeth along fold. Stitch along pencil line. Clip into points; trim and turn. Hem ragged edge, using overcast stitch where hem meets back slit to form facing. Adjust to desired length, cut off excess material at waist, and make casing at waist for elastic. Run elastic through and stitch opening closed.

WEBBING BELT

Material:

Piece of webbing desired waist size, plus 2 inches
1 yard narrow bias tape
6 eyelets

Directions:

Turn under each end of webbing 1 inch and stitch. Space 3 eyelets evenly on each side, ½ inch from folded edge of belt. Attach eyelets according to package directions, and lace with bias tape.

POCKET TISSUE HOLDER

Material:

Scrap of material 10 × 5½ inches

Directions:

Fold under short sides of material ¼ inch and stitch. Fold stitched sides under 1 inch and press. Fold the sides to meet in the center, right side of material in, and press. Stitch across ends in ¼-inch seam. Turn right-side out and insert package of tissue.

CHILD'S EAR MUFFS

Material:

Red felt, 8 × 17 inches
White felt, 4 × 8 inches, and 3 × 5 inches
Green felt, 3 × 5 inches
Black and red embroidery cotton
White velvet ribbon, ½ inch wide and 1 yard long

Directions:

Cut out headband. Glue circles of white felt onto red headband. Glue green circles to white circles. When glue is dry, stitch end of velvet ribbon to green circle. Cut out and embroider kitten's faces, using black stitches for all features but the mouth. Sew mouth with red. Glue kitten's faces on top of green circle, covering sewn end of ribbon. Cut hanging ends of ribbon slantwise.

CLOWN PLACE MAT

Material:

Piece of felt, 12 × 18 inches
Piece of white felt
Scraps of red felt

Directions:

Cut felt for 12-X-18-inch mat with pinking shears. Cut face and hands from white felt. Glue face to mat. Glue wrist and knuckles of hands to mat leaving opening to hold napkin and silver. Glue on hat and clown's nose.

CHILD'S DOORSTOP

Material:

One brick
Felt to cover brick
Scraps of felt

Directions:

Glue felt to brick to cover, cutting away excess felt on ends to prevent overlapping. With felt scraps, decorate front of brick with clown, soldier, or animal, and glue in place.

DOORSTOP

Material:

New York telephone book or thick catalogue
Shellac

Directions:

Beginning with top cover page, fold half the pages into center; then reverse process and fold back half into center. The extra bulk near the binding causes catalogue to curl into soft, round doorstop. Coat with shellac.

PIGGY BANK

Material:

White-plastic bleach or ammonia bottle with handle, about 12 inches long and 6 inches in diameter
Four corks
Pipe cleaner
Felt scraps

Directions:

The side of the bottle with the handle becomes the top of the bank. With paring knife, cut a slit in center top lengthwise 1½ inches long. Widen slit enough to pass coins. Cut a piece of pink felt 1 inch wide and 2¾ inches long; cut both ends to points; slash center 1½ inches long and glue over slit. On bottom of bottle cut four holes for cork legs to fit in snugly. Insert corks and glue. Punch hole at center back and insert pipe cleaner for tail. Cut ears, mouth, and nose from pink felt and glue in place. Cut eyes and eyebrows from black felt and glue. Decorate remaining top and sides of pig with felt flowers, polka dots, or stars as desired.

CHILD'S BIB

Material:

Terry-cloth guest towel
Seam binding or ribbon
Felt rickrack braid or scraps of material for trim

Directions:

Fold end of towel over 4 inches. Cut neckline curve 4½ inches wide and 1½ inches deep at center. Bind edge, leaving 14-inch ties on each side. Sew on desired trim.

GLOVE-EYEGLASS CASE

Material:

6½-×-7-inch piece of white felt
Scraps of felt for trim

Directions:

Fold felt piece in half lengthwise. On one side draw glove outline: fingers equal in length and omitting thumb. Enlarge wrist to form cuff. Cut glove outline—do not cut between fingers and do not cut folded side. (Cut cuff bottom and cuff side with pinking shears.) Beginning just above cuff, stitch sides and bottom close to edge through both thicknesses, leaving cuff open. Draw lines between fingers with pencil, stitch along lines with colored thread, and decorate as desired with scraps of felt.

ONE-YARD KITCHEN SET

Material:

1 yard cotton material 36 inches wide
1 package wide bias tape
2 curtain rings
Stuffing for potholders (quilting or extra-thick material)

Directions:

Cut two 12-×-17-inch place mats, one 18-×-26-inch dishtowel, four 9-inch squares for potholders. Ravel all sides of place mats evenly. Ravel ends of dishtowel and make roll hem on each long side. Put quilting between potholder squares, quilt and bind with bias tape. Sew curtain ring to one corner of each potholder.

OCTOPUS

Material:

1 ounce white knitting worsted
Scraps of black and pink felt
1 Styrofoam ball
Pink ribbon

Directions:

Divide yarn into 2 parts. Put half the yarn over ball in one direction. Put rest of yarn over ball, covering it completely. Tie pink ribbon underneath ball to form bow tie, letting excess yarn hang down from ball. Divide hanging yarn into 8 parts and braid each part for legs. Tie ribbon bow at end of each leg. Cut pink and black felt into shape of eyes and sew in place. Cut pink nose and sew in place.

DECORATIVE BASKET FOR
CHRISTMAS GREENS OR CARDS

Material:

Tin-lined basket
Gold spray paint
Pine cones, artificial fruit, and ribbon
Glue

Directions:

Spray basket with gold paint and glue on spray of cones and fruit. Tie ribbon and bow and attach on one side.

BEACH BAG

Material:

Terry cloth
Scraps of white, black, and colored felt
Rickrack braid
Glue
Cord

Directions:

Cut two pieces of terry cloth 8 inches long and 12 inches wide. Cut one end into V shape for nose of "fish." Put two pieces together and sew up sides with rickrack between the edges for the "fins." Turn under wide end 6 inches and stitch twice, having the lines of stitching 1½ inches apart. Slit side seam at one side between the two rows of stitching and insert draw cord. Finish both sides of bag with eye, mouth, and tail fins cut from felt, and glue in place.

CHILD'S-DRESS APRON

Material:

½ yard printed cotton 36 inches wide
Scraps of contrasting plain material
Bias binding
1⅔ yards cotton ribbon

Directions:

Printed material will be a rectangle 18 inches wide and 36 inches long. Stitch ¼-inch hems along each narrow edge. At bottom edge, turn under 2-inch hem and stitch. At top edge, turn under 1-inch hem and stitch. Along top edge, stitch bias binding and run cotton ribbon through space between binding and bottom of the 1-inch hem for a draw string. Fold material in half and cut semicircles in material 5½ inches long for armholes. Bind with bias binding. The center of these semicircles should be located about 8 inches from center front of apron and 6 inches down from top. Cut two pieces of plain material 6 × 7½ inches for pockets. Fold top under 1 inch and stitch. Fold side and bottom under ¼ inch and stitch pockets into place on apron.

SMOCKED APRON

Material:

1-inch checkered cotton 48 inches wide
Embroidery cotton
Apron hoop

Directions:

Cut cotton 22 inches in length or the length you wish apron to be. Make ¼-inch hems on both narrow sides, a ½-inch hem at bottom, and a 1-inch hem at top. The squares make this a very easy material to smock. Smock 6 rows at top of apron, beginning 1 inch below top edge, pulling together and fastening with embroidery cotton every other square in row and alternating squares in each succeeding row. Insert apron hoop into top hem.

WOVEN PLACE MAT

Weave 1-inch-wide satintone self-adhering ribbon into size of place mat desired. Two-toned or two or more different-colored ribbons may be used. Turn under ends on all four sides and glue to felt, cardboard, or plastic backing. Decorate with artificial flower or bow.

TRAY

Buy or make a simple wooden frame, and attach decorative drawer pulls for handles. Mount attractive prints on board backing, cut to size of frame. Finish bottom of tray with felt, cut to fit, and past on board backing. If desired, make a mat at top and bottom of prints with colored ribbon.

CHEESEBOARD

Cut light and dark wood into equal-size strips and glue together, alternating light and dark strips to form a striped board. Let dry for 24 hours, then cut across the board into equal-size strips and reform, again alternating light and dark wood to make a checkerboard effect. Let dry, then sand thoroughly and rub with olive oil.

POMANDER BALL

Stud a large navel orange thickly with large cloves. This is easier to do if the orange is first punched with an ice pick. Tie with ribbon and a bow. If possible, sell fresh pomander balls rather than the dried. Do not make them further ahead than one week, and store in the refrigerator until time of the fair.

CHAPTER 8

Miscellaneous Fund-raising Events

If a comprehensive fair or bazaar is beyond the scope of your organization, many of the individual booth ideas, presented in the chapter on *Bazaars and Fairs,* can be projected into a special fund-raising event, without all the work that a fair entails. And there are many other ways of turning talents and crafts into a profit for your organization, whether you measure the profit in terms of good fellowship, education, or money.

For example, the pastor of a church in Indiana was concerned about the happiness and welfare of the aged and aging in his congregation. In an attempt to provide its older members with worthwhile free-time activities, he suggested turning the old coalbin into a hobby room. His members were delighted, and several women volunteered to instruct classes in various crafts, such as knitting, painting, ceramics, and leathercraft. One member of the congregation donated a small kiln for baking clay, and the dirty coalbin was converted into a well-lighted workshop.

At the end of three years the walls were covered with paintings, mosaics, and patchwork quilts, and display stands exhibited hand-tooled belts and purses, tiny water colors, crocheted afghans, and ceramic vases, representing the work of more than 250 hobbyists, ranging in age from five to eighty-five years. For, when the young people found out how much fun and pleasure the oldsters were getting out of their hobbies, they clamored for admittance to the workshop. Latent talents were developed and new friendships blossomed, and a potluck dinner, served to about two hundred people, has become the happy climax to the annual display of arts.

COOKBOOKS

Untold numbers of churches and other organizations have found it worthwhile to compile and print their own cookbooks. It's a big undertaking and should not be attempted by any group that cannot count a great many good cooks among its members or does not have one or more experienced persons willing to check and edit the recipes, put them into logical order, and write introductory copy.

A group of women belonging to a Greek Orthodox Church in Hempstead, New York, had mutual culinary interests, and they met at monthly intervals to sample some special Greek dishes and to exchange recipes. Soon they decided to compile a cookbook to help with the erection of a newer and larger church. At the end of two-and-a-half years of compiling, sorting, testing, and editing, their Greek cookbook was privately printed.

Because the book was well done and contained new, unusual and interesting recipes, it captured the fancy of the food editors of two large New York newspapers, and editorials on the food pages of these newspapers praised the book and the Greek cuisine so vividly detailed in its pages. Letters and orders poured in from all over the country. People who had bought one, ordered more—sometimes as many as a dozen. The book had immense appeal for all food-conscious people, for gourmets, experimental cooks, and for tourists, who wished to duplicate in their own kitchens some of the exciting dishes they had experienced on recent trips to Greece. The end of the success story is that the book was bought by a publishing firm. It was enlarged and published in a handsome hardcover edition in the fall of 1963 by Doubleday.

A charity organization in New York compiled, edited, and had printed a small but charming hard-cover cookbook. Every step along the way was supervised by the very capable food editor of a leading woman's magazine. Because the book was attractive, the format original and decorative, and the recipes good, over twenty thousand copies were distributed, resulting in an income of more than twenty-five thousand dollars that was used for underprivileged girls.

There is always a demand for new recipes and cookbooks, but they must be worthwhile. They must be able to stand up to the many cookbooks written each year by professionals in the food field. Collect your members' best recipes, test each one thoroughly, and type them in an easy-to-follow style that is consistent throughout. The recipes should not be copied from *Fannie Farmer* or from *The Joy of Cooking* but should be original dishes, reflecting the flavor and special ingredients indigenous to your section of the country. Or they may contribute a special cuisine as made today by second-generation ethnic groups. The number of recipes, whether set in type or offset from handwritten pages, whether illustrated or not, makes little difference; the quality and originality of the contents are what determine its success.

Select a title for your book that includes the name of your organization. Shop around among local printers for estimates on size, format, and costs, or write to the North American Press, 918 Broadway, Kansas City, Missouri (one of the largest publishers of Organization and Church Cookbooks), for information on one of several types of cookbook projects in which they specialize. On request they will send you a booklet with a very long title, "How to Have Fun Publishing Your Own Cookbook, and Make Money for Your Group at the Same Time."

There are a few other considerations to discuss before embarking on a cookbook project. Should you solicit local advertising to cover printing costs? How many copies can you afford to order and where will you store them? How will you publicize and merchandise the book? If you plan to fill orders by mail, who will handle the wrapping and mailing?

A COUNTRY STORE

Once or more often during the year, many organizations offer for sale a variety of merchandise—old, refurbished, new, and hand-made. If you can find an empty store in a good shopping area that is awaiting a new tenant on a lease basis, you might be able to persuade the owner to let you use it for a very small rent, but preferably for nothing. The number of days you will need to use the premises will depend on the amount of merchandise you have to sell and the season of the year. If you have concentrated on gift merchandise designed to appeal to holiday shoppers, and have a sufficient supply, you may want to run your store for several days; if, on the other hand, your group has specialized in outdoor wares, one lovely spring day may be all that is needed for you to be cleaned out of everything.

One club in Westchester, New York, held their Bonanza Bazaar for two days in early November; the variety of wares included wearing apparel, paper goods, toys, books, jewelry, as well as personal- and home-gift items. Another club runs a Nearly New shop each year for ten consecutive days, including Thursday evening and all day Saturday. New and used merchandise of all categories are sold.

You can dispense food, gifts, crafts, and household items, or practically anything you feel will have a demand among your special clientele. Be sure to advertise the event well in advance of the scheduled dates. Keep track of the most popular and profitable items. Change your theme each year, but repeat the "big sellers." Save any left-over merchandise; give it a new look and offer it for sale the following year.

SWAP SHOPS

These can be conducted in very much the same way as the Country Store. Trade items such as children's outgrown clothing, toys, and equipment. Charge a fee for each transaction completed.

AMATEUR NIGHT

There is hidden talent in any group. Appoint someone who has had experience, no matter how limited, to stage an entertainment program. If no stage is available, perform "in the round." Have as much variety as possible: a dancer, a singer, a musician, a monologist, a comedian. You can have, if desired, a series of short skits or sketches. Charge admission and serve coffee and cake at a short social hour at the end of the program.

PLAYS AND MUSICALS

These can be big fund-raisers for a community, providing they are well done, but one wonders if the profit is ever commensurate with the work that goes into such a project. Everybody gets into the act and everybody has fun and tension continues to mount as the moment for raising the curtain approaches. Men are set designers, carpenters, painters, prop men, and stage managers. Women sew, make costumes, sell tickets, usher, and publicize the event. Even children are enlisted to help where they can. By all means get some professional help to direct activities and actors. Even children's Christmas plays need a professional touch.

For copyright laws and royalties on plays, contact Samuel French, Inc., 15 West 45th Street, New York 36, N.Y. For musicals, contact Jerome J. Cargill Producing Organization, Inc., 140 Fifth Avenue, New York 11, N.Y.

PROFESSIONAL ENTERTAINMENT

There's much less work and almost as much profit in sponsoring the appearance of a group of professional entertainers, even if you have to hire a hall. Select the kind of entertainment that will appeal to your particular community—a musical quartet, a pianist, violinist, or harpist, an Elizabethan choral group, puppeteers, a well-known actress to read poetry or Shakespeare. Publicize the event in every way possible, and sell as many tickets in advance as you can. A social hour at the end of the entertainment, gives the audience a chance to meet the entertainers. For a list of talent agencies, who specialize in touring entertainers, see your classified telephone directory.

ART SHOWS

It takes from three to six weeks to organize an art show where professionals exhibit their work. There should be a range of mediums and styles—oils, water colors, drawings, sculpture, and the less-expensive but popular woodcuts, etchings, and lithographs. If well selected, you should expect to sell about one third of the works exhibited. The prices of the art are decided on by the artists. The organization takes one third of the selling price. If pictures are borrowed from galleries, the commission is shared with them, the sponsoring organization receiving from 10 to 20 per cent of the sales price.

The chairman of the show should be a person with an art background and she, with the help of three or more assistants, should select the pictures. The advice of an art dealer is also helpful in evaluating the canvases chosen for display.

You will need a transportation committee to pick up, pack, and crate the art, when necessary. This same committee might be responsible for the physical labor of hanging the pictures in the "gallery." All canvases and works of art should be insured from the time of pickup to their return to artist or gallery.

Because of the trucking and handling costs of the pictures and other expenses, try to hold the show in a rent-free building or hall. Libraries, school auditoriums, hotel suites are all suitable, provided that they are well lighted and the pictures can be displayed to their best advantage. The artists, whose work is selected for exhibit, should sign a release giving the organization permission to show their pictures on consignment.

Your show can be completed in one day, or can last through a weekend or for an entire week. With plenty of advertising, publicity, and a preview, chances are you'll sell as many paintings over a weekend as you will if your show lasts longer. Don't forget the show must be manned. There should be at least two people on duty every hour that the exhibit is open. They should be well versed in art and able to answer questions about the show, the artists, the prices, and keep an eye on the pictures to see that no harm comes to them.

The entrance fee should cover the cost of the printed program.

Art books can also be on sale, and you might have an artist present, making quick portrait sketches.

Refreshments can be served for a nominal consideration.

CALENDARS FOR SALE

There are many sources from which an organization can buy decorative calendars for resale to their group or to the community. Select one that appeals to your particular organization—religious, culinary, or scenic, or you might decide on one of the pretty ones with pictures of cats, dogs, or birds. When attractively boxed, calendars make charming gifts for holiday presents.

ANTIQUE SHOWS

If you live in a community where people appreciate antiques, you may wish to stage an antique show. Legally, a piece of furniture or other item must be made prior to 1830, although most people will go along with the current meaning that, anything over a hundred years old is an antique. If you sell antiques, it is best to get professional advice on identifying and pricing the genuine articles. If you sell reproductions of popular antiques, be sure to label them for what they are.

Rather than become involved in soliciting and collecting antiques for sale or display, you might prefer to sell space in your hall or auditorium to dealers on an outright price basis or on a percentage of any sales they might make. You can conduct the show on one or several evenings during the week, with a special preview night for the immediate members of your society. In order to attract a crowd, this type of affair needs advertising. You can sell refreshments and other items if you wish, and it is wise to charge admission, for more people come to see antiques than to buy them.

CANDY AND BAKE SALES

Many kinds of very good candy, cookies, dried or glazed fruits and nuts, and fruitcakes can be obtained at wholesale prices from manufacturers who pack especially for individual organizations. Profits amount to about 50 per cent. Unless the manufacturer will accept return merchandise, don't overestimate your sales. It's far better to begin modestly and, if the results are successful, make it a yearly event and increase the amount of your order. Station salespeople at busy corners, outside a supermarket, or in heavily trafficked places. Be sure to let the buyer know what charitable organization will benefit from their purchase. See *Directory of Sources* at back of book under specific foods.

Homemade candy and baked goods can net even bigger profits for an organization. They have more appeal to buyers, providing they look attractive and professional. It takes more work, however, and lots of co-operation on the part of the people in your organization.

A church in Roseville, Illinois, sold 1068 cans of homemade candy one year, clearing $1000 after expenses. In view of the fact that the population of Roseville was, at the time, only 1065 and many of the church members lived up to ten miles out of town, their candy sale was a phenomenal success.

One way to insure consistency and quality is to set up a sort of chain candy-making operation. Who has the most perfect recipe for chocolate-nut fudge? Ask her to invite five or six people in for an evening to show them how to make a batch of five pounds of fudge. During the evening they will also package it attractively and set it aside for the day of the sale. On the following evening, each of the five or six women could invite a few of their friends to their homes for similar instructions, make a five-pound batch and package it. You now have from twenty-five to thirty pounds of packaged candy ready for sale. Each person has devoted two evenings to the project and has supplied the cost of the ingredients of one five-pound batch. If your organization is a large one, think how much candy could be made in this way over a ten-day period! Even if a few links in your chain flounder, you can produce many hundreds of pounds of packaged candy. You don't have to restrict the candy-making to one recipe. You might decide to make five one-pound batches of five different candies, rather than a five-pound batch of just one.

Traveling bake sales are always sure-fire moneymakers. Decorate station wagons and load them with attractively boxed homemade goodies. Put drivers and hostesses in bright costumes and let them take off for all points in the city. If you can arrange to equip each wagon with a loud-speaker, announce what goods are for sale and what charity you are helping. If the baked goods are of excellent quality, your community will look forward to your sale each year.

FASHION SHOWS

Fashion-show teas and luncheons are becoming an increasingly popular way of putting money in the treasury of your favorite charity. There are many kinds of shows that can be staged and many different ways of going about it, but they all take a lot of work. Whatever you do, make the show specific and select the one most likely to draw a good audience from your community. Try to have an experienced commentator, if possible. Charge a fee for admission and refreshments. Award door prizes or raffle off other merchandise if you wish.

Children's Fashion Show

Let children from the age of three to eleven parade in costumes made by members or borrowed from the latest collection of a local department store. Children's toys and dolls, ranging in price from one to ten dollars can also be sold. Children might carry life-size dolls modeling layettes and baby fashions.

Teen-Age or Career-Girl Fashion Show

Members of your organization model school, college, and career fashions from a local store.

Suburban Fashion Show

This might be staged from either home-sewn or from designer fashions. If home sewn, award prizes for the best designs in various categories. Aprons, kitchen towels, place mats, and other household home-sewn items can be sold.

Bride's Fashion Show

Members model wedding costumes from early American days through the years to the ultramodern. The show might feature a display of a wedding party, complete with bridesmaids, flower girl, and ring bearer.

Professional Fashion Show

Individual designers as well as leading department stores often welcome the opportunity to exhibit their latest collection. They select the clothes and supply their own professional models and commentator. The organization sponsoring such an event is responsible for staging, publicity, and refreshments. If you have the facilities, serve tea or luncheon during the show in your own hall or auditorium. Otherwise you can arrange to stage the show at a local hotel but, as always, more profit is derived for your charity, if you are able to provide accommodations and refreshments yourself.

EDUCATIONAL FILMS

Hundreds of fascinating films of interest to both men and women are available without charge, except for postage and insurance. The films, 16 millimeter, usually run from fifteen to twenty minutes. Rent or borrow a projector and screen, charge a nominal fee, and serve refreshments.

A good source for a variety of films on wild life, fishing, and cooking, can be obtained by writing to the Department of the Interior, Washington, D.C. Two salmon films, one on catching the fish and another on various ways to cook it, for example, make a good hour show. Attractive recipe booklets with color illustrations can also be purchased for resale. A 13½-minute color-sound film entitled *Coffeetime* may be obtained by writing to Coffee Brewing Institute, 120 Wall Street, New York, N.Y. Some leading manufacturers of food products also have films for private showing. Your school or library might have a list of sources.

KITCHEN TOURS

If you can find as many as half-a-dozen interesting kitchens in your community, a tour of inspection appeals to women. The kitchens need not be the "latest word" in equipment and modernity, but should all have charm in their individual ways. Try to select widely different and unique approaches to kitchen arrangement and décor: a real, old-fashioned, country or early-American kitchen; a living-cooking-eating kitchen; a professional chef's kitchen; and so on. You could arrange to have packaged food for sale at one or more of the kitchens, and serve simple refreshments, such as dainty sandwiches, cake, cookies, and a cup of coffee at the conclusion of the tour.

OPEN-HOUSE AND GARDEN TOURS

These never fail to bring a response in a community, but take a lot of advance preparation and hard work. The gardens or houses must be selected with care, and you need more than the owners' permission; you need their wholehearted co-operation and enthusiasm. Don't put the entire responsibility on the owners, however. Give them as much help as possible in supplying refreshments and providing hostesses. You should have maps printed and also post signs along the route. Advance publicity will do much to make this event a success.

Often organizations combine a tour of this kind with a sort of progressive bazaar, with open houses exhibiting different merchandise. In small towns, arrange houses within walking distance from each other. In larger communities, or when houses are well spaced from each other, some means of transportation should be arranged. Supply shopping bags.

TREASURE HUNTS

These can be a great deal of fun for adults as well as for children. They are most successful when conducted in an attractive countryside, on a crisp spring or fall day. Specify comfortable walking shoes, for exercise is one of the main reasons for participation in the "hunt." You can divide hunters into groups and give different instructions to different groups, letting them all end up at a central depot for refreshments—a private house, a club, or a country restaurant. Charge a fee for participation and refreshments and, if possible, have the treasures and prizes donated.

RECIPE TESTING

Large manufacturers of food frequently enlist the services of homemakers in various sections of the country to test recipes or new products, and fill out a questionnaire. The cost of the ingredients is supplied, and a fee per recipe is donated to a specific charity. Soap and household products are sometimes tested in this way.

For further information, write the home economics department of the company whose products you would like to test.

CHAPTER 9

The Joys of Christmas

The special joys of Christmas set it apart from the other days of the year. Like Thanksgiving, Christmas calls for a prayer of thanks and a bountiful feast; like the New Year, it offers hope for a better world and a promise of peace; like Easter, it reminds us of God's love for man; like a birthday, it is a day to shower with gifts and good wishes. But Christmas is more than the sum of wishes and gifts and feasting; it is more than a reminder of love. It is Love itself, coming to the hearts and minds of us all.

Perhaps the most important thing for everyone to remember, as you plan your group festivities for the Christmas season, is that Christmas is a religious holiday and commercialism is the quickest way to spoil the spirit that Christmas should convey. This doesn't mean that you won't be having fund-raising drives for Christmas. Money is necessary; there are the sick, the homeless, and the aged to think about at this time of year, and every group will want to do its share to see that no person is too young or too old to miss the joys of Christmas. But emphasis should be on the good you will do, not on the money you want to raise. How much you contribute in thoughtfulness and time is often more important than how much you give. It's relatively easy to peel off a dollar bill to donate to charity; harder by far to give of yourself ˊat this, the busiest time of the year. The sensitive heart need not be reminded of this, but in the hustle and bustle of committee meetings, the fast pace of ideas presented and acted on, it is possible to get far away from the whole point of Christmas, the festival of Love.

In addition to fund-raising activities, there are all the wonderful traditions of Christmas that make this season of the year the merriest and most beautiful. There are trees to trim and carols to sing. There's mistletoe and holly, jingle bells and Santa Claus. There's plum pudding and Dickens' *Christmas Carol*. There's the Christmas Star that shone over Bethlehem. There are the shepherds, the wise men, and the angels, who are part of the Christmas scene. There are cranberry strings and popcorn balls, a source of fun in the making and the eating. There are fruitcakes and Clement Moore's *The Night Before Christmas*. There are reindeers (especially Rudolph) and Christmas trees and Christmas cards.

What other Christmas symbols are there to set your plans in action? Most of all, there's the Spirit of Christmas—may it shine through every one of your plans and make your Christmas happy.

DON'T PLAN TOO MUCH

Choose one activity and make it the best of its kind. If you plan a tree-trimming party, *and* a Christmas-carol songfest, *and* a Christmas party, you will add to the general exhaustion that all your members feel in a too-busy season, and take away from the peace and serenity that should be part of the holiday. By concentrating on one activity, you can devote all your efforts to it.

BEGIN WELL IN ADVANCE

October is none too early to begin thinking of Christmas, making plans, and getting some activities started. It's the time to make Christmas fruitcakes and plum puddings to give them time to age. If you are planning a Christmas-cake and cooky sale, you might begin now to take advance orders for the fruitcakes and

For instructions for making items in figures 106 to 116, see Chapter IX.

Christmas food items can be edible as well as decorative.

106. Cooky Tree Ornaments   107. Merry Christmas Gingerbread

108. Cookymobile

109 and 110. Three-dimensional Cooky Stars are easy to make by following the how-to pictures. Roll out a very firm sugar cooky dough thinly and cut out, following design of a cardboard cutout. Put two together and decorate with decorator's frosting colored with food coloring.

111. Cooky Trees

112. Cake Candles

113. Snowballs

114. Frosty the Snowman

115 and 116. Empty coffee and one-pound shortening cans, copper molds, even flowerpots are good for packaging fruitcake. The cakes can be baked directly in the containers before they are decorated.

For instructions for making items in figures 117 to 121, see Chapter VI.

117. Gourmet kitchen equipment for booth at a fair can be more appealing when combined with a suitable recipe and one of the ingredients for making the dish.

118. Bake-'n'-Take Cakes make a handsome array at a cake booth or cake sale.

Attractive packaging of f[
in suitable containers a[
much to the food tables a[
fair. Use inexpensive chi[
wooden, or glass receptacle[

119.

120.

121.

122. Triangular arrangement reflects the Early Christian architecture with its columns and lintel opening. To be used in pairs. (For this and the following flower arrangements, see Chapter X.)

123. Round formation repeats the oval-shaped dome of Byzantine structure. To be used in pairs.

124. The semicircular lines of the Romanesque are reflected in a rhythmic arrangement. To be used in pairs.

125. The pointed arches and vertical lines of Gothic architecture are repeated in a classic composition. To be used in pairs.

126. The massive construction and horizontal lines of the Renaissance are felt in the combination of fruit, flowers, and foliage to be used as a single arrangement in back of the altar with flowerstands flanking either side.

puddings to give you some idea of how many you will need to supply the demand.

CHRISTMAS CARDS

There are many card companies that are glad to supply sample cards from which orders can be taken. There are others that will sell lots of cards wholesale, to be resold at a profit for charity. Some companies will refund money on cards returned in good condition. The children in your organization make good door-to-door salesmen, for few can resist the salesmanship of youth.

Perhaps the most lucrative and best way to make Christmas cards a group project is to design and hand-make your own attractive cards to sell. A talented artist might design a few simply made cards, which other members could copy, using production-line methods. If you have a way of displaying the sample cards and taking orders in advance, you will know how many of each design you are going to need. If the quantity warrants the cost of a line cut, you can have the outline of the design printed on card stock, and the design filled in later with water colors or crayons. A candid-camera picture, or a line drawing of your church, or the door of your club trimmed with a Christmas wreath, can be inexpensively reproduced. You might add hand touches of color to brighten it in suitable places, or have it printed in sepia, gold, or green.

GIFT WRAPPINGS

Everybody buys paper, ribbon, stickers, and tags for Christmas, so they might just as well buy from an organization as from the local department store. The profit can go toward making Christmas a happier time for many unfortunates in your community. Such items can be sold by a door-to-door canvass, selling on the spot or taking orders from samples and delivering a few days later. Or you might have a tea, where samples of attractive gift-wrapped packages would be displayed, and the appropriate paper, ribbon, baubles and bows sold. Be sure to supply shopping bags to make it easy for buyers to transport their purchases to their homes, and be sure to schedule the event early enough to catch people before they have done their gift-wrapping shopping elsewhere.

CHRISTMAS CANDLES

You can buy decorative candles wholesale and resell them for profit.

You can buy plain candles and add decorative touches to make them more attractive and worth a higher price.

You can plan a Candlelight Service outdoors in front of the community tree.

You can ask each house in your community to place a candle in their window as an expression of each and everyone's desire for peace, and supply a certain kind of a candle—tall and slim, or fat and squat, red or green or white—for their donation to your charity.

CHRISTMAS DECORATIONS

Early in October you might schedule a lecture by a garden enthusiast on decorating homes for Christmas. Or you might ask one of your garden-club members to instruct your group in the making of door and mantel decorations. Decorative pieces constructed of dried and artificial flowers and greens can be made well in advance. Those made of fresh greens should not be put together until two weeks before Christmas, but can be designed and orders can be taken for specific shapes and sizes. If you plan some combining cones or nuts, plain or gilded, part of the work can be executed early and the fresh greens added later.

Members with skillful fingers might enjoy making small Christmas corsages to distribute or sell at Christmastime. Use tiny cones, sprays of evergreen, little holly berries, even tiny Christmas balls. A local florist might volunteer his help, donating corsage wire and pins as his contribution to your Christmas fund.

You can sell Christmas trees from the lawn or steps of your church or clubhouse. Within the building or parish house, might be for sale tree ornaments, small decorated trees, as well as door and mantel decorations. Serve hot chocolate and doughnuts to your customers.

You can organize a progressive Christmas-Tree Tour, arranging in advance for people to allow a group to see their tree and other home decorations. Many people go to tremendous expense and trouble to decorate their homes lavishly at Christmastime and spend months developing a novel theme and color scheme for their tree. They are pleased and flattered to be asked to be included in the Christmas Tree Tour.

THE CHRISTMAS TREE

Ask members to each contribute a small sum toward the purchase of a huge Christmas tree to be set up on the village green, in front of your church, Scout headquarters, school, or hospital. Also ask each member to contribute one tree ornament and invite all to gather for a grand tree-trimming party, with hot milk punch and cookies for all. The "admission price" to a tree-trimming party or other Christmas event within your church or clubhouse, might be a Christmas gift, decoratively wrapped. Each gift should be labeled according to the contents, on a removable slip—then distributed according to the nature of the gift. These presents need not be expensive, but they should be useful, and geared to the purpose: a hospital patient might welcome a paperback book or a small bottle of cologne; the aged might prefer a box of candy or a package of cigarettes. If these gifts are to be displayed at the base of your indoor tree for several days prior to distribution, you can ask members to wrap their gifts in a specific color: all white, all red, etc., or in a combination of selected colors to blend with other Christmas decorations within the church or hall.

TOY ROUNDUP

Ask members of your organization to donate any good but used toys from the attic and deliver them to a central depot at a given date. Or arrange for members to pick them up from the various homes in station wagons. Men, women, and children can spend many happy group evenings, repairing, painting, and wrapping the toys for a local orphanage or for hospitalized children.

PRE-CHRISTMAS ACTIVITIES FOR CHILDREN

Encourage the children in your group to make Christmas gifts for their family and friends, rather than buy them. With supervision, older girls can sew aprons, baby bibs, felt mittens, and bake cookies. Boys can make simple wood projects, such as chopping boards, napkin holders. Even little tots are able to cut out bookmarks of felt and decorate them with felt appliqués.

Have children gather pine cones. Then, at a cocoa-and-cooky party, they can paint the cones with silver and gold paint for mantel or door decorations, or place them in hand-woven baskets for a gift for a friend or neighbor.

Children will love decorating tiny trees for the birds with seeds, tiny bits of suet, and bright-red apples tied with gay ribbon.

At an early December meeting, ask each member to bring a bag of lollipops. Use them to decorate a lollipop tree at a children's Christmas party. Let admission to the Lollipop Tree Party be one used but good toy, to be refurbished by club members and distributed to less-fortunate children.

CAROLING

One of the nicest customs of the Christmas season is the group singing of Christmas carols. There are many individual ways of working this out, but it remains a pleasant occasion for people who enjoy singing, to carry the Christmas message from door to door and add to the spirit and charm of Christmas.

Groups of traveling carolers should be kept small. It is better to organize several small groups, than one very large one. One group might specialize in the nostalgic Christmas carols like "Silent Night" and "We Three Kings"; another might rehearse the carols that are especially appealing to the children; still another might contribute Elizabethan carols. When possible, add a musical instrument to your group—a violin, an accordion, or a guitar. In suburban and urban areas, carolers should carry flashlights to light the way from home to home, but once they have reached their destination, it is more effective to extinguish the flashes and let each singer hold a lighted candle in one hand.

Larger caroling groups are more impressive when conducted from platform or church steps.

CHRISTMAS IS A TIME TO REMEMBER

You can compile a list of servicemen, shut-ins, or faraway former members of your group and send a round-robin Christmas greeting letter to each.

If your town has a college or other institution where people are parted from their own families at Christmas, sponsor a Guest-for-Christmas Movement. Encourage families to each invite at least one person to be their guest at Christmastime. Foreign students and servicemen are appreciative candidates.

You can pack goody boxes for children in your crippled-children's hospital or local orphanage, for those confined in older-citizen homes, etc. Make it everybody's concern to let no one be forgotten.

Several days before Christmas, have a Sharing-of-the-Greens. Ask members to bring sprays of greens, holly, wire, and tools, and make wreaths and decorations for a hospital or institution. Remember to wear old leather gloves, and do have someone visit the place you will decorate to plan exactly what decorations are needed. Make sure that no other organization has selected the same institution for the decorating project.

CHRISTMAS FOOD

Christmas is such a busy time that many members of your community would welcome the opportunity of buying their Christmas cookies, cakes, candies, and puddings, than to make them, PROVIDING they are sure that these commodities are truly homemade by expert cooks in your organization. If your group has a large, well-equipped kitchen, the making, baking, and packaging of Christmas foods can be group projects and lots of fun. Otherwise, they can be made in individual kitchens around town. Groups can meet in the town hall, parish house, or Sunday-school room for sessions of assembly-line packing in gaily decorated cans and pretty boxes.

Empty coffee cans or 1-pound shortening cans make excellent containers in which to package cookies, candy, and fruit cake. Empty containers should be solicited early in the fall. Collect bits of ribbon, Christmas cards, wrapping paper, decals, and buy lots of spray paint. Spray the cans gold or silver and let people use their own techniques and imagination in decorating them. The prettier the cans, the easier it will be to sell your wares. Sell as much as possible by advance order. Sell the rest from street corners with a "merry Christmas" to passers-by, or by a door-to-door canvass.

Food for a Christmas Fair should be traditional. Stick to all the recipes that spell Christmas—the pfeffernuss and springerle cookies, the gingerbread men, penuche and peanut brittle, the Christmas stollen, mincemeat pies or packaged mincemeat filling, and many other holiday treats.

In addition to selling Christmas food items to be taken home for personal enjoyment or for gift giving, have miniature pieces of certain items to give out as samples. Also sell cookies, slices of cake or pie right on the spot. You might have a table selling wedges of mincemeat pie with a big dollop of hard sauce and cups of steaming coffee to be enjoyed by the visitors to your sale.

Some of the Christmas food items can be designed to be not only decidedly edible but to double as table or mantel decorations.

COOKY-TREE ORNAMENTS
(See photo 106.)

Bake cookies in the shapes of stars, moons, wreaths, balls, and bells. Make a stiff cooky dough and, before baking, make a hole in the top of each "ornament" with a sharp instrument such as an ice pick, ¼ inch from outer edge of cooky. After baking, decorate with tinted decorator's icing and silver shot or sugar crystals, and cinnamon candies. Insert string or wire through holes in top of cookies. Package a dozen cooky-tree ornaments to a box. Have a cooky tree on display to show a variety of ornament designs.

MERRY CHRISTMAS GINGERBREAD
(See photo 107.)

Gingerbread cooky dough can be rolled out and cut into Christmas-tree ornaments or into more ambitious shapes, such as a gingerbread sled. Decorator's icing is used to "glue" the various parts of the sled together. Lettered gingersnaps can be "glued" onto ribbon to carry a sweet message from a small table centerpiece tree or from the mantel. Package cooky letters 14 to a box, each box spelling "Merry Christmas." For smaller boxes of 9 cookies each, use the abbreviation, "Merry Xmas."

COOKYMOBILE
(See photo 108.)

Sugar cookies in the form of musical angels and stars, or other symbols of Christmas, can be hung from holes in the cookies with string onto sugar-cooky "comets." Hang one for display and package all edible parts for the mobile. Let children buy and assemble their own cookymobile to dangle from chandelier or mantel.

THREE-DIMENSIONAL COOKY STARS
(See photos 109 and 110.)

Cooky stars are great fun to make and are easy enough if cardboard cutouts are used. Make them in a variety of sizes for Christmas-tree ornaments or for a centerpiece or mantel display. Frost them attractively with tinted decorator's icing.

COOKY TREES
(See photo 111.)

Graduated sugar-cooky stars are threaded on wooden dowels or long, thin pencils. Sugar-cooky rings give separation to the stars. The little cooky trees make attractive edible decorations for table centerpiece or mantel. Sell them singly, but show displays where the trees are used in pairs or an arrangement of three or more.

CAKE CANDLES
(See photo 112.)

Squares of cake are sandwiched together with frosting to build a candle of desired height. Frosted and decorated with green borders, holly leaves, and cinnamon-candy "berries," they make attractive table decorations to enjoy throughout a holiday meal and for dessert, after the main course is finished. Insert small candles in top of each cake candle.

SNOWBALLS
(See photo 113.)

Frosted cupcakes, rolled in coconut, make a pretty centerpiece. Edible, too. Arrange several on a bed of pine sprays and insert a small candle in top of each.

FROSTY THE SNOWMAN
(See photo 114.)

Cake batter is cooked in two small bowls for the body of the snowman and flat sides put together with frosting. The head is baked in either a smaller bowl or a coffee can. Fluffy frosting rounds out the head and body. Because Frosty is coated with fluffy meringue frosting, he is difficult to transport. Better use him as the centerpiece for a children's Christmas party. Serve him with ice cream.

CHRISTMAS FRUITCAKES
(See photo 115.)

Christmas cakes can be baked right in empty coffee or 1-pound shortening cans. When cool, remove cakes and decorate the cans with attractive gift paper, decals, gold trim. Top the cakes with a thick layer of almond paste and decorate the paste with nuts or candied fruit. Wrap decorated cakes in transparent film, replace in the cans, and top with a colorful bow.

Fruitcakes may be baked in other receptacles, such as ceramic flower pots or metal molds. Be sure to take into consideration the cost of the receptacle when pricing the cakes for sale. *(See photo 116.)*

CHAPTER 10

Church Flowers and Gardens

FLOWERS IN THE CHURCH

Flowers have played an important part in all religions of the world. From the first Christian churches in A.D. 300, palms, branches, garlands, and flowers have been used to decorate temples and churches, and in medieval times, monks cut single flowers from their gardens to adorn their chapels. During the Renaissance, the flower arrangements became more elaborate in keeping with the architecture of the cathedrals.

The custom has come down through the ages, and flowers have taken a place in churches equal in enjoyment to music, stained-glass windows, paintings, and sculpture.

In planning flower arrangements, the first consideration should be the architecture of the church; the flower arrangements should follow the structural lines of the interior of the building, and be harmonious with the surroundings.

Most of our churches in the United States have been adapted from five types of architecture: Early Christian, Byzantine, Romanesque, Gothic, and Renaissance. All these styles are represented throughout our country, but there are probably more adaptations of Gothic than any other form.

In California, the first churches were influenced by the Franciscan monks, who built their missions of thick adobe, with white plaster ceilings and wood carvings, patterned from the churches of the Spanish Renaissance. Churches in New England, at the time of the Pilgrims, were primitive meetinghouses constructed of hand-split logs, unadorned inside and out. Later, the early settlers built their churches of white clapboard with a tall steeple. The early churches of Virginia were similar to those in New England states.

As our country progressed, and world trade made available marble, silks, glass, silver, and exotic woods, our churches became more elaborate, until today we have magnificent churches that compare favorably with religious architecture in Europe. Today's architects of contemporary churches are using the most modern material—glass, metal, plastic—and are designing dignified, functional churches with simple lines, but lines that still reflect the vertical columns of the Gothic and the horizontal lines of the Renaissance.

COLOR OF FLOWERS

In considering the color of flowers to be used for a service, one should bear in mind the color of the vestments and the meaning of liturgical colors. Colors are symbolic, and an understanding of them is helpful in selecting suitable flowers for special occasions: white for purity, red for divine love, blue for truth, violet for suffering, purple for penance, and green for longevity. Yellow means deceit and is not generally used in an altar arrangement, but is frequently used in other rooms in the church or parish.

In addition to understanding the symbolic meaning of colors, one should be familiar with major feast days, how they are celebrated, and their legends; a liturgical calendar is most helpful as a reference.

Two kinds of color combinations are most suitable for flower arrangements in the church: the monochromatic and the analogous. The monochromatic is beautiful and formal. In it, flowers of different values are used to create a shaded effect, beginning with lighter tones at the top and shading to the darker tones at the base. The analogous color scheme is also lovely and is designed by arranging colors in the sequence found on a color wheel.

A complementary color scheme, consisting of an arrangement of contrasting colors, is likely to strike a blatant note and is not as harmonious or as suitable for a church as the monochromatic or analogous. An altar arrangement that contrasts with the background is most pleasing, but the flowers themselves are not attractive when strong contrasting colors are used.

A mixed-color bouquet is apt to appear fussy and ineffectual when viewed from a distance, yet an altar arrangement of fruit, such as purple or green grapes–combined with foliage and flowers, can be very effective. Suitable, too, at the time of the harvest and Thanksgiving are sheaves of corn, wheat, autumn leaves, and seed pods to suggest the rejoicing of the season.

Bright- and light-colored flowers complement most church interiors and show up to better advantage in the dim light than the darker ones, and greenery should be as light as possible to avoid becoming too somber and overpowering.

Many colors, particularly lavenders, purples, and blues, fade in artificial light, so flowers should be taken into the illuminated chapel to be judged for their true color effect. Consideration, also, should be given to the particular spot in which the flower arrangement is to be placed. If in front of a window, for example, through which a good deal of daylight or sunshine penetrates, darker flowers may be used, as lighter ones may appear too garish. If they are to be near a stained-glass window, they should be of strong colors, harmonizing with the colors of the glass itself. Most stained-glass windows consist of vivid blues, reds, and golds, and therefore white, yellow, and shades of red are best, because too delicate or pastel shades of flowers are lost against such a background.

A church floral arrangement must have unity, simplicity, emphasis, and appropriateness. Unity in the selection of container and plant material. Simplicity in the clean, natural, and uncontrived use of flowers and greenery. Emphasis in stressing a focal point, either with flowers, form, or color. Appropriateness in suitable flowers for the occasion and the place they will occupy. Flower arrangements should never overpower, and always be subordinate to the church service.

FLOWERS AND KINDS OF ARRANGEMENTS

Flowers should be large and have form so they can be seen by people sitting far back in the church and on the sides. Lilies, single-stemmed dahlias, and peonies are "form" flowers, while phlox and spray chrysanthemums are effective, because of the cluster formation of the blooms. If small-headed flowers are used, they should be grouped together to form a mass for a center of interest. Flower heads, such as roses and ranunculuses, should be arranged as a focal point with greens as background. Shrubs, such as bridal wreath, syringa, trumpet vine, honeysuckle, weigela, may also be used and will create beautiful effects with little effort on the part of the arranger.

PLACEMENT OF FLOWERS

It is important to know where flowers can and cannot be placed in a church. There are some places where no decorations are permitted. Flowers may not be placed in front of the cross, or on the cross, or at the corners of the altar, or too close to the lighted candles. Flowers may not be placed on the altar rail, the chancel, or rood screen, the handrail leading to the pulpit, or on the pulpit's shelf itself.

Flowers should never be placed on the altar table, as they distract from the service, but may be placed on the shelf behind the altar with extra candlesticks, or may be placed in niches at the sides of the altar. Flowerpots on chancel or sanctuary steps are unwise, for they may lead to accidents. Flowers are not permitted on the tabernacle or in front of the tabernacle door.

All attention should be focused toward and on the altar itself, therefore floral decorations should accent the entrance to the chancel, the sanctuary, the sides of the altar, and, finally, the cross itself. The pulpit and lectern may be decorated and, for special occasions—such as Easter, Christmas, and weddings—the arches, pillars, choir stalls, and the center church aisle may also be decorated, providing the decorations in no way interfere with the service. (*See photos 122–126.*)

FLOWERS OF THE MONTH

January	*Carnation*
February	*Violet* or *Primrose*
March	*Jonquil* or *Daffodil*
April	*Sweet Pea* or *Daisy*
May	*Lily of the Valley* or *Hawthorne*
June	*Rose* or *Honeysuckle*
July	*Larkspur* or *Water Lily*
August	*Poppy* or *Gladiolus*
September	*Aster* or *Morning Glory*
October	*Calendula* or *Cosmos*
November	*Chrysanthemum*
December	*Holly*

SEASONAL FLOWERS BY COLOR

The following chart of flowers, divided into seasons and colors, may be helpful as a guide in selecting floral decorations for churches. There are many more, but these are the ones with the best-lasting qualities. Many wildflowers can be made into charming arrangements, but make sure they will stay fresh through the desired time.

WHITE

SPRING	SUMMER	AUTUMN	WINTER
Azalea	Bouvardia	Aster	Carnation
Hyacinth	Daisy	Chrysanthemum	Cyclamen
Lilac	Phlox	Dahlia	Gardenia
Lily	Gerbera	Hydrangea	Poinsettia
Narcissus	Stock	Queen Anne's	Rose
Peony	Snapdragon	Lace	
Tulip	Tuberose		

YELLOW

Daffodil	Coxcomb	Dahlia	Rose
Iris	Daisy	Goldenrod	
Narcissus	Gladiolus	Chrysanthemum	
Tulip	Rose	Marigold	
	Snapdragon	Rose	
	Tiger Lily	Zinnia	
	Zinnia		

ORANGE

Day Lily	Amaryllis	Dahlia	Bird of
Daffodil	Coxcomb	Marigold	Paradise
	Tiger Lily	Zinnia	Bittersweet
	Zinnia	Bittersweet	Rose
		Bird of Paradise	
		Chrysanthemum	

RED

Tulip	Amaryllis	Dahlia	Carnation
Peony	Coxcomb	Rose	Cyclamen
	Gladiolus	Torch Lily	Poinsettia
	Snapdragon	Zinnia	Rose
	Zinnia		

PINK

Hyacinth	Amaryllis	Aster	Carnation
Peony	Gerbera	Dahlia	Cyclamen
Rhododendron	Rose	Chrysanthemum	Rose
Tulip	Snapdragon		
Lilac	Stock		

SYMBOLISM OF FLOWERS

Acacia	Deathlessness	Hyacinth	Constancy
Anemone	Christ's Blood	Iris or Fleur-de-lis	The Sorrow
Arbutus	Hope		of Mary
Azalea	Devotion	Ivy	Immortality
Bleeding Heart	Fidelity	Laurel	Victory
Camelia	Contentment	Lily	Innocence
Carnation, Pink	Nuptials	Lotus	Truth
Carnation, Red	Love	Magnolia	Virtue
Chrysanthemum	Modesty	Myrtle	Long Life
Clover	Good Luck	Narcissus	Self-love
Cyclamen	Bleeding Nun	Orange Blossom	Purity
Daffodil	Joy	Palm	Victory over
Daisy	Innocence		Death
Dandelion	Wisdom	Pansy	Remembrance
Dogwood	Penitence	Poppy	Forgetfulness
Ferns	Humility	Rose	Martyrdom
Forget-me-not	Faith	Syringa	Fidelity
Gardenia	Purity	Violet	Humility
Holly	Protection		

SYMBOLISM OF FRUIT OR FRUIT LEAVES

Almond	Acceptable to the Lord	Olive	Peace
Apple	Original Sin	Orange	Generosity
Cherry	Chivalry	Peach	Wisdom
Chestnut	Crown of Thorns	Pear	Christ's Love
Fig	Fertility	Plum	Fidelity
Grape	Blood of Christ	Pomegranate	Resurrection
Lemon	Fidelity		

PRESERVATION OF FLOWERS

Select flowers before they have fully opened; they will keep longer and their color will not fade. Put flowers into deep containers filled with cool water and let them remain for one or two hours. Remove most of the lower leaves on the stems before arranging the flowers, as the leaves quickly contaminate the water. Cut the stems diagonally, so the flowers can absorb more water. Flowers with a tough, woodlike stem, such as poinsettias, should have the ends of the stems burned before placing them in water. The stems of dahlias, chrysanthemums, and zinnias should be dipped in boiling water, then allowed to stand in cold water, before being arranged. Roses should be placed in a vase or container with water to a depth of one third the length of the stem. The stems of irises, tulips, and hyacinths should be split about one inch, so water can circulate more readily.

The water, for all flowers, should be at room temperature since extremely cold water shocks the blossoms.

To hold needles on the branches of any trees in the pine family, add about ½ cup sugar per gallon of water.

PRESERVATION WITH GLYCERIN

Any broad-leafed bush or tree is suitable for the glycerin method of preservation. Place stems in a solution of 1 part glycerin to 2 parts water. Add more solution as the leaves soak it up. Keep in a cool room for two to six weeks. Watch for desired shades and coloring in the leaves, and remove from the solution when best coloring is achieved. Arrange in a vase without water, combined with any desired dried flowers. If fresh flowers are used with the glycerined leaves, they should be set into a small container of water and inserted into the larger container of leaves.

Leaves Suitable for Glycerin Preservation

Laurel	*Aspidistra*
Magnolia	*Celosia*
Eucalyptus	*Crape-Myrtle*
Croton	*Seed Pods*

PRESERVATION BY DRYING

Place flowers to be dried in a dry container in a dark place where air is able to circulate.

Suitable Flowers and Weeds for Drying

Acacia	Cattail	Pepper Berries
Acanthus	Caladium Leaves	Pittosporum
Anthurium	Date-Palm Seeds	Pomegranate
Artichoke	Dock	Pussy Willow
Aspidistra	Forsythia	Rose Hips
Babies'-Breath	Hollyhock	Salvia
Bayberry	Iris Pods	Smoke Tree
Bells of Ireland	Joe-pye Weed	Spoon Plant
Bittersweet	Manzanita	Yucca
Bottle Bush	Milkweed	
Castor-Bean Pods	Oriental Poppy	

The following plants should have their stems tied together and should be hung upside down in a cool, dark, airy place to dry:

Astilbe	Larkspur
Cryptomeria	Monkshood
Desert Holly	Tamarisk
Goldenrod	Veronica
Heather	

THE CHURCH GARDEN, A LIVING MEMORIAL

A garden can be a happy and beautiful addition to the grounds surrounding a church, as well as an inspiration and interest for the members of the congregation. If there is an existing garden, perhaps an expansion or renovation is in order. If there is none, however, but space is available, a garden project on the part of the members of the parish will be a rewarding undertaking.

Several types of gardens are suitable for adjoining a church, ranging from a simple cutting garden to a most ambitious biblical garden. The selection of a particular one will depend on available space and the time that can be devoted to its supervision and continual care. A cutting garden is a nice way of insuring for the church continuous blossoms for floral arrangements. If space permits, a charming covered summerhouse, surrounded by shrubs and evergreens, might be constructed where church gatherings, such as teas, suppers, lectures and musical evenings could be conducted. Or perhaps you might decide on a rose or herb garden, where members of the congregation can find solitude and sanctuary, or a biblical garden consisting of trees, shrubs, herbs, and flowers mentioned in the Bible. This latter project is rich with symbolism and biblical lore.

The combined help of a nurseryman and capable members of the church is necessary for the realization of a garden. Money, too, is necessary. This might be raised by various activities among the women's groups or by functions planned and executed by the men. One or more members of the congregation might be inspired to donate a starting fund, and many people who feel the urge to make a gift to a church, cannot afford anything as expensive as a stained-glass window or a pew, and hesitate to offer a more modest contribution. With a garden project, no gift would be too small. Donors would find gratification in subscribing to the purchase of a tree, plant, shrub, statuary, pool, or fountain in memory of a loved one.

Garden committees should be set up to supervise the physical layout, the selection of plants and flowers, and, most important, the maintenance and continued upkeep.

A ROSE GARDEN

A rose garden is always a thing of beauty, and there is not as much work or care involved in it as there are when many varieties of flowers, shrubs, and trees are planted. The pruning, feeding, and spraying of all the plants can be done at regular intervals during the year. And if quality roses are planted (your gardeners need not have a "green thumb"), they will bloom continuously from June to November.

In planning a rose garden, several aspects should be considered. The enclosure should not be too small or confined and must have good circulation of air. At the same time it must be sheltered against strong winds. A stone or brick wall gives protection and a feeling of security. A geometric design with flagstones or pebble paths will provide beauty of its own, in addition to the beauty of the flowers.

Roses lend themselves to either formal or informal planting. The garden need not be lavish. A few well-planned beds and borders can be a source of pleasure throughout the season and the blossoms can be used for arrangements within the church. They will be a constant reminder of Divine Love.

A rose bed may be laid out in a design around a focal point, such as a bird bath, pool, fountain, or garden benches. Since there are so many sizes, shapes, and colors of roses, numerous effects may be achieved.

A basic rose for any rose garden is the hybrid tea rose. It is excellent used along both sides of a path and may be planted two or more deep. The plants, arranged along a stone wall or in a circular-planting design, make a magnificent display.

The Florabunda is a perfect rose to plant in groups or for a hedge, as it produces many flowers and masses of color. It ranges in height from medium to tall and can therefore be planted against the side of a building or fence, in a graduated pattern.

Climbing roses are particularly beautiful against pillars or a wall, and lend color and warmth to a dark, austere building.

Tree roses may be used for garden accents or breaking up areas, or one can stand alone as a terminal plant at the end of a row.

A BIBLICAL GARDEN

There are many references to gardens and to specific plants, flowers, and trees in the Bible. We know that Jesus and his disciples went often to a garden to rest and pray. Jesus was laid to rest in a sepulcher in the garden of Joseph of Arimathea, and Jeremiah told the children of Israel to "plant gardens and eat the fruit of them."

A biblical garden would be a most suitable addition to the grounds of any church and an inspiration to all members of the congregation, a source of knowledge for the children and the young, a place of beauty, and a sanctuary of living symbolism.

Such a garden should seem to be a part of the church itself, but there is a great deal more to it than simply planting some bushes and trees. You'd be wise to enlist the services of a landscape gardener to help with the over-all plan and design; whether the garden is to be formal or informal depends greatly on the physical structure and architecture of the church. The size of the garden will depend on the available space, the enthusiasm of the members, and the money available for such a project. A pen-and-ink sketch will help determine the relative sizes and shapes of the plants to be selected.

The starting point of a church garden should be the consideration of a tree or trees. Trees were used to worship under before the first churches were constructed in A.D. 300.

From Bible passages we read that the olive and the pine were used in the building of the Temple of Solomon, and the Italian cypress was used by the Phoenicians and Greeks in building their ships. The cedar of Lebanon is mentioned in Ezekiel and in the First Book of the Kings, and the mulberry tree is mentioned in the Book of the Chronicles, when David was told by God to come upon the Philistines "over against the mulberry trees." Branches from the myrtle tree were gathered by the children of Israel and, in a land so dry that part of the year there was practically no vegetation, the oak, cedar, olive, bay, cypress, and mulberry were appreciated for the shade they afforded throughout the year.

Any of these trees would make an interesting focal point for a garden, and all of them would grow well in the United States.

In the time of Jesus, the land was unusually fertile in Palestine and, after the rains, the hillsides were covered with tulips, narcissi, hyacinths, lupins, poppies, and anemones. The people of the Bible referred to all flowers as lilies, roses or, simply, flowers of the fields. Their flowers are now our flowers, having been preserved and cultivated over these many hundreds of years. Anemones, which Jesus called the lilies of the field, is an excellent flower to plant for a border. It grows from six to eighteen inches high. Hyacinths, jonquils, narcissi, and red tulips are all bulbs that require a minimum of care and were referred to in biblical times as the lilies of Solomon's garden. The star-of-Bethlehem is another bulb that does well in a present-day garden and is good for a border. Larkspur, which blossoms continuously from May to August and grows about eighteen inches tall, is ideal for cutting for the church. So are blue and yellow lupins, which grow from one to three feet tall and bloom from early spring to July. White, pink, and red peonies, planted in groups make a dramatic display. They blossom lavishly in May and June, and are one of the most easily grown of flowering plants in a garden.

No biblical garden would be complete without herbs, and there are several, mentioned frequently in the Bible, that would happily intermingle with flowers. The delicate pink, blue, and white of flax, with its lovely pale-green leaves, will bloom from spring until the first frost. It grows about eighteen inches tall. This plant was used not only for making linens but for medicinal purposes.

References to linen are found in Exodus in making curtains and wall hangings for the tabernacle, and "garments of fine linen" for Aaron and his sons.

The caper plant, which grows in great profusion on the hills of Jerusalem, is an ideal covering for a wall. It has large white flowers with yellow stamens.

The mint plant lends a feathery appearance to a garden with its tall spikelike growth and small lavender flowers. It grows anywhere from one to two feet tall, and its growth from one year to the next must be strictly curtailed, because it has a tendency to take over the whole garden. Our common variety of spearmint is thought to be the same species referred to in St. Luke when the Lord said to the Pharisees, ". . . ye tithe mint and rue and all manner of herbs. . . ."

Rue is an herb with blue-green leaves and yellow flowers, growing about two feet high. It blooms from June to August, and would make a lovely hedge along a garden wall.

There are several varieties of wormwood, any of which is a fine plant for background planting. Some are tall bush plants with silky gray leaves and yellow flower heads. The tallest variety, growing as high as four feet, is the one that biblical botanists believe to be the herb referred to in the Bible as "bitter as gall." It is a medicinal herb, a little reminiscent of sweet basil, and its oils are used in the making of perfume.

Only a very few of the trees and flowers and herbs suitable for a church garden have been mentioned. There are many more. Some are difficult to grow in the United States; others require so much care and attention that they would not be practical. Each plant should contribute to the over-all effect of the garden and, in addition, be suitable for flowers and foliage within the church.

Flowers of the Bible: Anemone, Crocus, Cyclamen, Hyacinth, Iris, Ivy, Jonquil, Lily, Myrtle, Narcissus, Peony, Ranunculus, Rose, Star-of-Bethlehem, Tulip, Violet, and Water Lily.

Trees of the Bible: Ash, Bay, Box, Cedar of Lebanon, Chestnut,

Cypress, Elm, Fir, Hemlock, Holly, Juniper, Mulberry, Oak, Olive, Palm, Pine, Poplar, and Willow.

Herbs of the Bible: Anise, Caper, Castor, Coriander, Cumin, Flax, Garlic, Hyssop, Leek, Marjoram, Mallow, Mandrake, Mint, Mustard, Onion, Rue, Sage or Salvia, Saffron Crocus, and Wormwood.

CHAPTER 11

Purchasing Food for Fifty Servings

This chapter is reprinted by permission of the New York State College of Home Economics, a Contract College of the State University, Cornell University, Ithaca, New York. "Purchasing Food for 50 Servings," Cornell Extension Bulletin 803, was written by Marion Wood Crosby and Katharine W. Harris.

In using the information in this chapter, the authors suggest that:

1. A suggested serving size is given.

2. The "amount to buy" is for 50 servings of this size, not necessarily for 50 people.

3. The amount to buy for 50 servings will be adequate only if each serving will be the same size as that indicated in the column headed "Approximate size of serving."

FROZEN FRUITS AND VEGETABLES

Frozen fruits and vegetables are purchased by the pound. Regardless of the kind of material from which the container is made or the size of the package:

Allow 10 pounds of frozen fruit for fifty 3-ounce (½ cup) servings of fruit.

Allow 7½ pounds (three 40-ounce packages) of frozen vegetables for fifty 2½-ounce (⅓ cup) servings.

Allow 10 pounds (four 40-ounce packages) of frozen vegetables for fifty 3-ounce (½ cup) servings.

CANNED FOODS

General Information[1] Average net weight per can	Average cups per can	Average servings per can	Can size	Principal use for
14 to 16 ounces	1¾	2 or 3	No. 300	Specialty items such as pork and beans; cranberry sauce
16 to 17 ounces	2	4 or 5	No. 303	Vegetables, peaches, pears, fruit cocktail, applesauce
1 pound 4 ounces (20 ounces)	2½	4 or 5	No. 2	Vegetables, fruits, pie fillings, fruit and vegetable juices
1 pound 13 ounces (29 ounces)	3½	4 to 6	No. 2½	Peaches, apricots, pears, plums, fruit cocktail; s a u e r k r a u t, pumpkin, and some tomatoes
46 ounces	5¾	12 (approximately ½ cup each)		Fruit and vegetable juices

[1] Adapted from "Purchase and Use of Canned Foods," American Can Company, New York, New York.

CANNED FRUITS AND VEGETABLES, NO. 10 CANS
(INSTITUTIONAL SIZE)[2]

Fruits or vegetables	Average count: number per can	Servings per can	Size of serving	Cans to buy for 50 servings
Apples	Pie pack	3 pies	⅙ or ⅛ pie	2 to 3
Applesauce	. . . .	25	½ cup	2
Apricots, halves	83 to 108	25 to 30	3 or 4 halves	2
Cherries, sweet	306 to 378	30	½ cup (10 to 12 cherries)	2
Fruit cocktail	. . . .	25	½ cup	2
Grapefruit	. . . .	25	½ cup	2
Peaches, halves	36 to 54	24 to 27	1½ or 2 halves	2
Pears, halves	36 to 54	24 to 27	1½ or 2 halves	2
Pineapple slices	28 to 50	25 to 28	1 or 2 slices	2
Plums, purple	50 to 90	25 to 30	2 or 3 plums	2
Beans, green or wax	. . . .	20 to 23	3 to 3½ ounces	2¼ to 2½
Beets	. . . .	22 to 26	3 to 3½ ounces	2 to 2¼
Corn, cream style	. . . .	27 to 30	3½ to 4 ounces	1¾ to 2
Corn, whole kernel	. . . .	22 to 26	3 to 3½ ounces	2 to 2¼
Peas	. . . .	25 to 29	2½ to 3 ounces	1¾ to 2
Potatoes, sweet				
Sirup pack	. . . .	20 to 25	4 to 5 ounces	2 to 2½
Dry pack	. . . .	20 to 25	4 to 5 ounces	2 to 2½
Tomatoes	. . . .	25 to 29	3½ to 4 ounces	1¾ to 2

[2] Weight: 6 pounds 2 ounces to 6 pounds 12 ounces; measure: 12 to 13 cups. If more than one but less than two No. 10 cans are required, use No. 2 or No. 2½ cans to supplement the amount needed.

MEATS

MEAT[1] Kind	Size, weight, measure, or count per unit	Approximate size of serving	Servings per pound Number	Amount to buy for 50 servings Pounds	Notes
Beef: roast[2]					
Rib, rolled, boned	7 rib, roast weighs 12 to 15 pounds	2½ to 3 ounces cooked	2½ to 3	17 to 20	May use sirloin butt, boned
Rib, standing	7 rib, roast weighs 16 to 25 pounds	3 to 3½ ounces cooked, 4 to 5 ounces cooked	2 to 2½ 1⅓ to 1⅔	20 to 25 27 to 36	
Chuck, pot-roast (bone in)	Top chuck, 9 to 12 pounds; cross arm, 6 to 9 pounds	3 to 3½ ounces cooked	2 to 2½	20 to 25	Top chuck more tender
Beef: round steak		4 to 4½ ounces clear meat uncooked	2½ to 3	17 to 20	Bottom round requires longer cooking than top round
Beef: stew Chuck and plate —clear meat		5 ounces of stew	3 to 5	10 to 17	Yield per pound of raw meat depends on amount of vegetables added to the stew
Lamb: roast[2] Leg	6 to 8 pounds	2½ to 3 ounces cooked	1½ to 2½	20 to 35	Great variation due to difficulty in carving
Shoulder, boneless	4 to 6 pounds	2½ to 3 ounces cooked	2½ to 3	15 to 20	
Lamb: stew Shoulder and brisket—clear meat		5 ounces of stew	2½ to 3	17 to 20	Yield per pound of raw meat depends on amount of vegetables added to the stew

Pork: roast[2]				
Loin, trimmed	10 to 12 pounds	2½ to 3 ounces cooked	2 to 2½	20 to 25	
Ham:				
Fresh (bone in)	12 to 15 pounds	3 to 3½ ounces cooked	2 to 2½	20 to 25	Smoked shoulder may be substituted for ground or cubed ham in recipes
Smoked, tenderized (bone in)	12 to 15 pounds	3 to 3½ ounces cooked	2½ to 3	17 to 20	
Canned, boneless, ready-to-eat	2 to 9 pounds	3 ounces cooked	4 to 5	10 to 12	
Veal: roast[2]				
Leg	15 to 20 pounds	3 to 3½ ounces cooked	1½ to 2½	20 to 35	Great variation due to difficulty in carving
Shoulder, boneless	8 to 14 pounds	3 to 3½ ounces cooked	2½ to 3	17 to 20	
Veal cutlet	1 pound of raw meat measures 2 cups of meat packed	4 to 5 ounces un-cooked	3 to 4	12 to 17	May use frozen cutlets
Meat cakes	1 pound of raw meat measures 2 cups of meat packed	4 to 5 ounces un-cooked 1 or 2 cakes	2½ to 3	17 to 20	One kind of meat only or combinations may be used such as 10 pounds of beef and 5 pounds of veal or pork, or 10 pounds of fresh pork and 5 pounds of smoked ham
Meat loaf or extended meat patties	1 pound of raw meat measures 2 cups of meat packed	4 to 4½ ounces cooked meat loaf	3½ to 4	12 to 15	

[1] Unit of purchase: pound.
[2] A 2½- to 3-ounce slice of roast meat measures approximately 3½ to 4½ inches.
[3] A 2½- to 3-ounce slice of roast meat measures approximately 3½ to 4 inches.

MEATS (concluded), FISH

MEAT[1] Kind	Size, weight, measure, or count per unit	Approximate size of serving	Servings per pound (Number)	Amount to buy for 50 servings (Pounds)	Notes
Bacon:					
Sliced	30 to 36 medium or 15 to 20 wide strips per pound	3 strips / 2 strips	10 to 12 / 7 to 10	5 to 6 / 5 to 7	1 pound when cooked and diced measures 1½ cups
Canadian, sliced	12 to 16 slices per pound	2 or 3 slices	5 to 8	7 to 10	
Liver		4 ounces cooked	3 to 4	13 to 17	
Sausage:					
Links	8 to 9 large per pound	3 links	3	17 to 20	Yield varies with proportion of fat that fries out in cooking
Cakes		6 to 8 ounces raw meat—2 cakes	2 to 2½	20 to 25	
Weiners	8 to 10 per pound	2 weiners	4 to 5	10 to 11½	
FISH[1]					
Fresh or frozen fish fillets		4 to 5 ounces	3 to 4	14 to 17	
Oysters:					
For frying	24 to 40 large per quart	4 to 6 oysters		7 to 8 quarts	
For scalloping	60 to 100 small per quart			4 to 5 quarts	
For stew	60 to 100 small per quart	4 to 6 oysters		3 quarts	

[1] Unit of purchase: pound.

POULTRY

POULTRY — Kind	Dressed weight[1]	Eviscerated weight (ready-to-cook)	Approximate size of serving	Servings per pound		Amount to buy for 50 servings	
				Dressed weight[1]	Eviscerated weight (ready-to-cook)	Dressed weight[1]	Eviscerated weight (ready-to-cook)
	Pounds	Pounds		Number	Number	Pounds	Pounds
Chicken:							
Fryers	2½ to 3½	1¾ to 2½	¼ fryer			35 to 40	25 to 30
Fowl:							
Fricassee	3½ to 6	2½ to 4½	4 to 6 ounces including bone	1 to 1½	1¼ to 2	35 to 50	25 to 35
For dishes containing cut-up cooked meat			1 to 2 ounces of clear meat	2½ to 3	3 to 4	17 to 20[2]	13 to 17[2]
Turkey:[3]							
Young toms	12 to 23	10 to 18	2 to 2½ ounces of clear meat	1 to 1½	1½ to 2	35 to 50[4]	25 to 35[4]
Old toms	20 to 30	16 to 25					

[1] Dressed weight means blood and feathers removed.

[2] Fowl. Four pounds of dressed or 3 pounds of eviscerated fowl yield approximately 1 pound of cooked meat removed from the bone.

[3] Yield of meat depends on type and size of bird. Broad-breasted birds yield a larger amount of clear meat than the standard-type bird. Larger birds yield a greater amount of clear meat than smaller birds.

[4] Turkey. One pound of dressed weight yields from 4 to 5 ounces of sliced clear meat, or from 5 to 6 ounces of cooked boned meat.

VEGETABLES

Kind[1] and unit of purchase	Weight, Measure, or count per unit	Approximate size of serving	Servings per pound as purchased	Amount to buy for 50 servings	Additional Information
Asparagus Pound or 2 to 2½ pound bunches	1 bunch = 32 to 40 stalks	Cooked: 3 ounces or 4 or 5 stalks	3 to 4	12 to 16 pounds	Yield may be increased if tough part of stalk is peeled
Beans, green or wax Pound	1 pound measures 1 quart	Cooked: 2½ to 3 ounces or ½ cup	4 to 5	10 to 12 pounds	1 pound yields 3 cups cut up, raw
Beets Pound	4 medium beets per pound	Cooked: 2½ to 3 ounces or ½ cup	4 to 4½	12 to 14 pounds	1 pound raw yields from 1½ to 2 cups cooked and diced
Bunch	4 to 6 medium beets per bunch				
Broccoli Pound or 1½ to 2½ pound bunches		Cooked: 2½ to 3 ounces	2½ to 3	17 to 20 pounds	Yield may be increased if tough part of stalk is peeled
Brussels sprouts Quart basket	1 to 1¼ pounds per basket	Cooked: 2½ to 3 ounces	4 to 6	10 baskets or 12 pounds	
Cabbage Pound		Raw: 1 to 2 ounces Cooked: 2½ to 3 ounces or ½ cup	8 raw 4 cooked	8 to 10 pounds 12 to 15 pounds	1 pound raw yields 4 to 6 cups shredded 2 quarts raw, shredded, weighs 1 pound

[1] Before food is prepared.

Vegetable	Weight	Average serving	Servings	Quantity	Yield
Carrots, Pound	6 medium carrots per pound	Cooked: 2½ to 3 ounces or ½ cup / Raw: 2 to 3 inch strips	3 to 4	14 to 16 pounds	1 pound yields 2 cups cooked and diced
Cauliflower, Head, trimmed	1 to 3 pounds each	Cooked: 3 ounces or ½ cup	2	2 to 2½ pounds for raw strips / 28 to 32 pounds	3½ cups diced, raw, weighs 1 pound, 3¾ cups diced, cooked, weighs 1 pound / 1 3-pound head yields 3 quarts of raw flowerettes
Cucumbers, Single	1 cucumber weighs 10 to 14 ounces	Raw: 5 to 7 slices (¼ cup)		8 to 9	1 medium yields 1¾ to 2 cups of peeled slices
Celery, Pascal, Bunch	1 medium bunch weighs 2 pounds	Cooked: 2½ to 3 ounces or ½ cup	Cooked: 3 to 4 / Raw: 8 to 10	7 to 10 bunches / 3 to 4 bunches	1 medium bunch yields 1½ quarts raw, diced / 1 quart raw, diced, weighs 1 pound
Eggplant, Single or dozen	1 small eggplant weighs 1 pound	Cooked: 2½ ounces (1½ slices)	4	10 to 12	1 1-pound plant yields 8 or 9 slices
Lettuce, head, Head	1 medium head weighs 1½ to 2½ pounds before trimming	Raw: ⅙ to ⅛ head		4 to 5 heads for garnish / 6 to 8 heads for salad	10 to 12 salad leaves per head / 1 head untrimmed yields 1½ to 2 quarts shredded / 2 quarts shredded weighs 1 pound

VEGETABLES (continued)

Mushrooms Pound Basket	1 basket weighs 3 pounds				1 pound of sliced tops and stems measures 7 cups, and when sautéed, measures 2½ cups
Onions Pound	4 to 6 medium	Cooked: 3 to 3½ ounces or ½ cup	3 to 4	14 to 16 pounds	1 pound yields 2½ to 3 cups chopped 1 cup chopped weighs 5 ounces 1 cup sliced weighs 4 ounces
Parsley Bunch	1 bunch weighs 1 ounce				1 medium bunch yields ¼ cup finely chopped, 1 cup chopped weighs 3 ounces
Parsnips Pound	3 to 4 medium parsnips per pound	Cooked: 2½ to 3 ounces	3 to 4	15 pounds	
Peppers Pound Single	5 to 7 peppers per pound				1 pound yields 2 cups finely diced 1 cup chopped weighs 5 ounces
Potatoes: Sweet Pound	3 medium potatoes per pound	3½ to 4 ounces	2½ to 3	17 to 20 pounds	
White Pound	3 medium potatoes per pound	4 to 4½ ounces or ½ cup mashed or creamed	2 to 3	15 to 20 pounds	1 pound yields 2¼ cups diced

Bushel	1 bushel = 60 pounds				
Bag	1 bag = 50 pounds				
Rutabagas					
Pound	1 to 2 per pound	Cooked: 3 to 3½ ounces or ½ cup	2 to 2½	20 to 25 pounds	1 pound yields 1½ cups mashed or 2½ cups diced
Spinach					
Bag	10 or 20 ounces per bag	Cooked: 3 to 3½ ounces or ½ cup	2½ to 3	17 to 20 pounds homegrown	1 10-ounce bag yields 1½ quarts raw, coarsely chopped for salads
Bushel				12 to 15 10-ounce bags cleaned	
Squash:					
Summer		Cooked: 2½ to 3 ounces or ½ cup	3 to 4	13 to 16 pounds	
Pound					
Winter		Cooked: 3 ounces or ½ cup mashed	2	25 to 30 pounds	
Pound					
Tomatoes					
Pound	3 to 4 medium tomatoes per pound	Raw: 3 slices	5 sliced	10 pounds fresh for slicing	1 pound yields 2 cups diced or wedges
8-pound basket, 10-pound carton					
Turnips, white					
Pound		Cooked: 3 ounces or ½ cup	3 to 4	15 to 20 pounds	

FRUITS

Kind and unit of purchase	Weight, measure, or count per unit	Approximate size of serving	Amount to buy for 50 servings	Additional Information
Apples		½ cup sauce	15 to 20 pounds for sauce or pie	1 pound before peeling yields 3 cups diced or sliced, 4½ to 5 cups pared, diced, or sliced weighs 1 pound, 1 peck (12 pounds) makes 4 or 5 pies, 4 to 5 quarts of sauce, 7 to 8 quarts of raw cubes
Pound	2 to 3 medium apples per pound			
Peck	1 peck weighs 12 pounds			
Bushel	1 bushel weighs 48 pounds			
Box	1 box contains from 80 to 100 large or 113 to 138 medium apples			
Bananas		1 small	15 pounds	1 pound yields 2 to 2½ cups sliced thin or 1¼ cups mashed. For 1 cup sliced or diced, use 1⅓ medium bananas. For 1 cup mashed, use 2¼ medium bananas
Pound or Dozen	3 to 4 medium bananas per pound			
Cranberries		¼ cup sauce	4 pounds for sauce	1 pound makes 3 to 3½ cups of sauce or 2¾ cups of jelly
Pound	1 pound measures 1 to 1¼ quarts			
Grapefruit				1 medium-small grapefruit yields from 10 to 12 sections or 1¾ cups of broken sections
Dozen	Fruit per box:			
Box	Medium = 54 to 70			
Half-box	Small = 80 to 126			
Lemons			25 to 30 lemons (1¼ quart juice) for lemonade for 50 glasses	1 medium lemon yields ¼ cup of juice and 1 teaspoon of grated rind, 4 or 5 medium lemons yield 1 cup of juice
Dozen	Fruit per box:			
Box	Large = 210 to 250			
Half-box	Medium = 300 to 360			
	Small = 392 to 432			

Kind and unit of purchase	Weight, measure, or count per unit	Approximate size of serving	Amount to buy for 50 servings	Additional Information
Oranges Dozen Box Half-box	Fruit per box: Large = 80 to 126 Medium = 150 to 200 Small = 216 to 288	½ cup of sections	4 to 6 dozen medium oranges (6 quarts juice) for 50 4-ounce glasses 40 to 50 oranges	Use medium oranges for table and salad, 1 medium orange yields from 9 to 12 sections, and from ½ to ⅔ cup of diced fruit 1 dozen medium oranges yields 1 to 1½ quarts of juice
Peaches Pound Peck	3 to 5 per pound 1 peck weighs 12½ pounds	3 ounces or ½ cup	10 to 12 pounds for slicing	1 pound yields 2 cups peeled and sliced
½ bushel	½ bushel weighs 25 pounds			
Pineapple Each	1 medium pineapple weighs 2 pounds	½ cup cubed	5 medium	1 medium yields from 3 to 3½ cups of peeled and cubed fruit
Rhubarb, fresh Pound		½ cup sauce	10 pounds	10 pounds yields 6 quarts of sauce
Strawberries Quart		½ cup	10 to 13 quarts	1 quart yields 3 cups, hulled 1 quart yields from 4 to 5 servings of fruit
Quart		⅓ cup for shortcake	8 to 10 quarts	1 quart yields 1 pint hulled and crushed, which yields 6 servings of sauce for shortcake

STAPLES

Items	Equivalent weights and measures	Proportions for use
Baking powder	1 pound measures 2½ cups 1 ounce measures 2½ table-spoons	
Chocolate	1 bar equals 8 1-ounce squares	
Cocoa	1 pound measures 4 cups 1 cup weighs 4 ounces	2 cups of cocoa for 50 cups of beverage (2½ gallons)
Coconut	1 pound measures from 6 to 7 cups	
Corn-meal	1 pound measures 3 cups	
Cornstarch	1 pound measures 3 cups 1 ounce measures 3 table-spoons	½ cup to thicken 1 quart of liquid for pudding
Flour: White	1 pound measures 1 quart 1 cup weighs 4 ounces	
Graham or whole-wheat	1 pound measures 3½ cups 1 cup weighs 4⅘ ounces	
Gelatin: Granulated	1 pound measures 3 cups 1 ounce measures 3 table-spoons	2 to 3 tablespoons per quart of liquid
Flavored	1 pound measures 2½ cups 1 ounce measures 2½ table-spoons	1 to 1¼ cups per quart of liquid
Rice	1 pound measures 2⅛ cups 1 pound after cooking measures 1¾ quarts and yields 20 No. 16 scoops or 15 No. 12 scoops	2½ to 3 pounds for 50 servings
Shortening, vegetable	1 pound measures 2½ cups (2⅓ firmly packed)	
Sugar: Light brown Packed to hold shape of cup	1 pound measures 2 to 2¼ cups	Note: It is difficult to measure brown sugar accurately
Loosely packed	1 pound measures 3 to 3½ cups	
Confectioners'	1 pound measures 3 cups 1 cup weighs 5⅓ ounces	Note: Used for frosting
Cube	1 pound equals 50 to 60 large or 100 to 120 small cubes	

STAPLES (*continued*)

Items	Equivalent weights and measures	Amounts for 50 servings
Sugar (*cont'd*) Granulated	1 pound measures 2⅛ cups 1 cup weighs 7 ounces	¾ to 1 pound to sweeten 50 cups of coffee (1½ teaspoons per cup)
Bread: White and whole-wheat	1 1-pound loaf = 18 slices 1 2-pound club loaf = 24 slices 1 2-pound Pullman (sandwich) loaf = 36 slices	Usually allow 1½ slices per person to accompany meal
Rye	1 1-pound loaf = 17 slices 1 2-pound short loaf = 29 slices 1 2-pound long loaf = 36 slices	
Crumbs, fine, dry Soft, chopped	1 pound measures 5 cups 1 quart weighs from 6 to 7 ounces 1 pound measures 2½ quarts	
Butter: For table	1 pound measures 2 cups 1 ounce measures 2 table-spoons 1 pound cuts 48 to 60 squares	1 to 1½ pounds (available in wholesale units cut into 48 to 90 pieces per pound; 60 count gives average size cut)
Cheese: Cheddar (store or American) Brick	1 pound chopped measures 1 quart 1 brick weighs 5 pounds 1 pound yields 16 thin slices (1 ounce each) 1 pound cuts 20 cubes for pie (⅘ ounce)	3¼ pounds sliced for sandwiches 2½ pounds for pie
Cottage	1 pound measures 2 cups 1 pound yields 8 to 9 No. 10 scoops; 12 to 13 No. 16 scoops; 25 No. 30 scoops	6 pounds for 50 average servings (No. 10 scoop, approximately ½ cup)
Cream	1 box = 3 pounds 1 pound measures 2 cups 1 small package weighs 3 ounces and measures 6 table-spoons	

STAPLES (*continued*)

Items	Equivalent weights and measures	Amounts for 50 servings
Coffee:		
Ground	1 pound drip grind measures 5 cups	1 pound coffee and 2½ gallons of water for 50 cups
Instant		2½ cups instant coffee and 2½ gallons of water for 50 cups
Cream:		
Heavy (40 per cent) to whip	Doubles its volume in whipping	1 pint yields 1 quart whipped and 50 servings of 1 rounded tablespoon
Light (20 per cent) or top milk (for coffee)	1 quart = 64 tablespoons	1¼ quarts for 50 servings; 1½ tablespoons per serving
Eggs	Medium eggs: Whole = 6 per cup Yolks = 14 per cup Whites = 9 per cup 1 dozen hard-cooked and chopped measures 3½ cups	Note: 1 case = 30 dozen
Fruit or vegetable juice	1 46-ounce can measures approximately 1½ quarts 1 can, No. 10, measures 13 cups or 3¼ quarts	4⅓ 46-ounce cans, or 6½ quarts; 4-ounce glass or ½ cup per serving
Fruits, dried:		
Dates, pitted	1 pound cut fine measures 2½ cups	
Prunes	1 pound contains 40 to 50 medium prunes	5 to 6 pounds for stewed fruit; 4 or 5 prunes per serving
Raisins	1 pound of seedless raisins measures 3 cups 1 pound seeded raisins measures 2½ cups	
Honey	1 pound measures 1⅓ cups	5 pounds, 2 tablespoons per serving
Ice cream:		
Brick	1 1-quart brick cuts from 6 to 8 slices	7 to 9 bricks (available in slices individually wrapped)

STAPLES (*continued*)

Items	Equivalent weights and measures	Amounts for 50 servings
Bulk	1 gallon yields from 25 to 30 servings dipped with a No. 10 scoop	2 gallons
Lard	1 pound measures 2½ cups firmly packed	
Lemonade		2½ gallons (25 to 30 lemons for 1¼ quarts of juice) 1 8-ounce glass (¾ measuring cup) per serving
Margarine	1 pound measures 2 cups 1 ounce measures 2 tablespoons	
Meat:		
Cooked, ground	1 pound measures 3 cups	
Cooked, diced	1 pound measures 1 quart	
Uncooked, ground	1 pound measures 2 cups	
Milk:		
Evaporated	6-ounce can measures ⅔ cup 14½-ounce can measures 1⅔ cups	
Powdered or dry:		
Instant	1⅓ cups instant and 3¾ cups water = 1 quart reliquified milk	
Regular	1 cup (4 ounces) and 1 quart water = 1 quart reliquified milk	
Peanut butter	1 pound measures 1¾ cups	4 pounds for sandwiches
Potato chips	1 pound measures 5 quarts	2 pounds, ¾ to 1 ounce serving
Salad dressings:		1 to 1½ quarts for mixed salads
Mayonnaise		3 to 4 cups of garnish, 1 tablespoon for each salad
French		¾ to 1 quart
Sandwiches:		
Bread	1 2-pound loaf (14-inch) cuts from 30 to 35 medium or from 35 to 40 very thin slices	3 14-inch loaves
Butter		¾ pound to spread 1 slice of 50 sandwiches

STAPLES (*concluded*)

Items	Equivalent weights and measures	Amounts for 50 servings
Butter (*cont'd*)		1½ pounds to spread both slices
Fillings		1¾ to 2 quarts, 2 tablespoons or 1 No. 30 scoop per serving 2½ to 3 quarts, 3 tablespoons or 1 No. 24 scoop per serving
Tea	1 pound measures 6 cups	Hot—50 individual tea bags or Iced—3 ounces bulk tea to 2½ gallons water and chipped ice
Vegetables, dried: Beans, navy	1 pound measures 2⅓ cups	5 to 6 pounds

CHAPTER 12

Quantity Recipes

GUACAMOLE (*Avocado Dip*)
Yield: 2 cups

Ingredients:

2 avocados, peeled, seeded, and sliced

2 tablespoons lemon juice

4 tablespoons salad oil

1 clove garlic (*optional*)

1 tablespoon chopped green-onion tops

1 teaspoon salt

1 teaspoon dill weed

Dash hot pepper sauce

Method:

Put all ingredients into container of an electric blender, cover and blend on high speed until smooth, stopping to stir down if necessary. Store in refrigerator until ready to serve.

CREAM CHEESE AND RED CAVIAR CANAPES
Yield: 64 canapés about 1¼ inch square

Ingredients:

1 pound soft cream cheese

2 tablespoons grated onion and juice

½ cup minced parsley

⅔ cup red caviar (6-ounce jar)

Salt and freshly ground pepper

64 canapé bases

Method:

Mix all ingredients.

Spread on toast squares or melba-toast rounds or on strips of pumpernickel bread. Serve 2 canapés per person.

Refrigerate until serving time.

CHEESE BALLS

Mash cream cheese with a little blue cheese, or grated Cheddar to taste. Season, if desired, with Tabasco or chopped chives. Form into tiny balls and roll in chopped nuts. Chill on baking sheets in refrigerator. Serve 2 or 3 balls per person, depending on size.

MOLDED CHEESE BALL
Yield: 1 ball to serve 8

Ingredients:

½ cup walnuts
2 tablespoons warm milk
½ cup (1 stick) soft butter
½ cup crumbled blue cheese

½ cup diced semisoft cheese such as Bel Paese or cream cheese

Method:

Into container of the electric blender put walnuts. Cover and blend on high speed for 6 seconds, or until nuts are ground. Empty onto waxed paper.

Into container put warm milk and butter. Cover and blend until mixture is smooth. Uncover and, with motor on, add piece by piece the blue cheese and the soft cheese. Blend until smooth, stopping to stir down when necessary.

Scrape mixture out onto the ground nuts. Put hands under waxed paper and shape into a ball, coating it with the nuts. Wrap in foil and chill. Serve with crackers or with thin slices pumpernickel bread.

CUCUMBER APPETIZER
Yield: Serves 24

Ingredients:

12 medium cucumbers, peeled and thinly sliced
Salt
20 green onions, chopped (2 bunches)

¼ teaspoon pepper
1 teaspoon cumin
1 teaspoon cloves
4 cups yogurt

Method:

Put cucumbers in large crock or stainless-steel bowl and sprinkle with salt.

Combine green onions, pepper, cumin, cloves, and yogurt. Mix well and chill both sauce and cucumbers.

Serve cucumbers on individual plates, topped with the yogurt sauce.

PIROSHKI
Yield: 24 2-inch turnovers

Ingredients:

1 cup (2 sticks) butter or margarine
2 3-ounce packages cream cheese

2 cups flour
½ teaspoon salt
Filling (see below)

Method:

Cut butter and cheese into flour until very fine. Blend thoroughly, using fingers to work butter and cheese into flour. Wrap dough in waxed paper and refrigerate overnight or freeze for a couple of hours.

Cut dough into small pieces, roll out one piece at a time, on well-floured board with a well-floured rolling pin. Cut into 4-inch squares.

Put a dab of fish, cabbage, mushroom, or meat filling on each square, fold into a triangle, and press edges firmly together with tines of a fork. Prick top crust. Bake in a preheated 450° F. oven for about 12 minutes, or until golden in color. Reheat before serving.

FISH FILLING:
(for 24)

Ingredients:
    1½ *cups cooked fish fillet*
        (*flounder, cod, or*
        whitefish)
    2 *hard-cooked eggs, chopped*

    4 *tablespoons medium*
        cream sauce or may-
        onnaise
    Salt and pepper to taste

Method:
Flake fish and mix with other ingredients.

CABBAGE FILLING:
(for 24)

Ingredients:
    2 *tablespoons shortening*
    ½ *teaspoon curry powder*
    ½ *teaspoon salt*

    2 *cups finely shredded cab-*
        bage
    2 *tablespoons minced onion*
    4 *tablespoons sour cream*

Method:
Heat shortening in skillet with curry powder and salt. Add cabbage and onion; cook, stirring, until cabbage is wilted. Remove from heat and stir in cream.

MEAT FILLING:
(for 24)

Ingredients:

1 tablespoon shortening   ½ teaspoon chili powder
½ pound ground meat   ½ teaspoon salt
2 teaspoons grated onion

Method:

Heat shortening in skillet. Add all ingredients and cook, stirring, until meat loses color. Cool.

MUSHROOM FILLING:
(for 24)

Ingredients:

4 tablespoons shortening   ½ teaspoon salt
2 small onions, minced   Freshly ground pepper
½ pound mushrooms, finely   2 tablespoons flour
    chopped   ¼ cup heavy cream
2 pinches thyme

Method:

In skillet heat shortening and in it brown onion lightly. Add mushrooms; cook, stirring, for about 5 minutes. Add thyme, salt, pepper, and stir in flour. Stir in cream and cook, stirring, for about 2 minutes longer.

QUICHE LORRAINE (*Cheese Tart*)
Yield: 54 2-inch squares

Ingredients:

4 cups flour	1½ pounds shredded Swiss
2 teaspoons salt	cheese
1½ cups shortening	4 cups cream
Water	8 eggs, lightly beaten
1 egg, beaten	1 teaspoon salt
½ pound bacon	½ teaspoon nutmeg
3 medium onions, minced	

Method:

In mixing bowl combine flour and salt. Cut in shortening and stir in enough water to hold mixture together. Roll out on large floured pastry cloth and line a 12-X-18-inch pan. Brush with the beaten egg and refrigerate.

Cook bacon until slices are crisp and crumble into bottom of pastry.

Sauté onions in about 4 tablespoons of bacon fat remaining in pan until tender; sprinkle over bacon in pan. Sprinkle onions with the grated cheese.

To bake: Remove pastry from refrigerator. Scald cream and gradually stir it into the eggs. Stir in salt and nutmeg.

Put the pastry-lined pan in a preheated 450° F. oven. Pour cream mixture into pan, and bake for 10 minutes.

Reduce oven temperature to 325° F. and continue to bake for 20 minutes, or until custard is set. Serve warm, but not hot.

CHINESE PEPPER STEAK
Yield: 24 servings

Ingredients:

1½ cups shortening or oil
6 onions, minced
12 green peppers, seeded and
    cut into 1-inch squares
6 pounds round steak cut
    into thin slices
1½ cups soy sauce
1 tablespoon salt

1 teaspoon pepper
1 tablespoon sugar
6 cups canned bean sprouts
6 cups canned tomatoes
3 tablespoons cornstarch
¾ cup cold water
2 bunches green onions,
    minced

Method:

In large skillet heat ½ cup of the oil and in it sauté onions until barely tender. They should still be crisp.

Lift onions with slotted spoon into 2 large baking pans.

Add another ½ cup oil to skillet and in it cook green peppers for about 2 minutes. Divide into pans and mix with onions.

Add remaining oil to skillet and in it cook the meat over high heat until it is seared on both sides. Divide with onions and green peppers in pans.

Add soy sauce, salt, pepper, sugar, bean sprouts, and tomatoes, dividing equally into pans and cook, stirring, for 5 minutes. Keep warm.

Before serving, mix cornstarch and water, stir into juices in pans and cook, stirring, until sauce is slightly thickened. Serve sprinkled with chopped green onions. Serve with cooked rice.

BRAISED BEEF A LA MODE PARISIENNE
Yield: 50 4-ounce portions

Ingredients:

25 pounds beef rounds, tied
Flour
Salt and pepper, to taste
1 pint oil
1 pound celery, coarsely
    chopped
1 pound carrots, coarsely
    chopped
1 pound onions, coarsely
    chopped
1 No. 10 can tomatoes,
    crushed
2 quarts beef stock

Herb bag containing 1 tea-
    spoon thyme or mar-
    joram and 1 bay leaf
100 silver-skin onions
100 potatoes, diced
100 carrots, diced
100 turnips, diced
2½ pounds frozen peas
¼ cup tarragon vinegar
2 tablespoons Worcester-
    shire sauce
12 tablespoons cornstarch or
    arrowroot
1½ cups water

Method:

Dredge meat in flour seasoned with salt and pepper.

Heat oil in roasting pans, add meat and brown well on all sides.

Add chopped celery, carrots, and onions; sauté until vegetables are browned.

Add tomatoes, beef stock, and herb bag.

Bring to boil, cover and bake in 400° F. oven for about 3½ hours.

Cook all vegetables and keep warm.

When meat is done, remove from roasting pan and strain sauce. There should be about 3 quarts.

Add tarragon vinegar and Worcestershire sauce.

Return to heat and bring to a boil.

Dissolve arrowroot or cornstarch in the 1½ cups water, stir into sauce and blend until thickened.

Slice meat slightly less than ¼ inch thick. Serve one slice per person, garnished with vegetables. Serve 2 ounces sauce per portion.

SAUERBRATEN
Yield: 50 4-ounce portions

Ingredients for Marinade:

2 quarts cider vinegar
2 pounds onions, sliced thin
1 pound carrots, sliced thin
½ pound celery, sliced thin
½ pound brown sugar
6 cloves garlic, chopped

2 ounces salt
6 bay leaves
1 teaspoon peppercorns, crushed
Water

Remaining ingredients:

25 pounds beef rounds, tied
1 cup oil

1 pound crushed gingersnaps

Method:

Put all ingredients for marinade into a large crock and stir well. Place meat in crock, add enough water for liquid to cover, and let stand in cool place for 24 hours.

Remove meat, wipe dry, and brown in hot oil in fry pan or skillet.

Remove to large heavy kettle. Strain the marinade and add vegetables and spices to the meat. Add 5 quarts of marinade.

Cover, bring to boil, and cook over a low heat for 2½ hours, or until tender.

When meat is done, transfer to dry pan, cover with damp cloth and keep warm.

Whip crushed gingersnaps into the sauce and let stand until gingersnaps are soft and blended with the sauce. Strain and keep hot until servingtime.

Slice meat across grain less than ¼ inch thick and serve 1 slice per serving with 2 ounces sauce.

NEW ENGLAND BOILED DINNER

Yield: 48 servings (2½ ounces corned beef and 4 ounces or ½–⅔ cup vegetables)

Ingredients:

13 pounds corned-beef brisket

2¾ gallons water

2¼ quarts cooked, peeled, and sliced beets

6 heads cabbage, each cut into 8 wedges

3 quarts sliced or 7 pounds small, whole carrots

50 medium potatoes

1 No. 10 can whole beets

Method:

Place brisket in large kettle and add water. Bring to a boil, cover and simmer for 3½ to 4 hours. Fork should be inserted and withdrawn with ease. Do not overcook.

Cook each vegetable (except beets) separately in corned-beef stock. Heat beets in liquid from can; drain.

Slice brisket diagonally across grain, turning meat as necessary. Serve 2½-ounce slice of corned beef over wedge of cabbage, accompanied by other vegetables.

HUNGARIAN GOULASH WITH NOODLES

Yield: 48 8-ounce servings

Ingredients:

16 pounds beef rump or round, boned and cut into 1-inch cubes

1⅓ cups suet or drippings

3 quarts sliced onions

2 cloves chopped garlic (optional)

1 tablespoon dry mustard

¼ cup paprika

⅛ teaspoon red pepper

2 bay leaves

2 to 4 tablespoons salt or to taste

1 quart tomato paste

2 gallons water

1⅓ cups flour

2 cups water

3½ pounds noodles

3 gallons water

¼ cup salt

2 cups bread crumbs

½ pound butter

Method:

Brown meat in suet or drippings.

Add onions and garlic and cook for 10 minutes.

Add mustard, paprika, pepper, bay leaves, and salt to taste.

Combine tomato paste with the 2 gallons of water and add.

Simmer in a closely covered, heavy-bottomed kettle for two hours, or until meat is tender.

Stir in flour mixed with the 2 cups water. Keep over low heat until ready to serve, stirring occasionally.

Cook noodles in the 3 gallons water with the ¼ cup salt until tender. Drain. Pour cold water over to remove excess starch.

While noodles are cooking, brown bread crumbs in butter.

Mix bread crumbs and butter with the noodles and reheat.

Serve separately. Place one half cup of noodles on each plate and cover with meat and gravy.

BEEF STROGANOFF
Yield: 24 servings

Ingredients:

1 *cup shortening*	⅔ *cup flour*
8 *pounds round of beef,*	1⅛ *cups beef consommé*
thinly sliced	2 *tablespoons salt or to*
3¾ *quarts water*	*taste*
1 *6-ounce can tomato paste*	1 *tablespoon paprika*
1 *quart chopped onions*	2 *quarts warm sour cream*
3 *pounds mushrooms, sliced*	

Method:

In heavy kettle melt 3 tablespoons of the shortening and in it brown meat over high heat.

Add the water and tomato paste. Bring to a boil and simmer for about 2 hours or until meat is tender.

In a large saucepan sauté onions and mushrooms in remaining shortening until onions are tender. Strain hot liquid from meat into vegetables and bring to a boil. Stir in flour mixed to a paste with the beef consommé; cook, stirring, until sauce is smooth and thickened. Stir in salt to taste and paprika.

Add meat and reheat.

Just before serving, stir in the sour cream.

Serve with hot cooked rice or buttered noodles.

●

SWEDISH MEAT BALLS

Yield: 50 portions (3 meat balls each plus ¼ cup gravy)

Ingredients:

2 cups ground or minced on-ion	½ teaspoon cayenne
¾ cup beef fat	½ teaspoon black pepper
2 quarts ground, lean pork	6 cups milk
4 quarts ground beef	8 eggs, beaten
6 cups crumbs, fine	1 cup flour
2 tablespoons salt	1 quart hot meat stock
1 tablespoon nutmeg	2 quarts hot cream
1 tablespoon allspice	Salt and pepper to taste

Method:

Cook onions in beef fat until transparent and add to ground pork and beef.

Mix crumbs and seasonings thoroughly and work into the meat mixture with hands.

Add milk and eggs and mix thoroughly.

Using a level No. 30 scoop or other measure, place balls in rows on heavy-bottomed baking pans and cook in a 400° F. oven for about 15 minutes. Reduce oven temperature to 350° F. and continue to bake for 1 hour.

Remove meat balls from pans and keep warm.

Remove all but 1 cup drippings from baking pans. Stir in flour and gradually stir in meat stock and cream. Season with salt and pepper; cook, stirring for 5 minutes.

Serve 3 balls per serving with ¼ cup gravy.

TEXAS HASH
Yield: 50 10-ounce servings

Ingredients:

12 onions, chopped
12 green peppers, finely cut
12 cups chopped celery
12 pounds ground lean beef
1 pound margarine or vegetable shortening

6 teaspoons chili powder
12 teaspoons salt
2 teaspoons pepper
6 cups raw rice
6 No. 2½ cans tomatoes

Method:

Brown onions, peppers, celery, and meat in shortening.

Add seasonings and transfer meat mixture to large baking dishes.

Sprinkle rice over top. Do not stir.

Add tomatoes. Cover baking dishes, and bake in a 350° F. oven for 2 hours.

TAMALE PIE
Yield: 54 2-inch squares

Ingredients:

3 quarts water
3 tablespoons salt
3 cups evaporated milk
2 pounds corn meal
6 pounds ground beef

3 cups chopped onion
½ cup cooking oil
1½ quarts canned tomatoes
1 tablespoon salt
2 teaspoons pepper

Method:

In large saucepan combine water, salt, and milk. Bring to a boil and gradually stir in the corn meal. Cook, stirring, until mixture thickens. Cover and cool.

In heavy kettle sauté beef and onions in the oil until browned.

Add remaining ingredients and cook over low heat for 20 minutes.

Spread half the corn-meal mixture in bottom of a greased 12-X-18-X-2-inch baking pan. Cover with meat mixture and spread remaining corn-meal mixture on top.

Bake in a preheated 375° F. oven for 45 minutes, or until top is lightly browned. Cut into squares and serve hot.

CHILI CON CARNE
Yield: 18 servings, 8 ounces each

Ingredients:

6 *pounds ground beef*	8 *dried chili peppers*
2 *cups chopped onions*	1 *tablespoon salt*
6 *tablespoons oil or drippings*	1 *tablespoon chili powder*
4 *6-ounce cans tomato paste*	1 *teaspoon ground cumin*
6 *cups water*	½ *ounce* (½ *square*) *bitter*
2 *cloves garlic, minced*	*chocolate*

Method:

In large kettle brown meat and onions in the oil or drippings.

Add remaining ingredients and simmer for 3 hours. Taste occasionally for flavor and remove the peppers if chili begins to get too hot. Add more water if necessary.

Skim oil from top before serving. Serve with cooked rice or kidney beans.

BLANKET OF VEAL

Yield: 24 portions, 8 ounces each

Ingredients:

8 pounds shoulder of veal, cubed	½ bunch parsley
	4 sprigs celery with leaves
4 quarts water	1 leek
4 dozen small onions	4 pounds mushrooms
12 carrots, cut into julienne strips	2 cups water
	2 teaspoons salt
2 tablespoons salt	Juice of 2 lemons
2 bay leaves	½ cup flour
2 cloves garlic	½ cup soft butter
1 teaspoon peppercorns	8 egg yolks
½ teaspoon thyme	1 quart cream

Method:

Put veal, the 4 quarts water, onions, carrots, the 2 tablespoons salt, bay leaves, garlic, peppercorns, thyme, parsley, celery, and leek into a large kettle. Bring to a boil and simmer for 1½ hours, skimming surface several times during the first half hour of cooking.

Wash mushrooms and simmer in the 2 cups water with the 2 teaspoons salt and the juice of the lemons for 5 minutes. Let stand in their broth.

When meat is tender, remove meat and onions and carrots and keep warm. Cook the broth until reduced to 1½ quarts. Discard the parsley, celery, and leek.

In saucepan combine flour and butter to a smooth paste; cook, stirring, until lightly browned. Stir in broth from the meat and mushrooms; cook, stirring, until sauce is smooth and thickened. Cook over low heat for 15 minutes, stirring occasionally.

Beat egg yolks and cream with 2 cups of the hot sauce. Stir into remaining sauce and heat without boiling. Add meat and vegetables and mix lightly.

RAGOUT OF VEAL WITH MUSHROOMS
Yield: 48 servings, 6 ounces each

Ingredients:

2 sticks (1 cup) butter	1½ quarts water
12 pounds veal, cubed	3 pounds mushrooms, sliced
3 cups minced onions	3 cups water
2 tablespoons salt	3 cups warm sour cream

Method:

Melt half the butter in heavy kettle and in it brown meat.

Add onions and brown lightly.

Add salt and the 1½ quarts water. Cover and simmer for 1 hour, until meat is tender.

Meanwhile cook mushrooms in remaining butter with the 3 cups water. Cover and simmer for 5 minutes.

When meat is tender, add mushrooms and the mushroom liquid. Keep stew hot until servingtime.

At last minute stir in the sour cream first mixed with a little of the hot gravy.

VEAL BIRDS
Yield: 48 servings, 6 ounces each

Ingredients:

12½ pounds round of veal, sliced ¼ inch thick	3 cups shortening
1 gallon bread stuffing	8 stalks celery, coarsely cut
¼ cup salt	6 medium onions, sliced
1½ cups flour	3 quarts water

Method:

Trim and cut veal into pieces about 3½ to 4 ounces each; pound into rectangular pieces.

Grind or finely cut the meat trimmings and add to bread stuffing.

Sprinkle meat with salt and cover with dressing. Roll up and fasten with toothpicks.

Roll birds in flour and brown in hot shortening.

Arrange birds in single layer in baking pans with celery and sliced onions. Add water. Cover and bake in a 325° F. oven for 1½ to 2 hours. Uncover during last ½ hour to brown.

Remove picks from birds, place in serving dishes, and strain gravy over.

Serve 2 birds per person with 3 tablespoons gravy.

LAMB STEW A LA GRECQUE
Yield: 24 servings

Ingredients:

¾ cup cooking oil
12 lamb shanks, each split into several pieces
4 cloves garlic, minced
8 medium onions (3 pounds), sliced

3½ quarts canned tomatoes
1 tablespoon salt
2 teaspoons oregano
2 teaspoons thyme
4 tablespoons cornstarch
2 cups water

Method:

In large kettle heat oil and in it brown the lamb shanks on all sides.

Add garlic and onions; brown lightly.

Add tomatoes, salt, herbs. Cover and bring to a boil. Cook over low heat for 2 hours, or until meat is so tender it is ready to fall from bones.

Cool and remove fat.

To serve, reheat to simmering and stir in cornstarch mixed to a paste with the water. Keep simmering until servingtime.

HAM STEAK HAWAIIAN
Yield: 50 portions

Ingredients:
50 pullman ham steaks, 4
    ounces each
50 pineapple slices

1 cup sugar
1 teaspoon cinnamon
Oil

Method:
Arrange ham steaks on lightly greased sheet pan.
Broil about 3 inches from heat for 3 to 5 minutes.
Turn ham and broil for 3 minutes longer. Remove from broiler and keep hot.
Arrange pineapple rings on buttered sheet pan.
Combine sugar and cinnamon and sprinkle over pineapple.
Place pineapple under broiler and glaze.
Place a pineapple slice on each ham steak to serve.

FISHERMAN'S PLATTER
Yield: 50 portions

Ingredients:
    Breading materials
2½ pounds shrimp, shelled
    and cleaned
½ gallon fresh oysters, shelled

6 pounds scallops
5 pounds of fillet of sole,
    cut into serving por-
    tions

Method:
Bread all items with egg wash and crumbs or meal.
Fry at 365° F. until golden. Drain on absorbent paper and keep hot in warm oven.
Serve with tartar sauce and garnish each serving with lemon wedge and parsley sprig.

LOBSTER NEWBURG
Yield: 50 portions (⅔ cup or 5¼ ounces)

Ingredients:

1 pound butter
3 tablespoons paprika
10 pounds cooked, diced lobster meat, or half lobster and half white fish

2 gallons light Cream Sauce
Salt and pepper
Juice of 1 lemon

Method:

In a large saucepan melt butter with paprika.

Add lobster meat and sauté for 5 minutes or until lobster meat is heated through.

Mix lobster meat with cream sauce, using a wooden paddle or spoon. Bring to boiling point; season to taste with salt and pepper. Add lemon juice.

Serve in individual casserole dishes with toast points.

BRUNSWICK STEW
Yield: 24 servings

Ingredients:

24 chicken parts
Flour
¾ cup bacon drippings
3 quarts water
1 tablespoon salt
2 cups chopped onions
6 No. 2½ cans tomatoes

2 bay leaves
1 tablespoon Worcestershire sauce
4 boxes frozen okra
4 boxes frozen lima beans
4 boxes frozen corn kernels

Method:

Dust chicken parts in flour and brown on all sides in bacon drippings in a heavy skillet.

As pieces brown transfer to large kettle or stewpot.

Add water to cover chicken, and the salt, onions, tomatoes, bay leaves, and Worcestershire.

Bring to a boil and simmer for 2 hours. This may be cooked on the day before or early in the morning.

Before serving, bring back to a simmer, add okra, limas, and corn. Simmer for 5 minutes. Serve 1 piece chicken with ¾ cup vegetables and gravy per serving.

CHICKEN PAPRIKASH

Yield: 24 servings, ¼ chicken each with ½ cup sauce

Ingredients:

6 3-pound chickens, cut into serving portions	3 cups minced onion
Flour	4 cloves garlic, minced
1 tablespoon salt	3 tablespoons paprika
6 tablespoons butter	12 tablespoons flour
1 cup vegetable shortening	6 tablespoons tomato paste
3 green peppers, minced	9 cups water (2 quarts, plus 1 cup)
6 pimientos, finely chopped	1½ cups warm sour cream

Method:

Sort over chicken pieces and put necks, wing tips, backs, and giblets in saucepan. Cover with salted water, bring to a boil, and simmer for 1 hour covered. Strain and reserve stock. It should measure 3 cups.

Dust pieces of chicken in flour mixed with half the salt. In heavy skillet melt half the butter and shortening and in it brown chicken pieces on all sides.

As each piece is browned, remove to large kettle.

When all pieces are browned, melt remaining butter and shortening and in it sauté green peppers, pimientos, onions, garlic, paprika, and the remaining salt until onion is tender. Stir in flour and tomato paste.

Add to kettle with chicken and slowly stir in the water.

Add strained stock and bring to a boil.

Cover and simmer for 1 hour, stirring occasionally.

Cool and remove fat from surface.

Reheat and, just before serving, stir in the sour cream, mixed with a little of the hot gravy.

CHICKEN CACCIATORE

Yield: 50 portions, ½ chicken each with 3 ounces sauce

Ingredients:

25 chickens (2¼ to 2½ pounds), halved

4 cups flour

2 tablespoons salt

2 teaspoons pepper

1 quart oil

3 pounds onions, thickly sliced

3 pounds mushrooms, sliced

2 pounds green peppers, sliced

2 tablespoons minced garlic

2 No. 10 cans crushed tomatoes and juice

1 pint chicken stock

1 teaspoon oregano, crushed

Salt to taste

Pepper to taste

Method:

Roll chicken halves in flour seasoned with salt and pepper.

Fry chicken in ⅛ inch hot oil in fry pans or heavy skillets until lightly browned on both sides. Place in roasting pans.

Cook onions, mushrooms, green peppers, and garlic in large saucepan in remaining oil for 15 minutes.

Add crushed tomatoes with juice, stock, and seasonings.

Blend well, pour sauce over chickens and bake, covered, in 350° F. oven for 45 to 60 minutes.

Serve ½ chicken for each portion, using both white and dark meat. Serve with 3 ounces sauce.

CHICKEN MARENGO

Yield: 50 portions, ½ chicken each with about ½ cup sauce

Ingredients:

25 chickens, 2¼ to 2½
    pounds, halved
Salt and pepper to taste
1 *quart salad oil*
¼ *pound butter*
3 *cloves garlic, minced*

½ *gallon chicken stock*
½ *gallon tomato sauce*
½ *gallon brown gravy*
½ *pound butter*
4 *pounds mushrooms, sliced*

Method:

Salt and pepper the chickens. Sauté in oil in skillets until golden brown.

When browned place in roasting pans.

Deglaze skillets with 1 quart water and reserve liquid for the sauce.

Melt the ¼ pound butter in skillet, add garlic, and cook for 30 seconds.

Add chicken stock and cook until it is reduced to 1 quart liquid.

Add tomato sauce and brown gravy.

Simmer about ½ hour. Strain over chickens.

Heat the ½ pound butter in skillet and add mushrooms. Sauté until done and spread over the chickens.

Cover roasting pans, bring gravy to boil on top of stove, then transfer to preheated 350° F. oven and cook for 45 minutes, or until tender.

CHICKEN TETRAZZINI

Yield: Serves 10. A good dish for women to make at home and bring to dinner, providing facilities for reheating are available.

Ingredients:

1 5-pound plump hen	1 cup light cream
1 pound thin spaghetti	½ teaspoon salt
3 tablespoons butter	½ teaspoon oregano
½ pound mushrooms, sliced	⅛ teaspoon nutmeg
3 tablespoons flour	½ cup grated Swiss or Parmesan cheese
2½ cups chicken broth	san cheese

Method:

On day before, cook chicken according to general directions. Cool. Remove chicken from broth, reserving broth, and cut meat into bite-size pieces. Strain broth and measure 2½ cups.

Cook spaghetti according to package directions. Drain and rinse.

Grease a large roasting pan and line bottom and sides with about ⅔ of precooked spaghetti.

In large skillet melt butter and in it cook mushrooms for 5 minutes.

Stir in flour. Gradually stir in measured chicken broth and cook, stirring, until sauce is thickened. Stir in cream, salt, oregano, and nutmeg.

Add chicken and mix.

Pour most of the chicken mixture over spaghetti and top with remaining spaghetti.

Add rest of chicken, cover with grated cheese.

Bake in preheated 375° F. oven for 45 minutes.

JAMBALAYA
Yield: Serves 12

Ingredients:

¼ cup fat	1 quart water
2 3-pound chickens, cut into serving portions	1 teaspoon salt
	½ teaspoon marjoram
1 cup chopped onions	½ teaspoon thyme
2 cloves garlic, minced	1 bay leaf
2 cups rice	1 cup diced ham
2 cups canned tomatoes	12 small sausages

Method:

In large skillet or saucepan melt fat and in it brown chickens. Remove.

Add onion and garlic to fat remaining in pan and cook until onion is transparent.

Add rice and stir to coat each grain with fat.

Add tomatoes, water, salt, herbs, and ham. Place chicken on top.

Cover and set aside.

Half an hour before serving, turn heat on under pot. Bring liquid to a rapid boil, cover pot tightly, turn heat very low and cook for 40 minutes on top of stove or in a preheated 375° F. oven for 40 minutes.

While Jambalaya is cooking, brown sausages separately and add as garnish before serving.

RICE PILAF
Yield: 50 portions, ½ cup each

Ingredients:

1 pound butter or margarine	3 pounds raw rice
3 medium onions, chopped	2 teaspoons salt
3 cloves garlic, minced (optional)	2½ quarts chicken stock or beef broth

Method:

In heavy saucepan melt butter and in it stew onions and garlic until vegetables are transparent.

Add rice and cook, stirring, until rice turns golden.

Add salt and chicken stock or beef broth and bring liquid to a rapid boil.

Cover saucepan, reduce heat to very low, and cook without removing cover for 30 minutes.

Directory of Sources for Quantity Supplies

A great deal of money can be saved by church and club organizations by wise buying. When possible, it is suggested that local merchants be patronized; most are anxious to co-operate and be part of a community affair, and will make special prices on quantity buying. For unusual merchandise, not available in your area, consult this *Directory of Sources*. The companies listed have indicated their willingness to give consideration to fund-raising organizations. The list is in no way complete but will, it is hoped, be of help in some areas. In places where the *Directory* is incomplete, see local listings for brokers and wholesale supply houses in the yellow pages of your telephone directory.

BASKETS OF STRAW

Round the World Basket and Gift Shop
444 Third Avenue
New York, New York

Everything imaginable in straw: baskets, hampers, magazine racks, trays, planters, animal-shaped purses, bird cages. Write for catalogue and order blank.

BOOKS FOR CHRISTMAS

Ideals Publishing Company
11315 Watertown Plank Road
Milwaukee 1, Wisconsin

Special Christmas books for group selling plus books of inspiration. Easter and other holidays. Write for catalogue and order form.

BULBS

Michigan Bulb Company
Grand Rapids, Michigan

Imported tulip bulbs. Guaranteed blooms for five years. Shipped post paid. Write for details and order forms.

CANDIES

The Country Store
at Centerville
Cape Cod, Massachusetts

Penny-candy assortment, old-fashioned lemon drops, honey drops, coffee crunch, old-fashioned rock candy on a string, old-fashioned horehound drops, old-fashioned molasses-peppermint drops, and stick candy, just to name a few. Special consideration given to church groups for quantity orders. Write for catalogue.

Gilmores
104 Crestmont Street
Reading, Pennsylvania

Fancy-filled hard candies at quantity discounts. Sample tin mailed on request, $1.59. Write for information and order form.

Katharine Beecher
Manchester, Pennsylvania

Katharine Beecher butter mints are made with pure creamery butter. Beautifully packaged for gifts or resale. Write for brochure.

Kathryn Beich
Bloomington, Illinois

Old-fashioned confections made especially for fund raising. Golden crumbles, butter toffee, katydids, almonds 'n' chocolate, krumble krunch, party nuts. Minimum order 12 cases; packed 12 tins to a case, combination cases if desired. Write for catalogue and order form.

Lekvar-by-the-Barrel
H. Roth & Son
1577 First Avenue
New York 28, New York

Rum beans, chocolate cat tongues, fruit-filled chocolate bottles, pischinger torte, Christmas-tree bonbons, chocolate Tobler bars, and many others. World-famous German and Hungarian Christmas items. Write for catalogue.

Mrs. Leland's Kitchens
330 South Wells Street
Chicago 6, Illinois

Golden Butter-Bits, Chocolate Covered Butter-Bits and Holiday Candies in decorative, reuseable canisters. Also big, thick bars of Rich Milk Chocolate, personalized with name of organization and fund-drive purpose. 60 days credit. Write for further information and order forms.

Manganaro Foods
488 Ninth Avenue
New York 18, New York

A complete line of imported cakes and candies from Italy. Sold individually or assorted in gift baskets. Torrone, marrons glacés, amaretti, caramels, gianduiotti, cremini, and Milanese assortment. Write for candy and cake-basket catalogue. Consideration given to church groups on large orders.

Mason Candies, Inc.
P.O. Box 549
Mineola, New York

Chocolate mints, assorted jellies, almond coconut, boxed. Personalized labels if desired. 30 packages per carton, minimum order 15 cartons, shipped on consignment. Write for information and order form.

New Hampton General Store
R.F.D. Hampton, New Jersey

Sweets—a feature of the general store. The most popular are old-fashioned candy in striped bags, glass toys filled with candy, old-fashioned rock candy, true lemon drops, horehound and molasses-peppermint drops. Send for the General Catalogue.

Paprikas Weiss Importer
1546 Second Avenue
New York 28, New York

Finest, imported bulk candies from Vienna, Austria: milk-chocolate bars, imported cookies from West Germany, biscuits from France, Christmas candies beautifully boxed. Send for catalogue.

Pennsylvania Dutch Candies
Mount Holly Springs, Pennsylvania

Pennsylvania-Dutch bite-size pillows with peanut butter center, in decorative tin. Wholesale prices. Write for information and order form.

Priester's Pecans
Fort Deposit, Alabama

Southern-hospitality pecan candies, such as chocolate-toasted pecans, crunch 'n' nut, chocolate-pecan wilkies, pecan fudge, pecan-stuffed dates. Pecan pralines are creamy and full of pecans; also pecan brittle packaged in small attractive tins. Write for catalogue.

Vrest Orton
The Vermont Country Store
Weston, Vermont

Old-fashioned candy sold three ways—mixture in gift boxes, same mixture in striped bags, or one kind in a gift box (23 varieties), or coffee-bean candy, striped candy sticks, licorice, and horehound candy made of the real horehound herb. Big box maple country candy, and Vermont maple-butternut fudge. Write for catalogue and order form. All prices f.o.b. Weston. No orders accepted for less than $2.00.

CANDLES

The Little Candle Shop
Box 94
Huntington, Long Island
New York

Beautifully designed candles for all occasions. Candle vases—dainty, hollow, clear-plastic cylinders that hold flowers at the base of the candle, also many other candle decorations. Special consideration given to church groups. Write for catalogue.

Mona Shops, Inc.
5 West Third Street
New York 12, New York

Candles in unlimited colors and candle lamps. Order must be 1 dozen of any style and no less than 6 dozen for total order. Write describing type of candle desired.

Royal Candle Company, Inc.
Union City, New Jersey

Candles in glass for all occasions. Some with Christmas motifs and stories. Some with stripes, sequins; also frosty and pearl finish. Very attractive. Minimum order $50.00. Write for catalogues and order sheets.

CARNIVAL

Charles Shear, Inc.
150 Park Row
New York 7, New York

Buttons, pennants, balloons, carnival goods, party favors, parade specials, and a wide assortment of novelty hats. Complete line of St. Patrick's Day specialties. 25 per cent deposit on all C.O.D. orders, special prices on quantity orders, f.o.b. New York. Write for brochure and order form.

Karl Guggenheim, Inc.
159–07 Archer Avenue
P.O. Box 510
Jamaica, New York

Consolation prizes or give-away items, five-cent grab bag or fish-pond items to more expensive prizes. Game equipment and balloons. Minimum order $10.00. Write for price list and order form.

Baron, Rott and Samuels, Inc.
233 Park Avenue South
New York 3, New York

Listed among adult games and extravagant bingo equipment are some good games of skill, such as cork clowns to shoot at with rifles that shoot corks, hoopla boxes and hardwood hoops, Huckley Buck outfits, fish ponds, dart games, etc. All good quality, designed to last through many fairs. Prices range from $6.50 to $200. Write for catalogue.

CHEESE

Phil Alpert, Inc.
Cheese of All Nations
235 Fulton Street
New York, New York

One of the largest cheese emporiums in the country featuring varieties of cheese from all over the world. The original cheese-of-the-month club. Send for catalogue.

Berkshire Farms
945 Yonkers Avenue
Yonkers, New York

Cheese packaged in colorful boxes and baskets. Swiss, Austrian, Danish, and Italian cheese in handsome tray baskets; also a wonderful array of gourmet gifts. Send for catalogue.

Manganaro Foods
488 Ninth Avenue
New York 18, New York

Thirty cheese specialties, fine grating cheese, mild Italian, strong Italian, fresh Italian, plus all the favorite cheeses of the world. Write for shopping list and gift-basket brochure.

Old Denmark
135 East Fifty-seventh Street
New York, New York

Over 30 kinds of Danish cheese, all aged. Write for information.

CHINESE COOKING UTENSILS

Cathay's Hardware Corporation
49 Mott Street
New York, New York

All sorts of Chinese cooking utensils, layered steamers, meat cleavers, and Chinese *woks*. Send for catalogue.

CHRISTMAS CARDS

National Audubon Society
1130 Fifth Avenue
New York 28, New York

Bird prints, place mats and napkins, tea towels, hanging feeders for all birds, gifts for the members of the National Audubon Society. Christmas cards at a very reasonable price. Send for the gift catalogue.

COFFEE, FRESHLY ROASTED

House of Yemen
486 Ninth Avenue
New York, New York

An old established coffee-roasting house featuring ten major blends. Also unblended coffee, the favorite being Mocha and Java, strong flavor but not bitter. Special house blend called Gregorian, named after Mr. Gregory the founder. Send for free catalogue.

Schapira Coffee Company
117 West Tenth Street
New York, New York

One blend of coffee roasted three ways: American, French (sometimes referred to as New Orleans), and espresso. This company has been roasting coffee beans for over 60 years and uses the finest Colombian coffee beans with some mocha to make their blend. Also teas: oolong, jasmine, pekoe, to name a few. Tea may be ordered in bulk for repackaging. Write for catalogue.

COLONIAL GIFTS

Craft House
Colonial Williamsburg
Williamsburg, Virginia

Williamsburg reproductions of eighteenth-century antiques and one-of-a-kind gifts. Beautiful but expensive. All income derived from Craft House is used to maintain and develop Colonial Williamsburg and to carry forward its educational program. Send for the Craft House catalogue, price $2.00.

COOKIES AND CANDIES

Temple Tea Bags
P.O. Box 6104
Philadelphia 15, Pennsylvania

Quality Danish cookies in decorative tins at wholesale prices. Also butter-mints in four pastel colors. Write for information and order form.

COUNTRY STORE

Vrest Orton
The Vermont Country Store
Weston, Vermont

Woodenware, pewterware, tin and cast-iron match holders, deerskin gloves and moccasins, briar pipes, calico, hand-woven coverlets, iron trivets, old-fashioned Vermont aprons, historic tiles, old-fashioned candy, real licorice and horehound in gift boxes and bags, maple syrup, and soft maple sugar. Country Store exclusive foods and gift-food packets. Write for catalogue.

New Hampton General Store
R.F.D. Hampton, New Jersey

Early-American products for the home, old-fashioned penny candy, and country-style food products. Early-American mint tea and tea sampler of five gourmet favorites. Discount allowances for quantity orders, from 10 per cent to 25 per cent, depending on size of order. Check or money order must accompany order. Write for the general catalogue.

The Country Store
at Centerville
Cape Cod, Massachusetts

Typical country-store items. Penny candy, sharp cheese, and many Early-American products. Useful utensils for the kitchen (scoops, cutters, knives). Special consideration given to church groups that need items in quantity. Write for the "Country News," order form is on back page.

DUTCH PRODUCTS

John Monnikendam
20 West Twenty-second Street
New York 10, New York

Handsome gift items imported from Holland, souvenir spoons and novelties, silver and pewter. Royal Delft miniature vases and pitchers, windmills and mugs, lamps, teapots, spoonracks, and other Royal Delft blue-china items. Holland pewter soup bowls with spoons, candleholders, pitchers and porringers, wooden shoes, Dutch dolls. Write for catalogue sheets and prices.

EDUCATIONAL FILMS

Department of Church Building and Architecture
National Council of the Churches of Christ, U.S.A.
475 Riverside Drive
New York 27, New York

For the church with a new building in mind. Films of church planning. Films to be rented from $3.00 to $10.00, also color slides of American and European Buildings (more than 1000). Printed materials of annual conferences and retreat proceedings. Brochure of church building and architecture. Write for audio-visual and printed materials.

FELT

Beckmann Felt
Beckmann Building
120 Baster Street
New York 13, New York

Distributor of felt by the yard for display purposes, handicraft, and art needlework. An array of colors to inspire any craftsman. Will dye any color to order and cut to size or shape. Special consideration to church groups. Write for catalogue of samples.

FRUITCAKES

Tasso Plantation Foods, Inc.
335 Mohle Avenue
Arabi, Louisiana

Quality Duncan Hines fruitcakes, bursting with Southern pecans and fruits, made from an old plantation recipe. Wholesale prices in even-case lots. Send $1.00 for sample cake with supply of individual tasting pieces for members of your committee.

GERMAN SPECIALTIES

George Kern, Inc.
496 Ninth Avenue
New York, New York

Services New York State only. Delicatessen products, bratwurst, smoked ham, sausages, and other meat products (50 pounds minimum). No catalogue.

GIFT-WRAPPING IDEAS AND SUPPLIES

East House
134 Fifth Avenue
New York, New York

Colorful tissue wrapping papers in brilliant fashion colors. Color totes (shopping bags), color bags in assorted sizes. Gold enchantys ribbon. Fool's gold decorations. For gift wrapping or to sell. Ask for East House Products at your better department stores.

Hallmark

Available only through local stores. Also booklets available from Hallmark outlets at a nominal charge on gift-wrapping ideas.

Pride Gift Wrappings
2300 Logan Boulevard
Chicago 47, Illinois

Wholesale prices. Minimum shipment $100.00, f.o.b. Chicago. Cash only. Write for catalogue.

Tie-Tie
Chicago Printed String Company
2300 Logan Boulevard
Chicago 47, Illinois

The things you can do with satintone and ribbonette are limited only by your imagination—bows, flowers, bells, butterflies, wreaths, and chains. Send for the Tie-Tie gift-wrapping magic booklet, only 25 cents.

GRAINS BY MAIL—STONE-GROUND

Byrd Mill, Louisa, Virginia
Clarks Falls Grist Mill, North Stonington, Connecticut

Grist Mill of the Vermont Guild, Weston, Vermont
Mill O'Milford, Inc., Danbury, Connecticut
Mystic Seaport Stores, Inc., Mystic, Connecticut
Rose Mill, Milford, Connecticut
Vermont Country Store, Weston, Vermont

HAMS BY MAIL

Country Hams

Homestead Stock Farm, Trenton, Tennessee
Nicholson and Weede, Franklin, Virginia
Olde Salem Country Ham, 885 Northern Boulevard, Winston-
Salem, North Carolina

Virginia or Smithfield

Gwaltney, Inc., Smithfield, Virginia
Jordan's Old Virginia Smokehouse, 1435-L, East Cary Street,
Richmond, Virginia
V. W. Joyner, Smithfield, Virginia
Seven Day Shopping Center, Barracks Road and Route 29,
Charlottesville, Virginia
Smithfield Ham and Products Company, Smithfield, Virginia
Smithfield Packing Company, Smithfield, Virginia
Thalhimer Fine Food Shop, 7 Broad Street, Richmond, Virginia

HAWAIIAN PRODUCTS

Orchids of Hawaii, Inc.
305 Seventh Avenue
New York 1, New York

Everything for a *luau*, fresh-flower *leis*, *luau* table items, and
food specialties. Orchid corsages good for any time of the year;
and for Christmas, fresh mistletoe. Minimum order $10.00. Also
live baby palm trees for Palm Sunday for only 15 cents each.
Minimum order, 100, f.o.b. New York. Write for catalogue and
order sheet.

HUNGARIAN FOODS AND HOUSEHOLD ACCESSORIES

Lekvar-by-the-Barrel
H. Roth & Son, Prop.
1577 First Avenue
New York 28, New York

Hungarian gift items, candies, and Christmas items. For cooking: spices and herbs, paprika for goulash. A complete line of herb teas. Kitchen items for the gourmet: cutters, molds, graters, etc. A reasonable discount to church groups. Send for booklet called "A Continental Bazaar," and order form.

Paprikas Weiss Importer
1546 Second Avenue
New York 28, New York

Jams, jellies, and marmalades, imported spices and herbs, cheese delicacies, true fruit syrups, cookies, and candies, also imported teas. All kinds of kitchen utilities plus a wide variety of pepper mills. Good selection of gelatin molds and forms of all kinds. Send for catalogue and order form. Special consideration given to church groups.

INTERNATIONAL MERCHANDISE

New International Importing Company
517 Ninth Avenue
New York, New York

Food of all countries. Minimum order, $1.00. No catalogue.

Shopping International
25 North Main Street
White River Junction, Vermont

Attractive gift items from many countries in the world. Florentine gold picture frames, alabaster-heart paperweights, Danish wooden cheese mice, golden teakettles from Japan, Sumi water-color sets, taro doll pin cushions, Tyrolean woodcarved fawns, take-apart soldiers, and other toys, 10 per cent discount to church groups for orders over $10.00. Write for catalogue.

ITALIAN FOOD

Manganaro Foods
488 Ninth Avenue
New York 18, New York

Imported foods from many lands but mostly from Italy, 30 cheese specialties, cakes and candies, fruits and preserves, and other popular Italian foods. A special price on sizable orders to church groups. Write for catalogue and order form.

JAPANESE SPECIALTIES (see *Oriental Specialties*)

JEWELRY

Richard Downes
11 West Thirtieth Street
New York 1, New York

Jewelry you create yourselves for profit and enjoyment. No skill or experience needed. No tricky techniques to learn. Send for catalogue and order sheet. No minimum order; catalogue, 25 cents.

KITCHEN EQUIPMENT

Bazar Français
666 Sixth Avenue
New York, New York

Copperware, from the smallest pan to the largest pot, au gratin dishes and asparagus steamers, fish molds or anything for the French cook. Gadgets galore. Write for catalogue.

The Bridge Company
498 Third Avenue
New York, New York

Everything for the gourmet and kitchen. Pots, molds, and kettles, and all things needed for baking. Large equipment for the institutional kitchen. No catalogue. Write for information.

La Cuisinière, Inc.
903 Madison Avenue
New York, New York

Gifts for the homemaker: mostly in the cooking line. Special omelette pans, pots, cookbooks, molds, and copper items from this lovely shop. Send for brochure.

LEATHER GOODS

Ambassador Leather Goods
2222 Falls Street
Niagara Falls, New York

Credit-card organizers for men and purse-secretaries for women in English morocco top-grain cowhide and pin-seal vinby in all colors. All leather products available with free personalization in genuine 14-carat raised-gold plates. Send for brochure and order form.

MEXICAN PRODUCTS

The Phoenix
1514 Wisconsin Avenue N.W.
Washington 7, D.C.

Exquisite handcrafted items of silver with inlaid stones. Hand-woven scarves and *rebozos*, pottery and piggy banks. Send for catalogue.

NEAR- AND MIDDLE-EASTERN SPECIALTIES

Kassos Brothers
570 Ninth Avenue
New York, New York

All Greek foods imaginable. Minimum order, $10.00. No catalogue.

Sahadi Importing Company, Inc.
187 Atlantic Avenue
Brooklyn, New York

Specializing in Near East foods, sweets, and spices. Write for catalogue.

Trinacria Importing Company
415 Third Avenue
New York, New York

Cooking supplies for East Indian foods, and foods of the Far East. No catalogue.

NEEDLEWORK

Frederick Herrschner Company
72 East Randolph Street
Chicago 1, Illinois

Yarns and complete kits for afghans and other handicrafts. Hoops and frames for quilting, dress-me dolls, and sock toy kits. Write for Herrschners' catalogue.

Merribee Company
2727 West Seventh Street
Fort Worth 7, Texas

Yarn-craft kits, knit kits for sweaters and stoles, yarns and equipment for embroidering, knitting, rug making, weaving, crocheting, tatting, quilting, and needlepoint. Also plastic dolls with movable eyes, head, and arms, very reasonable and cheaper by the dozen. Discounts based on quantity purchases. Write for catalogue and order sheets.

Katagiri & Company, Inc.
224 East Fifty-ninth Street
New York 22, New York

A place to get all ingredients for sukiyaki. Special flour and rice products, dried vegetables, dried fish, dried seaweed; bottled and canned goods, Oriental spices and green teas. Also Japanese cooking utensils, chinaware, lacquerware, stationery, and chopsticks. Write for price list.

Miya Company, Inc.
373 Park Avenue South
New York 16, New York

Japanese gifts; teak snack trays, candy bowls, kiri flower vases, and porcelainware. Stone lanterns, pebbles, and other Oriental décor for house and garden. Write for catalogue.

Oriental Food Shop
1302 Amsterdam Avenue
New York, New York

Oriental and exotic food preparations from Japanese and Philippine, Chinese and Indian dishes. For catalogue, send 10 cents.

PAPER PRODUCTS FOR THE TABLE

The Grace Line Company
1134 Stinson Boulevard
Minneapolis 13, Minnesota

Over forty decorative table paper prayer napkins, available in luncheon, dinner, and miniature sizes at wholesale prices. One carton and postage free on orders of eight or more cartons; 5 per cent discount when cash accompanies order. Write for order forms.

Lily Tulip Cup Corporation

Look up local distributor in telephone directory. If not listed as such, check paper dealers, wholesale, in classified directory.

PECANS

Priester's Pecans
Fort Deposit, Alabama

Gifts of fancy pecans, fruitcakes, and candies including pralines, pecan rolls, and butter-pecan brittle. Pecans packaged many ways in tins and boxes; papershell pecans come in boxes and bags in 5 pounds to 25 pounds. Fancy, select pecan halves can be ordered roasted and salted fresh to order. Write for brochure and shopping form.

Schermer Pecan Company
Fairhope, Alabama

Jumbo whole pecan halves in 1-pound cellophane bags. Wholesale prices for resale. Write for details and order form.

Southland Pecans, Inc.
P.O. Box 1588
Mobile, Alabama

Choice shelled pecans, in cellophane bags, twenty-four per case. Shipment express prepaid on orders of four cases or more. Special case prices. Write for information and order form.

H. M. Thames Pecan Company, Inc.
P.O. Box 1588
Mobile, Alabama

Quality 12-ounce and 16-ounce cellophane packages and bulk pecans. Orders for assorted cases welcomed. Shipping charges prepaid. Write for information and order form.

PENNSYLVANIA-DUTCH PRODUCTS

The Pfaltzgraff Pottery Company
York, Pennsylvania

Pennsylvania-Dutch pie plate. Attractive pie plate with sticker in center with recipe of Pennsylvania-Dutch apple pie. Wholesale price of 55 cents each, based on a minimum order of 12 dozen. No catalogue.

PLATES

World Wide Art Studios
Covington, Tennessee

Custom-decorated ceramics at wholesale prices. Special keepsake plates in seventeen styles, 23-carat gold border on most styles. Staff artists work from snapshots of any picture that shows details of church. No extra charge for copy on backs of plates (history of church, etc.). No extra charge for art or engravings. Low minimum-order requirements. Also framed tiles for walls. Write for catalogue sheets and order forms.

RELIGIOUS ARTICLES

Morehouse & Barlow
14 East Forty-first Street
New York, New York

Fine religious jewelry, plaques, and books of inspiration are sold here. Also a vestment department and appointment department. Write for general catalogue or, at Christmas time, the Christmas catalogue.

SCANDINAVIAN SPECIALTIES

Nyborg & Nelson
937 Second Avenue
New York, New York

Small gifts from the Scandinavian countries plus foods from Sweden, Norway, and Denmark. Write for catalogue.

SCOTCH SPECIALTIES

Drewes Brothers, Inc.,
6815 Eighth Avenue
Brooklyn 20, New York

Gifts from Scotland plus a wonderful line of Scotch food. Scotch lorne sausages and beef links; black pudding and white pudding, Dundee cake, shortbread, and assorted cookies. In candies: Keelers' butterscotch, and imported English candies. Write for catalogue.

SMILING SCOT PRODUCTS

Smiling Scot
1266 Goodale Boulevard
Columbus 12, Ohio

Over 500 wholesale articles ranging from Christmas and other occasion card assortments, ribbons, novelties, to jewelry, household, and personal items. Aprons, kitchen towels, calendar towels, spray perfumes, stationery, first-aid kits, toys and puzzles, napkin and letter holders, pure vanilla, Christmas matches and candles, world Bibles, greeting cards and gift wrappings. Write for information and order form.

SPANISH FOODS

Casa Moneo
218 West Fourteenth Street
New York, New York

Spanish foods, Mexican, and South American foods can be purchased here. A small charge for mailing. No catalogue.

SPICES AND HERBS

Mrs. DeWildt
Lakeview Drive
Kinnelon, New Jersey 07405

Write to Mrs. DeWildt for Indonesian recipes. This mail-order house sells all spices and ingredients needed. Also Far Eastern and Holland foods, condiments and party snacks.

Keihl Pharmacy, Inc.
109 Third Avenue
New York 3, New York

A pharmacy established over a century ago with over 3000 items to cure what ails you. Herbs from all over the world for cooking; botanicals for making cosmetics. Wherever possible, herbs can be supplied in the following form: cut, sifted, granulated, or powdered. Write for the Kiehl's handy book of first aid; it has a listing of many items available.

Les Eschalottes
706 Lafayette Street
Paramus, New Jersey

Shallots by mail; write for information.

Manganaro Foods
488 Ninth Avenue
New York 18, New York

Many spices and herbs available at this store. Also, dry mushrooms, truffles, saffron, french mustard, pignoli, and flavoring extracts. Write for catalogue.

Paprikas Weiss Importer
1546 Second Avenue
New York 28, New York

Imported spices and herbs, nuts and flavors for baking. Jams, jellies, and marmalades imported from Switzerland. Finest imported rose paprika. Send for complete catalogue.

Ye Olde Herb Shoppe
46 Dey Street
New York, New York

Herbs of all kinds for every use. Minimum order $5.00. No catalogue; write for specific information.

STOCKINGS

National Wholesale Company, Inc.
Lexington, North Carolina

High-fashion hosiery in popular shades. Very reasonable per dozen. Unconditionally guaranteed. Write for details and order forms.

TABLEWARE

Corning Glass Works
Corning, New York

Pyrex Brand tableware, stain and chip resistant, can be used for both baking and serving. Does not warp or crack. Distinctive patterns in narrow-rim frame. Available in Fern Green, Grecian blue grass, and Revel. Also double-tough tumblers, thin yet sturdy, in four graceful shapes. Available through Corning distributors. The Pyroceram Brand tableware is available only through Corning Glass Works, Corning, New York. Write for catalogue sheets.

TEA

Lekvar-by-the-Barrel
H. Roth & Son, Prop.
1577 First Avenue
New York 28, New York

Twenty-one different herb teas plus coffees (green, roasted, chicory, malt), cocoas, and Ceylon Russian-mixture tea. Write for the booklet "A Continental Bazaar."

New Hampton General Store
R.F.D. Hampton, New Jersey

A five-tea sampler, five of the finest teas in all the world: Mandarin, Jasmine, Keemun, English-breakfast and Imperial Gunpowder. Also in the American tradition, mint tea. Write for general catalogue.

Paprikas Weiss Importer
1546 Second Avenue
New York 28, New York

Fifty-four different teas listed, many coffees and cocoa too. Write for catalogue.

Schapira Coffee Company
117 West Tenth Street
New York, New York

Tea may be ordered in bulk or in bags for repackaging. Oolong, jasmine, pekoe, to name a few. Write for catalogue.

TEA BAGS

Temple Tea Bags
P.O. Box 6104
Philadelphia 15, Pennsylvania

Blend of fine tea, 50 bags per attractive carton. The name of your organization imprinted on the box and on each tea-bag label at no extra cost with order of 200 or more boxes. In stock, boxes and tea bags imprinted with "Woman's Society of Christian Service," and others. Also family-size tea bags for hot or iced teas. Sixty-day credit. Write for free samples and order form.

TOYS

Creative Playthings Inc.
P.O. Box 1100
Princeton, New Jersey

"Learning-through-play" materials for children from 2 to 8 years, based on the revolutionary ideas of Maria Montessori and endorsed by leading child psychologists. Cost no more than ordinary toys. Prices range from $3.00 to over $50.00. Majority under $10.00. Discounts for church and school groups up to 20 per cent, depending on size of order. Write for special parents'-consumer catalogue.

VANILLA BEANS

L.A. Champon & Company
230 West Forty-first Street
New York, New York

Vanilla beans. No minimum, just write for amount needed. No catalogue.

Index of Recipes